The Dynamics of Strategy

The Dynamics of Strategy

Mastering Strategic Landscapes of the Firm

Duncan A. Robertson and Adrián A. Caldart

OXFORD

UNIVERSITY PRESS

OXFORD
UNIVERSITY PRESS

Great Clarendon Street, Oxford OX2 6DP

Oxford University Press is a department of the University of Oxford.
It furthers the University's objective of excellence in research, scholarship,
and education by publishing worldwide in

Oxford New York

Auckland Cape Town Dar es Salaam Hong Kong Karachi
Kuala Lumpur Madrid Melbourne Mexico City Nairobi
New Delhi Shanghai Taipei Toronto

With offices in

Argentina Austria Brazil Chile Czech Republic France Greece
Guatemala Hungary Italy Japan Poland Portugal Singapore
South Korea Switzerland Thailand Turkey Ukraine Vietnam

Oxford is a registered trade mark of Oxford University Press
in the UK and in certain other countries

Published in the United States
by Oxford University Press Inc., New York

© Duncan A. Robertson and Adrián A. Caldart 2009

The moral rights of the authors have been asserted
Database right Oxford University Press (maker)

First published 2009

British Library Cataloguing in Publication Data

Data available

Library of Congress Cataloging in Publication Data

Data available

Typeset by SPI Publisher Services, Pondicherry, India
Printed in Great Britain
on acid-free paper by the
MPG Books Group, Bodmin and King's Lynn

ISBN 978–0–19–923415–8 (Hbk.)
978–0–19–923416–5 (Pbk.)

1 3 5 7 9 10 8 6 4 2

⬚ CONTENTS

☐ LIST OF FIGURES

⎕ LIST OF TABLES

☐ LIST OF ABBREVIATIONS

ABMs	Agent-Based (Simulation) Models
EBO	Emerging Business Opportunities
ERP	Enterprise Resource Planning
GM	General Motors
HDTV	High Definition Television
HSC	Holland Sweetener Company
IO	Industrial Organization
JV	Joint Venture
OED	Oxford English Dictionary
OS	Operating System
S-C-P	Structure-Conduct-Performance Paradigm

1 Introduction

1.1 The dynamics of the management process

Modern firms and organizations can be seen as socio-technical systems that process information, continuously converting their ideas into action and action into ideas. Firms' actions in their competitive landscape are based on ideas or assumptions on which the whole firm has been built with the purpose of being successful in its competitive landscape. These ideas constitute the firm's 'view of their world' or, using Peter Drucker's expression, its 'theory of business' (Drucker 1994).

As firms act in their competitive landscapes according to their theory of business, on the one hand they influence such a landscape, and on the other they obtain new information in the form of, for instance, a certain degree of customer acceptance for the firm's products or competitors' responses to the firm's competitive initiatives. By processing such information, the firm generates new ideas, integrates these ideas with its knowledge base, and generates new action out of its (revised) set of hypotheses about its business. In this way, through a recursive process, firm's actions in the competitive landscape become the practical application of the firm's theoretical knowledge that, in turn, derives from previous action. In this way, theory (i.e. the firm's set of hypotheses about what works and what does not work in its competitive landscape) develops out of action, and action develops out of theory in a continuous cycle of learning (Simon 1969; Friscknecht 1993).

1.2 The distinctive nature of strategic decisions

The recursive logic of thought and action embedded in the management process is common to different levels of decisions, each of which deals with different problems and relies on different sources of knowledge. Social scientists have identified the existence of three different levels of decisions in organizations (Parsons 1960; Thompson 1967; Chaffee 1985; Newell 1990) that we will label here as technical, managerial, and strategic.

Technical Decisions. At one extreme, we find decisions supported by robust bodies of explicit technical knowledge. These decisions are based on a set of ideas with very precise and established relationships between them enabling the firm to find, given certain premises, programmed, algorithmic solutions through formal analysis or computational methods. This is the case of firm's standard operating procedures such as invoicing, issuing salary notifications, or problems of optimization, such as setting a stock policy. In all these cases problems are simple enough to enable us to find a 'one best' solution, given certain premises, out of the exhaustive exploration of all the space of possible solutions. Such decisions are usually labelled as Technical.

It is worth noting that when labelling a problem as technical, we assume that the firm has the knowledge to develop a program to solve such a problem. If the firm ignores the technology to solve the problem, it will be obliged to address it by applying alternative and less robust knowledge. For instance, finding the way to minimize the cost of manufacturing given a certain cost and availability of raw materials, labour and machinery capacity is a problem frequently soluble through a linear programming model. However, for firms that ignore how to work out this optimization technique, this problem is likely to be solved, normally less efficiently, through rules of thumb. In short, the categorization of a problem as technical has an objective dimension (whether there is a technical solution available for the problem) and subjective dimension (whether the subject dealing with the problem knows about the technical solution).

Managerial Decisions. A second decision level deals with situations for which the desirability of the range of possible alternative courses of action cannot be assessed exhaustively relying on 'packaged' knowledge (at least in a reasonable time frame). The complexity of the situation demands that we take 'short cuts' that we can identify only if we have experience dealing with similar matters. Decision makers need then to engage in a cognitive process that demands to create new solutions based on old experience in the form of heuristics, popularly referred to as rules of thumb, common sense, intuition, or educated guesses. This is the realm of the expert, a person, or a team of people with enough experience in a field to recognize familiar problems in almost every possible situation (Frischknecht 1993). Management consultants, forensic departments, architects, R&D teams, or medical doctors rely heavily on these sorts of heuristics in their everyday work. In the organizational context, the middle manager constitutes a clear example of the expert. As Mintzberg documented in his well-known work on the nature of managerial work (Mintzberg 1973), managers make most of their decisions applying common sense, rules of thumb, and intuition to deal with situations that typically require the balancing of multiple and dynamic criteria in the socio-technical environment they are responsible for. These decisions are usually referred to as heuristic or programmable ones and in business organizations they characterize the managerial level of the firm. Following Parsons (1960), we chose to label them as managerial decisions.

Strategic Decisions. Finally, firms face the need to make decisions on matters for which the 'theory' inspiring them is far from suitable for programming or even for the application of the heuristics of the expert. These decisions concern situations characterized by their high *complexity*, as they relate to problems with multiple and related dimensions and their high *uncertainty*, as they are characterized by the interdependent behaviour of different actors, making it highly difficult to choose the best course of action analytically. In the absence of certain cause-effect relationships or experience about how these dialectical processes between organizations will unfold, the firm can only hypothesize about the implications of different possible initiatives and learn more about them through interaction with other actors such as competitors, regulators, customers, suppliers, and partners in its competitive landscape. In these situations, managers face the extremely difficult problem in making decisions that demand a long-term perspective, committing the firm in the long run within a competitive landscape that is unlikely to stand still. We call these decisions Strategic decisions.

The high uncertainty characterizing strategic decisions can be reduced as actors implicitly agree on 'rules of the game' in their interaction in the marketplace. By doing this, they stabilize the competitive situation as the volatility of the variables that characterize competition in the industry is reduced. For instance, when the price structure within an industrial sector converges around certain reference values or 'focal points' typically established around the pricing policy of the market leader, the uncertainty related to the evolution of these firms' prices of products is reduced substantially, at least for some time (see Chapter 2). Conversely, when a new major competitor enters the market, as in the case of Microsoft's entry into the video-console market in 2001, risk increases as players are likely to engage in price wars or they may differentiate aggressively by offering new features (see Case Box 2.1).[1]

1.3 The dynamics of strategic management as a recursive process

This recursive view of the management process discussed earlier constitutes the cornerstone of the dynamic approach to the study of strategic management proposed in this book. Our main concern is, therefore, not so much the

---

[1] As we will show in detail in Chapter 7, the complexity of strategic problems increases with the number of competitors and the number of competitive dimensions characterizing their interaction and decreases when any or both of these are reduced.

analysis of strategic situations at a particular point in time, but the understanding of the evolution of such situations through the continuous and circular relationship between thought (strategic plans, mission statements, formulating strategic initiatives) and action (getting the strategic initiatives done).

1.3.1 FROM HYPOTHESES TO ACTION

We represent the dynamics characterizing strategic management in Figure 1.1. We characterized such dynamics as the interaction of three different but interrelated building blocks.

The first block of a firm's strategic posture is the Strategic Intent of the firm. The Strategic Intent (Hamel and Prahalad 1989) of the firm is an overall value proposition that the firm intends to develop in a way to secure a competitive position leading to attractive returns in its competitive landscape. The choice of the core business of the firm and the choice of its generic strategic position (low cost provider, prestige brand firm, technology edge, reasonable price for quality, etc) are examples of decisions concerning the strategic intent of the firm.

The choice of a strategic intent corresponds to the top level of the firm as it concerns policy choices that will have long-term consequences for the firm.

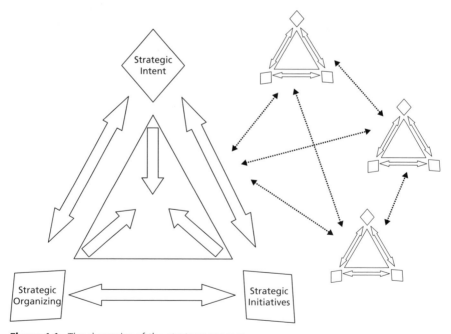

Figure 1.1. The dynamics of the strategy process.

Louis Vuitton's decision to position in the market for women's fashion accessories as a top design, premium quality player, or Asda's positioning in the British supermarket sector as a price leader with national scope constitute examples of a firm's strategic intent.

The value proposition embedded in the strategic intent is materialized through a set of strategic initiatives, the second building block of the strategic posture. Each of these initiatives contributes to specific dimensions of the value proposition of the firm, such as cost of manufacturing, R&D effectiveness, customer service, or pricing policy. Table 1.1 summarizes typical initiatives referred to different dimensions of a firm's activity.

The final building block is the Strategic Organization of the firm. This concerns major organizational decisions referred to the firm's structure, processes, systems and incentives. These decisions are also strategic as they are functional to the successful implementation of the strategic initiatives.

The development of strategic initiatives, and the organization design supporting them, are typically framed within the strategic intent of the firm. However, there are situations in which firms develop initiatives outside such a frame, as a result of managers' reactions to the market's feedback, or as a result of innovation emerging due to the particular way the firm is organized. Sometimes these initiatives eventually end up altering the whole strategic intent. We call these situations 'bottom up' strategies. Intel's migration from being a manufacturer of DRAM memories to become the world leader producer of microprocessors is an example of how an initiative from middle management eventually shifted the firm's strategic intent (see Section 6.4.2).

Once the strategic intent has been set, the strategic initiatives designed, and the organization enabling them has been built, we move from the realm of

Table 1.1. Examples of strategic initiatives

Strategic Initiative	Goal
Upgrade technology	Reduce cost, improve quality. and reliability
Outsource manufacturing	Increase flexibility of manufacturing
Off-shore activities (manufacturing, customer service, etc.)	Reduce cost of activity
R&D joint venture	Reduce cost and risk of innovation
Expand market scope	Achieve economies of scale
Diversify into a new but related industry	Achieve economies of scope (transfer skills, share activities)
Implement global sourcing processes	Reduce cost of sourcing
Centralize IT in a multibusiness firm	Achieve synergies through activity sharing
Create a venture capital unit	Organize innovation initiatives independently from the routine business processes
Buy our local distributor's business	Improve control over our operation in a key market
Acquire a licence for use of a prestigious brand	Rapidly improve our brand position
Joint venture with a local firm in a foreign market	Fast and low-risk entry into a new market
Investment in a major TV advertising campaign	Increase brand awareness, reinforce strategic intent

strategic decisions to those of managerial and technical decisions. These constitute the 'day to day' of the competitive battle along the lines set by the strategic initiatives the firm has chosen.

1.3.2 FROM ACTION TO (REFRESHED) HYPOTHESES

The Strategic Intent that leads to Strategic Initiatives supported by a suitable Strategic Organization inspires a firm's actions in its competitive landscape. As an outcome of such action, the firm receives feedback that enables it to reflect on the adequacy of its actions. Such feedback can be positive, for example customers may run to buy the firm's products at a high price, or competitors may fail to react effectively and lose market share. When the adequacy of the firm's strategic posture is validated in the competitive landscape, the firm will reinforce its strategic direction and focus on the exploitation of its current situation through careful attention to day to day management.

However, the feedback can also be less favourable. Clients' reluctant reception to new products, competitors' aggressive responses to the firm's actions in the form of price cuts or intense promotion efforts or even lawsuits, or the government's decision to block an intended acquisition on grounds of anti-trust policy are examples of market responses that question the validity of the firm's strategic posture. When facing these situations, the challenge of the firm's top management is to understand the causes of such failure and to take the appropriate corrective action. A first difficulty is to determine whether the problem is a strategic one or not, as the implications in terms of the nature of the corrective actions required are quite different.

1.3.2.1 Doing the right things wrong: problems not demanding strategic changes

Failure to achieve the firm's strategic objectives could be the result of poor management of the day to day aspects of the firm's strategy. In these cases, we do not need to review our strategy, but just need to fine tune its execution. Examples of this situation are the shortage of a sufficient number of well seasoned middle managers following a fast expansion period, ignorance of best practices related to core processes, or low morale due to dysfunctional control and incentive systems. Case Box 1.1 accounts some of the issues surrounding the integration of Morrison and Safeway, an example of how the right strategy can be negatively affected by management problems.

1.3.2.1.1 Problems in the strategic posture. While management and technical problems are frequently at the root of a firm's poor performance, problems can

Case Box 1.1 Management issues during an M&A integration: Morrison's acquisition of Safeway

By 2003, William Morrison was a highly successful supermarket chain comprising 119 stores, mostly located in the north of the United Kingdom. Its record of 37 consecutive years of sales and profit growth made it a favourite in the City, even when Sir Ken Morrison, the founder's son and firm's leader for half a century, was legendary for his disdain for the 'best practices' widely followed by most FTSE 500 firms.

As the firm was strongly interested in expanding to the south of England and facing difficulties to do it through internal development due to the difficulties posed by urban planning restrictions, the opportunity to acquire Safeway, a struggling supermarket chain with a strong presence in the south was seen as a very sensible strategic option by Morrison. This view was shared by industry analysts and the specialized press. The acquisition eventually took place in 2004. Morrison expected to reduce the operating cost of the new merged operation by £250 million a year due to synergies. Morrison also expected to develop synergies due to knowledge transfer of Morrison's management practices to Safeway. However, the two first years of the joint company proved to be very difficult ones, leading Morrison to incur unexpected and unprecedented losses of £263 million in 2005. The reason for this dramatic fall in the firm's performance was mainly the difficulties faced during the process of integration of the two chains, characterized by some well-known management problems. First, Morrison assumed that 'they knew better' on management issues only because their performance was stronger than that of Safeway. Based on this assumption, Morrison fired 60 per cent of Safeway's corporate office staff while the rest felt marginalized from major decisions. However, being a firm four times bigger than Morrison, Safeway was used to dealing with far more complex operational and administrative challenges than those usually faced by Morrison. As a consequence of these massive layoffs of Safeway's personnel, much of the knowledge related to Safeway's complex management processes was lost. This situation eventually created some severe management difficulties for Morrison. First, Morrison's 'mainly paper based' information systems could not cope with the massive increase in size resulting from the merger. Safeway relied on sophisticated IT systems for supply chain management that the staff of Morrison were not equipped to handle properly. This led to erratic ordering patterns widely reported by suppliers.[2] Morrison also faced serious difficulties in understanding Safeway's complex accounting system, making the firm unable to give profit guidance to investors.

Another key management issue was Morrison's inaccurate planning of store conversion. Morrison initially expected to convert 358 of Safeway's stores, leaving 121 small stores operating under the Safeway brand as convenience stores. However, the (unanticipated) requirement to sell stores from the Competition Commission and the difficulties associated to operate some mid-size stores with more tailored product ranges led Morrison to eventually keep only 220 stores of the 358 planned and sell the rest mostly to Somerfield.

Eventually the firm acknowledged the importance of the knowledge base from Safeway's executives for the success of the new venture. In 2006, two years after the merger, CEO Bob Stott expressed the importance of learning from the 'newer colleagues'. (Annual Report 2006)

[2] *Financial Times*, 18 June 2005, page 3.

sometimes transcend these levels and they then belong to the more complex realm of the firm's strategic posture. In these cases, the roots of the problem need to be found at the level of the building blocks of such strategic posture, identified in Figure 1.1. While all the building blocks of the Strategic Posture of the firm are intimately related, strategic problems are likely to have a 'centre of gravity' around one of these blocks.

1.3.2.1.2 Problems centred in Strategic Organization. On many occasions, failure to perform adequately is caused by dysfunctional organizational design. Poor organization of the effort supporting the strategic intent and initiatives of the firm may damage even the most brilliant strategic posture.

For instance, excessive bureaucracy, a culture focused in short-term achievement, and the lack of proper processes to support innovation hindered IBM's ability to develop new products and take its share of the rapid growth experienced in the technology sector during the 1990s (see Case Box 5.3). Case Box 1.2 analyses the experience of ABB during the late 1990s. By then,

---

Case Box 1.2 Strategic reorganizing: ABB after the matrix

The story of ABB under Percy Barnevik's leadership is arguably one of the most popular examples of audacious and innovative management. One of the central elements of this story was ABB's decision to organize its global operations under a matrix structure, in an attempt to equalize the power between the two forces that drove the success of their engineering business: local responsiveness and global industrial integration. Local responsiveness was imperative, as most of the orders for ABB's products were awarded at a national level, making close contacts with clients (mostly governments owning utilities) and quick, proactive decision-making crucial for success. Only the empowerment of local managers would make ABB, a firm controlling 1,300 companies in 140 countries, achieve such local responsiveness. Conversely, for such a big and complex firm, there were obvious economic forces that favoured integration such as economies of scale in R&D and purchasing, the need to optimize production and product allocation, high potential for cross-border knowledge transfer, the need of a worldwide market allocation strategy, and the need for integrated systems for clear accountability of the 4,000 profit centres worldwide.

However, the competitive landscape of ABB changed substantially by the late 1990s. After a strong global wave of privatizations of public sector firms, new projects started to be financed independently rather than publicly, and global tenders were organized by the new private owners of the firms, replacing the traditional process based on the local awards of orders by national or regional governments. In addition, the markets became cost based, while ABB was a high quality but rather expensive firm.

The new CEO Goran Lindahl stated that 'our business is now a global business and it is no longer appropriate to optimize on a local level with local P&Ls. The matrix makes ABB too cumbersome to run'. As a consequence, he removed the matrix structure replacing it by a more traditional divisional organization organized by industry with a total of seven industries. In this way the now unnecessary empowerment of the local national structures was eliminated making the firm simpler, easier to run, and reducing overheads.

the company engaged in a major reorganization effort as its well-known matrix-type organizational design was dysfunctional for the novel requirements of its competitive landscape.

Organizational problems may be easily confused with non-strategic problems, as poor structures are likely to damage the performance of middle managers creating the idea that they are responsible for the failures. In the case of IBM, the failure of several product innovation projects during the 1990s was attributed to the project leaders' lack of political skills to navigate its complex matrix structure. Managers who blamed the cumbersome structure for their failure to succeed in leading innovation initiatives were deemed 'weak' (Garvin and Levesque 2004). Eventually, after doing some thorough research the firm's top management realized that IBM's organization was inadequate for innovation to blossom. Its structure and processes rewarded only short-term incremental initiatives and discouraged the long-term radical thinking and experimenting that characterizes major innovation. Solving organizational problems demands the active intervention of top management, as in any other strategic problem, but also requires active participation of middle managers both in diagnosing the problems and in leading and supporting the implementation of the new organizational practices.

1.3.2.1.3 Problems centred in the Strategic Initiatives. The strategic problems that mean that the firm is unable to perform as expected in their competitive landscape may also have their source in a poor practical craft of the Strategic Intent around effective strategic initiatives. The efforts of British food retailers, such as Waitrose, Sainsbury or Marks & Spencer to strengthen their range of premium ready-meals have been undermined by the rise of food commodities prices which pushed food inflation in the United Kingdom to 13.7 per cent by mid-2008. Higher prices squeezed consumers' budgets and led them to trade down, choosing own brands, and moving towards value retailers, a situation that benefited players such as Aldi and Lidl.

Another example of a strategic failure at the level of the strategic initiative was Toshiba's strong endorsement of HD-DVD technology in its attempt to set the standard for the new wave of DVD players suitable for the requirements of High Definition Television (HDTV). Eventually, the rival standard Blu-Ray, backed mainly by Sony, prevailed obliging Toshiba to stop production of HD-DVD players dismantling the whole organization built around the business (see Case Box 4.4). The redesign of strategic initiatives is a problem concerning mainly the top and middle management of the firm. If the new initiatives demand changes in the organization's design, as is usually the case, middle managers need also to have a central role leading and supporting its implementation.

1.3.2.1.4 Problems centred in the Strategic Intent. This is the least desired scenario for any company, as it involves a fundamental reassessment of its more fundamental beliefs about the 'whats' and the 'hows' of its business. Decisions such as engaging important resources in a diversification move, divesting from a core business, expanding or shrinking the geographic scope of the firm substantially, or modifying the generic strategy of the firm constitute examples of alteration of its strategic intent. For instance, IBM's decision to sell its PC group to Lenovo in 2004 or Apple's diversification initiatives leading to the development of the enormously successful iPod digital music player in 2001 and the iPhone in 2007, constitute examples of changes in Strategic Intent. In these situations, the fundamental and usually complex political decisions leading to the firm's overall value proposition need to be revised as the firm realizes that the very first premises framing the whole effort of the firm are flawed. Decisions to change the Strategic Intent involve not only the top management but also the whole governance structure of the firm. The Board of Directors and eventually influential shareholders ('blockholders') or partners are involved in these decisions. Case Box 1.3 summarizes the situation faced by Ficosa International, a car component manufacturing firm, when it had to migrate from its position as a producer of relatively simple car components for the car plants operating in the highly protected Spanish market to become a designer and supplier of integrated components at a European scale.[3] As the account of Ficosa's hardships and recovery reveals, changing the Strategic Intent is always a painful, high risk decision that also involves a major reformulation of most if not all of the firm's strategic initiatives and a major re-organization.

Case Box 1.3 Redefining the strategic intent: Ficosa International S.A

After the end of the Second World War, Spain suffered an international economic embargo against General Franco's regime. The country lacked a local automobile industry, and isolation led to a severe shortage of spare parts for cars. This created an opportunity for local companies to enter this business by substituting for imports. In this context, in 1949 Ficosa was founded with the purpose of supplying brake, clutch, and speedometer cables for used cars. In the early 1950s, the Spanish state created SEAT, a car manufacturer, thus boosting the national demand for car components. Ficosa seized this opportunity to expand its business beyond the cable business, becoming a supplier for new automobiles and trucks. By 1986, Ficosa was the leader of the Spanish cable, windscreen wiper, and rear-view mirror markets. Thanks to protectionist Spanish legislation, the company faced no significant international competition.

Major changes in Ficosa's competitive landscape
A major shift in Ficosa's competitive landscape began in 1986 and lasted for nearly a decade. On 1 January 1986, a significant event drastically and definitively changed the Spanish

(Continued)

---

[3] An exhaustive account of Ficosa's transition from a local to a global status can be found in Caldart and Canals (2002).

economy when the government agreed the country's entry into the EU (then the EEC). This was the beginning of the end of Spain's isolation from Europe. Besides this regulatory breakthrough, which exposed Ficosa to international competition, the auto components sector also had been undergoing important changes since the late 1970s and early 1980s.

Traditionally, European car manufacturers had developed their components in the countries where they manufactured their vehicles. In the late seventies, however, this practice began to change. Car manufacturers began to centralize component development in their regional headquarters. They also gradually stopped developing the components entirely themselves; instead, they started to share the development effort and costs with component manufacturers, transferring the engineering costs to them. This meant that the car makers' traditional policy of working with a large number of national suppliers, selected on a short-term basis, was replaced by a policy of dealing with a smaller number of more highly specialized suppliers, working under long-term agreements.

These changes wiped out Ficosa's main advantages as a tier-one supplier to Spanish automobile plants. Once component design and development decisions began to be made near the car companies' headquarters outside Spain, Ficosa's strong local commercial relationships in Spain were no longer essential. Moreover, its previous position as 'King of Spain'[4] in the components industry would be threatened by EU deregulation in 1993.

In light of the drastic changes affecting its industry, Ficosa's Chairman and then also CEO, Mr Pujol, understood that, from then on, the strategic intent of the firm had to be reviewed for two main reasons. First, because the firm's market scope changed, making the EU their natural market space instead of just Spain. Second, because the centralization of the car manufacturers' component design and development decisions meant that component suppliers would have to have a presence close to the decision centres, located primarily in Germany, the United Kingdom, France, and Italy. Third, because in order to position itself as a partner of car companies' long-term component development programmes, a component supplier would need to have an image of technological strength, obliging Ficosa to develop new technological capabilities and to create its reputation from scratch.

These 'exploratory' moves, reviewed in Case Box 1.3, represented a higher risk for the firm as it abandoned its well developed, but obsolete, strategy to pursue new avenues that, while more adequate for the new competitive reality, obliged the firm to explore unchartered territory. A shareholders' meeting was called to consider whether to start a European expansion plan, to sell the firm, or to continue with the current position. The first option was chosen.

Mr Roig summarized the sensitivity of the moment: 'we realised the need to battle for at least five or six years in Europe, before knowing whether this strategy would lead us to success or to a definitive failure. The uncertainty associated to this move led some of our long time minority partners to sell their participations before we began our expansion in Europe.'

Luján's new strategic initiatives

To hold on to its tier-one supplier status, Ficosa would have to build a presence in the automotive industry's European decision centres, where as yet it was a rather unknown player. For Luján, expanding into Europe from Spain entailed many challenges. First, it would require a huge financial effort, particularly for a privately held company with a turnover of only 37 million euros. Second, there would have to be a change in the organization's mindset, from being a technology follower with hardly any R&D to becoming a technology partner of car manufacturers. Third, the company would have to absorb the organizational and cultural impact of becoming a multinational and competing in countries with highly dynamic business environments. 'Our people had to get used to the idea that there would be many non-Spaniards in high management positions', commented the CEO.

---

[4] An expression used by one interviewee.

(Continued)

Case Box 1.3 (*Continued*)

Finally, Ficosa would have to rebuild all of its customer relationships virtually from scratch, as it barely had commercial relations with the car makers' European headquarters in the past.

The new strategic intent was materialized in corporate vision and was given expression in an international expansion plan aimed at positioning the company as a major European component manufacturer for all its product lines. The tactic to create a presence close to the clients' decision centres was to open Engineering Centres in each target country, led by native engineers hired 'ad hoc', with the purpose of building the company's reputation as an innovative European manufacturer. The Chairman remembered that 'we had to overcome the negative image that Spanish products tended to have in Europe in those days if we wanted to convince customers that we could become their technology partners. We had the advantage of being low cost producers, as the Spanish labour cost was then much lower than the German, French and British ones'. The purpose of the Engineering Centres was to establish strong relationships with the car manufacturers' R&D centres. In this way Ficosa opened Centres in the United Kingdom, France, and Germany between 1987 and 1988 and opened factories in the UK and France shortly after once orders started to flow.

Gradually, the firm established a reputation in Europe as a reliable, flexible, low cost technology partner. During the period 1986–2001, the company pursued strong organic growth, at a two digit compound rate and continued expanding its operations, not only in Europe but globally.

1.4 **Preliminary reflections and a roadmap for the book**

Our discussion so far leads us to make some reflections on the dynamics of the firm's strategy process. These reflections constitute starting points of the discussion to be developed throughout the book.

1.4.1 STRATEGIZING IS BOTH AN ANALYTICAL AND A SOCIAL PROCESS

As seen in the example of Ficosa, firms may face periods of strategic stability that enable them to keep the building blocks of their strategic postures barely unchanged, concentrating their focus on the managerial and technical aspects of the business. In these cases the firm's strategic plans tend to be quite accurate, as the rules of the game in the competitive landscape are known and relatively stable, creating the illusion that a firm can strategize in an analytical way.

The illusion of control of the competitive landscape led to the emergence of a strong rationalist intellectual tradition in the field of strategic management from its origins in the 1960s. Scholars working under this perspective were mostly based in the United States and were highly influenced by the comfortable strategic position faced by American firms as they operated in a vast, growing local market with little foreign competition. These perspectives put the stress on the importance of strategy design and strategic planning, leading to bodies of work currently referred to as the Design and the Planning Schools of Strategy (Mintzberg et al. 1998). This perspective conceives strategy making as a linear process in which thought always precedes action, obscuring the recursive nature of strategic thinking and action.

Once we adopt a recursive view of the strategy process we develop a different view of the role of strategic planning. Strategic analyses and plans developed out of these are useful as tools that help to communicate, coordinate, and articulate the strategy. However they are not useful as long-term projections of 'what will happen', as the hypotheses they are based on need to be continuously contrasted with the dynamic reality in which the firm's actions are embedded.

In cases of high stability in the competitive landscape, it is not pure rational analysis that explains the firm's strategic success, but the fact that the main strategic variables characterizing the firm's environment have behaved predictably, enabling the firm to maintain its strategic posture unchanged. This stability may derive from exogenous reasons such as a stable and rather predictable macroeconomic environment, as it was the case of the European economy from 1994 through to 2006. Stability also may be the result of endogenous reasons. This is the case when the variables that characterize competition, such as product prices, raw material prices, the cost of labour, degree of customer service, quality, and regulatory framework fluctuate in a stable or at least a rather predictable way. In these highly desirable situations, we can permit ourselves the 'luxury' of running our business taking our strategic position for granted.

However, 'good things never last', and competitive landscapes are periodically shaken up by changes. These can be the result of factors such as technology breakthroughs (e.g. the development of digital technology in photography), a major regulatory change (e.g. the recent enlargement of the EU to 27 members), the entry of new players with new business models (e.g. online retailers), change in economic conditions (such as the 2007–8 'credit crunch' and skyrocketing increases and then decreases in commodity prices), or new social values (e.g. the rise of 'green' consciousness in Europe). In these situations, the key variables that characterize a particular competitive landscape become more volatile, obliging the firm to focus actively on a review of its strategic posture.

1.4.2 STRATEGY AS A SOCIO-POLITICAL ACTIVITY WITH ECONOMIC OBJECTIVES

A comprehensive understanding of the nature of the firm's strategy process demands a realization that, while the economic drivers and purposes of the firm's decisions need to be at the forefront of any analysis, it is also necessary to realize that the process of making decisions on strategic intent, strategic initiatives, and organization design is essentially a political one. As strategic decisions are open problems, not subject to 'programming' or formalization, any conflict related to how to craft the firm's strategic posture is settled on power grounds.

The interaction between firms in the competitive landscape is also a political process, as the firm's ultimate goal is to develop sustainable competitive advantages that enable the firm to exercise a degree of control over its market, reducing the uncertainty associated with its strategic posture.

In this book, we acknowledge this need for interdisciplinary fertilization, integrating the Industrial Economics tradition with several threads of thought derived from political science, psychology, sociology, and the complexity sciences that constitute the body of knowledge of modern Organization Theory.

1.4.3 ORGANIZATION OF THE BOOK

The chapters of the book have been organized along three different types of contents:

a) *Conceptual Content.* This content constitutes the core of each chapter. We focus on reviewing major contributions in the field of Industrial Economics and Organization Theory, as well as on introducing contributions developed out of the authors' research and practice.

b) *Conceptual Boxes.* We use these to 'zoom in' on certain theoretical topics to benefit the reader especially interested in the in-depth technical or conceptual background of the ideas developed in the conceptual content.

c) *Case Boxes.* These help the reader to put the conceptual concepts 'into action' by observing them in the context of 'real life' companies or industries.

In the first part of the book, 'The Competitive Landscape' (Chapters 2 to 4), we discuss extensively the dynamics of strategizing focusing on the Strategic Intent and the strategic initiatives focused on the external environment.

Chapter 2 strongly draws on the tradition of Industrial Organization (IO) economics and focuses on the discussion of formal models of competition. These models constituted the building blocks of any competition analysis during most of the past century, but recently their effectiveness at understanding dynamic conditions has been questioned. While IO models are at the core of the current controversy between different paradigms of strategy research, they constitute powerful analytical tools leading to potentially powerful insights.

Chapter 3 relies on recent advances in the field of Strategic Management to analyse theoretical approaches to devising strategy in turbulent and volatile market conditions, which oblige firms to enter into active rather than passive strategizing. New tools and techniques such as agent-based models can be used to model these dynamic conditions.

Chapter 4 takes a stronger network stance and reviews the strategic implications of social networks and other forms of organizational networks. While the analysis of social networks has a tradition spanning four decades in sociology and organization theory, its recent popularization is due to the widespread development of online social networks, which often remain elusive as a means of setting strategy within firms.

In the second part of this book, 'The Organizational Landscape', we start (Chapters 5 and 6) focusing on the third building block of the strategy process, the organization of the firm consistent with the firm's strategic intent and initiatives. In Chapter 5, we review the evolution of thought on organizations: analysing, contrasting, and integrating rational and natural systems paradigms. We also investigate work focused on the practice of organizing.

Chapter 6 is centred on the analysis of the tradition of work focused on the powerful idea of feedback thought, the cornerstone of any dynamic approach to organization and strategic studies. After reviewing the development of this concept, we focus in particular on two current theoretical traditions: system dynamics and complexity theory.

In Chapter 7, we integrate the analysis of the dynamics of the competitive and the organizational landscape using a co-evolutionary perspective. We rely strongly on the use of agent-based simulation models as a method that enables us to explore jointly the dynamics of the competitive landscape and those of the organization.

PART I
THE COMPETITIVE LANDSCAPE

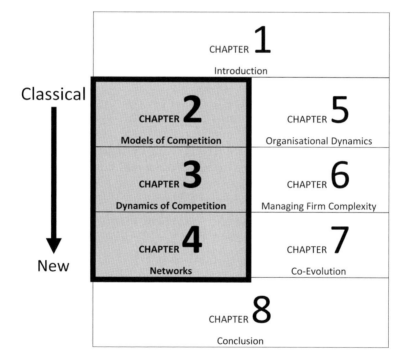

Introduction to Part I

Part 1 of the book concentrates on the interactions *between* firms, as shown in Figure 1.2. We focus particularly on the competitive nature of inter-firm competition. Competing firms constitute the *competitive landscape* of the industry (the internal or organizational landscape of the firm is covered in Part II). How firms are positioned and how firms move on this competitive landscape can be a source of sustainable competitive advantage.

Since the early days of strategic management, the dominant lens under which advances have been made is that of economics. The 'structure-conduct-performance' paradigm (Mason 1939; Bain 1956) originally developed in Industrial Organization Economics pervaded early work in strategic management. This focus has led to an over-concentration on finding an equilibrium state to investigate the attractiveness of industries or markets. In Chapter 2, we investigate some of these models, such as game theoretic models, industrial organization models of Cournot competition, and Hotelling's model of spatial competition. We consider how we can view firms competing on this competitive landscape, and how we can represent this competition in terms of firms' position on strategic landscapes, looking to understand how we can construct the dimensions of these landscapes on which firms compete – the 'strategy hypercube'. In Chapters 3 and 4, we introduce models that provide alternative perspectives, each with their own particular way of considering the dynamics of the competitive environment faced by firms. In doing so, we introduce new tools such as agent-based models and network analysis. This part of the book concentrates on the interactions *between* firms, as shown in the following chapters.

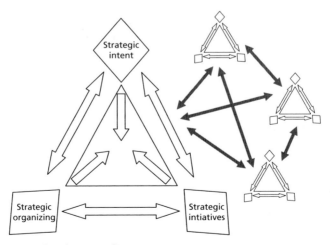

Figure 1.2. Interactions between firms

2 Models of Competition

2.1 Introduction

In this chapter, we review traditional approaches of inter-firm competition, concentrating on models that have their genesis in economics. Much of the early literature on strategic management was heavily influenced by this economic view. We set out a selection of the models and frameworks, and then discuss critically their suitability for analysing the dynamics of competition. This early view of strategic management field centred in Industrial Organization economics was based on models that have as their underpinning the notion of competitive equilibrium. In later chapters, we shall introduce alternative models that are able to go beyond the equilibrium-inspired view, but it is important to understand how equilibrium models work in order to see the need to extend these models and how to do it.

Economics as a discipline pervades strategic management, cutting across the external and the internal views of strategy: the external, industry-level analysis covered in this chapter of Porter (1980) traces its theory to industrial organization economists such as Bain (1956) and the 'structure-conduct-performance' paradigm, while the internal-facing paradigm of the resource-based view (Barney 1991; Wernerfelt 1984), covered in Chapter 3, traces its ancestry back to Penrose (1959). These views are characterized by their very general and robust (while somewhat heroic) assumptions regarding the behaviour of the firms. As such, we can explicitly formalize the firms' competitive environment, and formally model their actions and reactions. These neoclassical models assume that each actor (or firm) will maximize their own utility and behave *rationally*. This is a central theme of these models, and we set out the fundamental assumptions.

2.2 Utility and rationality

Firms maximize profits. Or at least that is what we are told by mainstream neoclassical economists. However, in the 1960s, along with the birth of strategic management, these fundamental views of the economic orthodoxy began to be challenged. Cyert and March (1963) proposed an alternate, behavioural theory of the firm. In this theory, the behaviour of a firm is such that, due to the multiple dimensions over which firms operate, they cannot maximize an overall utility function, rather they exhibit *satisficing* behaviour where they reach a satisfactory, acceptable level of performance rather than an optimal, 'profit maximizing' level. Later in this chapter, we shall even see, with the help of game theoretic models, that profit maximizing behaviour can actually be detrimental to performance. But before that, we will take a look at the concepts of utility and rationality that are assumed by neoclassical economics.

The concept of utility can be traced to the economist Edgeworth who in 1881 wrote in his book *Mathematical Psychics*, 'It is argued from mathematical considerations that the basis of arbitration between contractors is the greatest possible utility of all concerned.' The concept of utility was taken up by game theorists in the 1940s, with von Neumann and Morgenstern (1944) writing 'we feel ... that one part of our assumptions at least – that of treating utilities as numerically measurable quantities – is not quite as radical as is often assumed in the literature'. The concept of utility is that there is a quantifiable benefit of possessing goods or using services. We can measure this utility, and therefore rank differing options, for example which good or service to consume. This leads us to the concept of rationality.

Rationality is a term that pervades classical and neo-classical economics. It is based on the assumption that people behave like a *homo economicus*, or *Economic Man*. The homo economicus is a rational, perfectly informed, and *self-interested* agent who desires to possess wealth, avoids unnecessary labour, and has the ability to make precise judgements towards those ends. In terms of utility, this means that individuals will set out to maximize their utility, choosing between options on the basis of optimizing choices on the basis of a quantifiable measure, that of utility. However, this concept assumes, and is conditional upon, the belief that complete information is available for all individuals. If this is not the case, the decisions that will be made may not in fact maximize the individual's utility function – their decisions are, in the words of Herbert Simon, *boundedly* rational (Simon 1957a).

We review models of how firms are positioned in their competitive landscape through decisions on the price to charge, the quantity to be produced, or the choice of spatial location by building on two seminal models of economic competition: Hotelling's model of spatial competition, and Cournot and Bertrand's models that focus (indirectly) on price.

2.3 **Economic models**

Economic models are a fundamental component in the corpus of work on strategic management. In the following, we set out models from economics that consider two dimensions of competition: the Cournot model, where firms decide the quantity of goods to produce, Bertrand competition where firms decide the price to set, the Hotelling model where firms decide where to compete spatially, and game theory, where firms decide which 'strategy' to play. The Cournot and Bertrand models are models of *oligopoly*, that is to say idealized situations where there are few firms competing for many customers.

2.3.1 COURNOT AND BERTRAND COMPETITION

In this section we review the Cournot Model (Cournot 1838), a model of competitive industries in which firms make decisions by acting rationally, trying to maximize profits, and strategically, taking into account its competitors' decisions at the time of making their own. Augustin Cournot (1838) considered in his book *Researches into the Mathematical Principles of the Theory of Wealth* in the chapter 'On the Competition of Producers', the situation where two firms in a market compete solely on the grounds of what quantity of their product they should produce. The price of the goods produced (the goods from company 1 and company 2 are identical) is set by the market. We can assume that total costs to the producers are proportional to the quantity that they produce. For instance, if firm 1 produces Q_1 units of production, and the cost per unit is £10, then its total costs C_1 are $C_1 = 10Q_1$. If we assume that firm 2 has the same cost per unit, then the total costs of firm 2 are $C_2 = 10Q_2$. Cournot assumed that the market fixes the price of the goods (there is no differentiation between the products).

The strategic decision for each firm is the quantity to produce. But how should firms, behaving rationally, compute this amount? As they are behaving rationally, firms act to maximize their expected profits from production.

Under Cournot equilibrium, firms will satisfy the following three conditions:

- The price charged at equilibrium (denoted by an asterisk), P^*, is the market-clearing price $P^* = 100 - Q_1^* - Q_2^*$
- The quantity produced by firm 1 will be firm 1's profit-maximizing output given its estimate of firm 2's output, i.e. the quantity produced by firm 2; and
- The quantity produced by firm 2 will be firm 2's profit-maximizing output given its estimate of firm 1's output, i.e. the quantity produced by firm 1.

We know that the profit, π, for each firm will be the price multiplied by the quantity produced, minus the total cost of production. We know the formula for the price (set by the market) and the cost (related to the quantity produced by firm 1). Conceptual Box 2.1 shows the formal derivation of the Cournot equilibrium, where both firms are at equilibrium and there is no incentive for either firm to alter their quantity, as doing so would lead to a

Conceptual Box 2.1 Solving the Cournot model

The Cournot model can be solved as follows:

Total costs for Firm 1 and Firm 2 (C_1 and C_2) are

$C_1 = 10\,Q_1$

$C_2 = 10\,Q_2$

The price is set by the market in a downward sloping demand curve:

$P = 100 - Q_1 - Q_2$

Firms maximize their profits:

$\pi_1 = \text{revenue} - \text{cost}$

$= P_1 Q_1 - C_1$

$= (100 - Q_1 - Q_2)\,Q_1 - 10\,Q_1$

$= 100\,Q_1 - Q_1^2 - Q_2\,Q_1 - 10\,Q_1$

$= 90\,Q_1 - Q_1^2 - Q_2\,Q_1$

When profit is maximized, the derivative of the profit function is zero ($\partial\pi_1/\partial Q_1 = 0$)

Differentiating the profit function (assuming that Q_2 is constant):

$$\frac{\partial\pi_1}{\partial Q_1} = 90 - 2Q_1 - Q_2 = 0$$

$$\Rightarrow Q_1 = \frac{90}{2} - \frac{Q_2}{2}$$

This quantity level is the best response of Firm 1. We can plot this on a graph (below) and draw the reaction function of Firm 1.

Firms will both produce an output of 30, making a profit each of $90\,Q_1 - Q_1^2 - Q_2\,Q_1 = 90.30 - 30^2 - 30.30 = 2700 - 900 - 900 = 900$ (see Figure 2.1).

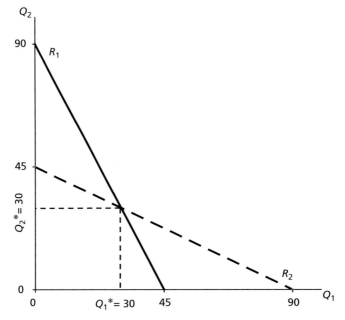

Figure 2.1. The Cournot model

(Continued)

Comparison with Monopoly Profits

We can calculate the monopoly profit, that is the price that a monopolist would charge if they were free to choose prices. As before, we have fixed marginal costs for the firms, and prices that reflect the supply in the market (we do not need a subscript 1, as there is only one firm)

$$C = 10\,Q$$
$$P = 100 - Q$$

We can calculate profits as given earlier:

$$\pi = \text{revenue} - \text{cost}$$
$$= PQ - C$$
$$= (100 - Q)\,Q - 10\,Q$$
$$= 100\,Q - Q^2 - 10\,Q$$
$$= 90\,Q - Q^2$$

As mentioned previously, we can calculate the quantity that maximizes profits. When profit is maximized, the derivative of the profit function is zero ($\partial\pi/\partial Q = 0$)

Differentiating the profit function:

$$\frac{\partial\pi}{\partial Q} = 90 - 2Q = 0$$

$$\Rightarrow Q = \frac{90}{2} = 45$$

We can then calculate the monopoly price and the monopoly profit:

$$P = 100 - Q = 100 - 45 = 55$$
$$\pi = 90\,Q - Q^2$$
$$= 90.\,45 - (45^2)$$
$$= 4050 - 2025$$
$$= 2025$$

Cournot Adjustment

The Cournot model is sometimes thought of as dynamic, as both firms can be thought of as 'adjusting' to the other firm's quantity. An example of how a firm, indicated in bold, may adjust is set out in the following (although later we shall see firms in the model jump immediately to the equilibrium quantities).

Starting Q_1	Starting Q_2	Firm Adjusting	Ending Q_1	Ending Q_2
40	40	Firm 1	**25**	40
25	40	Firm 2	25	**32.5**
25	32.5	Firm 1	**28.75**	32.5
28.75	32.5	Firm 2	28.75	**30.63**
28.75	30.63	Firm 1	**29.69**	30.63

reduced profit. As the firms are behaving rationally, they do not move from this level of output.

Firms will produce quantities that produce profits below the profit attainable if there was only one firm, the so-called monopoly profit. Firms will then be at equilibrium. Equilibrium industry output does not maximize industry profits: pursuit of firms' self-interest does not maximize the profits of the industry as a whole. The Cournot model, although seen as an adjustment process, is actually a static model – firms will anticipate their opponent's strategic move and jump straight to the equilibrium rather than sequentially change their quantities (and hence prices).

In such industrial organization models, economists assume that industries are such that, due to entry barriers, there is little scope for new entrants to undermine the competitive structure of the industry. Therefore, by setting their output to maximize profits, the market will determine prices higher than the perfectly competitive equilibrium price, and firms will benefit, in a sustained manner, from these industry conditions. Bain (1956: 3) defines these entry barriers as 'the advantage of established sellers in an industry over potential entrant sellers, these advantages being reflected in the extent to which established sellers can persistently raise their prices above a competitive level without attracting new firms to enter the industry'. The existence of entry barriers that cannot be surpassed by potential market entrants is the reason why Cournot equilibrium prices (and hence profits) can be maintained. If it were not for the entry barriers, other firms would enter the industry, lowering the industry's average profitability.

However, the equilibrium that exists under Cournot competition is interesting. If we compare the profits available to a monopolist (a single firm operating in the market), we find that the total profits of the firm are less than the monopoly profit. This Cournot equilibrium falls into the same trap as the Prisoner's Dilemma game theory model, which we shall review later in this chapter, in that firms are at an equilibrium that is sub-optimal. If the firms colluded, they could produce a quantity that allowed higher industry profits (we shall see later that this is called the Pareto optimal solution). Of course, if firms are generating higher profits, this means that someone – in this case consumers – are losing out. Therefore, as a matter of public policy, governments intervene to make this collusion between firms to exploit consumers illegal (see Conceptual Box 2.3).

Although the Cournot and the similar Bertrand (1883) model described in the following are sometimes considered as dynamic models, in that there appears to be a *path* to the equilibrium outcome which can be modelled as a response to the other firm's output decision, this trajectory is in fact an economic device to demonstrate how the equilibrium is achieved. The players in fact do not follow these trajectories, but jump instantaneously to the equilibrium point. As we shall see in Chapter 3, we can construct an agent-based model for a similar problem, that of the Hotelling equilibrium, that can show the individual actions and reactions of players, the equilibrium from the agent-based model being the same as the analytical equilibrium result from the economists' model.

2.3.1.1 Bertrand competition

Fifty years after Cournot had published his model, Joseph Bertrand reviewed Cournot's book, and proposed an extension to Cournot's model where, instead of firms setting the *quantities*, they adjust the *price* of the goods produced. Bertrand pointed out that there was a shortcoming in Cournot's argument: even though the solution holds in equilibrium, if one of the producers were to reduce their price by an infinitesimal amount, that producer would attract all buyers, which would then mean that the competitor would have to reduce their price to below the competitor's price, and so on leading to a 'price spiral' until the firms would be charging the cost of production. In this situation, no firm would want to reduce their price still further, as they would incur a loss. This is the price that would be charged under *perfect competition*, a situation characterized by the existence of many suppliers producing identical products. As we shall see later, this is an example of a Nash equilibrium.

It is interesting to note that even though the Bertrand and Cournot competition models have very similar assumptions, they produce vastly different outcomes: in the Cournot model, firms make profits, whereas in the Bertrand model, firms do not.

2.3.2 SPATIAL COMPETITION: HOTELLING'S MODEL

One of the most elegant models in economics, in which firms compete by setting their location, is the spatial competition model introduced by Hotelling (1929). Harold Hotelling pondered the situation where firms decide where to compete in the idealized situation represented in Figure 2.2.

In this model, customers are distributed uniformly along a space referred to as 'Main Street'. Two firms (the model assumes a duopoly) are competing for these customers. We can think of examples such as ice-cream sellers who tend to locate their carts strategically on a beach of length l in order to maximize their profits. Buyers transport their purchases home at a cost of c per unit distance. Firms set their prices to maximize their profits, and both

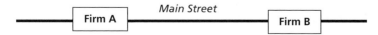

Figure 2.2. Hotelling's model

firms produce an identical good (as in models discussed earlier, no product differentiation is assumed).

This model can be thought of as a two-stage game where firms first choose their locations and secondly set their prices. Hotelling proposes an equilibrium, but subsequent authors have shown (Vickrey 1964: 323–34; d'Aspremont et al. 1979) that the strategies of firms (i.e. locations along the spatial dimension) chosen by the firms are not in equilibrium.

Hotelling's model can be thought of as strategic in nature – firms position themselves in space (albeit a one-dimensional space). Customers are considered fixed, and firms are able to change their prices. Hotelling asserts that there is an incentive for firms to move as close as possible to each other (in the example given earlier, firm A has an incentive to move to the right to capture more market share, and firm B has an incentive to move to the left to capture more market share, the equilibrium is obtained when A and B are located immediately next to each other. Hotelling asserted that if customers were not uniformly distributed, the equilibrium point for the firms would be at the location of the median of the distribution of customers so that both firm A and firm B each capture 50 per cent of the market share. Further extensions have been made to Hotelling's model, such as making the linear dimension circular so that there are no end points in the space (Salop 1979) and extending the model into two spatial dimensions (Christaller 1966, Lösch 1967).

What is interesting is that this problem, that of positioning, is not confined to economics: Downs' *Economic Theory of Democracy* (1957*a*, 1957*b*) extends Hotelling's model from a physical space (the 'Main Street' as used in Hotelling's model) to a space where the two actors, rather than being consumers and producers, are voters and political parties, hence the title 'economic' model of democracy. As we shall see in later chapters, the notion of the translation of models from one discipline to another is very worthwhile when analysing the dynamics of strategy. Rather than thinking that we should be confined to models from economics, there are many models from other natural or social sciences that can be of use in solving our management challenges. One of the characteristics of the Downs model is that it situates two different types of agents – in this case political parties and voters – within a space with the same dimensions. Even though voters and parties are clearly different, and even though intra-type variations may be large (e.g. two voters may have very different positions on other dimensions that are not included in Downs' formulation), they are both allowed to populate the same space. This will become important when we consider two different but similar agent types within strategic management, firms (analogous to parties in Downs' model), and customers (analogous to voters in Downs' model). Even though Downs places strong assumptions in his model (that there is only one strategy dimension along which parties position themselves, and the fact that in Downs' model there are only two political parties), this formulation can be extended further to more than two dimensions. The concurrence of two different types – voters and political parties – can be thought of as analogous to the product characteristics space envisaged by Lancaster (1966) where product dimensions required by customers (C-space) and those presented by firms (G-space) overlap. Even though voters and political parties may operate on several dimensions which are ignored by the other agent type, where there *is* overlap between types, the model can be constructed, and proves a very interesting and non-trivial problem. We shall see in Chapter 3 that the notion of having two different types of 'agents' will lend itself to being analysed by the use of agent-based models. Further research extending Downs' model has produced results that show that, when the assumption that there are only two political parties (or firms) is relaxed, there is no stable equilibrium. From an economist's or theoretical political scientist's perspective, this may mean that this model is no longer interesting, as it cannot be solved analytically. However, for us considering the situation where there are a (potentially large) number of firms competing for competitive advantage, we need to find alternative methods for analysing the problem. It can be noted that the problem of finding equilibrium with more than two parties has an analogue within the natural sciences. Where there are more than two 'bodies' in a system (e.g. three masses connected by springs), it may be impossible to determine the behaviour of the system; the system may become chaotic and intractable. This is a problem for economic modellers who try to analytically determine the equilibrium position of systems: it may be an impossible problem to 'solve'. This fascination with equilibrium can prevent further advances; such problems are seen as not 'important' from an economic perspective as they are unable to be solved analytically. This is what can set apart the domain of strategic management from that of economics – it is precisely the sort of problem that is seen as 'impossible' by economists that drives us to use new methods and techniques in order to analyse the problem.

As we shall see in Chapter 3, the number of strategic dimensions is a relevant feature of competition models. Real consumers are not restricted to one dimension of competition: they may have other attributes which are important when deciding where a firm should position itself. Lancaster (1966) refers to these dimensions as 'product space'. In Chapter 3, we shall use a model of spatial competition in two dimensions in order to investigate firm movement in multiple dimensions. We shall see that we can extend what essentially are static models by combining some of the features of the Cournot and Hotelling models in order to create a truly dynamic model of inter-firm competition.

The concepts of rationality and the idea that individuals can make decisions that maximize their utility, discussed earlier, are used extensively in the field of game theory. As we shall see, this rational behaviour can mean that in fact payoffs are *lower* than could be obtained if the players did not behave rationally. This seemingly perverse outcome is demonstrated later in the well known Prisoner's Dilemma game.

2.3.3 GAME THEORY

The concepts of rationality and the idea that individuals can make decisions that maximize their utility have been used extensively in the field of game theory. Game theory is concerned with understanding your competitor's reaction to your action. If we put ourselves in the mind of our competitor, particularly in a situation of few players, we are likely to be able to perform better than if we were to set our strategy with an assumption of *cerebus paribus*, or all other things being equal. The father of game theory, John von Neumann, first published his theory in 1928 in his paper 'Zur Theorie der Gesellschaftsspiele', translated as 'On the Theory of Games of Strategy'. The use of game theory is accepted widely as a tool throughout management (Ghemawat 1995) whereby more than one 'player' interacts with other players by playing certain strategies; the outcomes or 'payoffs' that are attributed to each player result from the interaction of these strategies.

We will illustrate the importance of considering our competitor's reaction to our strategy by reviewing one of game theory's best known problems, that of the 'Prisoner's Dilemma'.

2.3.3.1 The Prisoner's Dilemma

The Prisoner's (or Prisoners') Dilemma is a ubiquitous model within game theory, precisely due to the simplicity of the model and the interesting outcomes that are exhibited in the game. In the 'game', there are two 'players'. We can think of these players as being firms each with a strategy. In our simplified world of game theory, each has two possible strategies that they can 'play': to cooperate or to defect. We can think of these strategies as being to cooperate with an opponent or to compete with an opponent. We shall see that by *cooperating*, firms can in fact produce outcomes that are beneficial to both, 'win-win' situations. If however this presents a detriment to the con-sumer, where collusion is suspected, firms have to be attentive to anti-competitive and anti-trust legislation.

The outcomes from playing the game are called 'payoffs'. These are the profits, net income, or rents that both firms derive as part of playing the game. The crucial aspect of game theory is that your payoff *depends on the strategy of your opponent*. We can represent these payoffs in one or either of two ways, the 'normal' or 'extensive' representations.

The core assumptions of game theory are threefold. Firstly, the competitor will behave rationally and will try to win; secondly, the competitor is in an interdependent relationship with other competitors – the essence of the 'game'; and thirdly, competitors are aware of the interdependencies and of the moves that competitors could take. To benefit from game theory, strategists need to put

---

Conceptual Box 2.2 Game theory: The Prisoner's Dilemma

The Prisoner's Dilemma gets its name from the scenario where two suspects are accused of a crime. The 'payoffs' for the game can be represented as a *payoff matrix*, as follows:

Competitor A

Cooperate   Defect

		Cooperate	Defect

Competitor B

	Cooperate	2	3
		2	0
	Defect	0	1
		3	1

The payoff matrix shows, for each strategy adopted by Competitor A and Competitor B, the payoff (profit) derived by each of the players (which is in turn dependent upon each of the players' strategies).

The Prisoner's Dilemma represents a game of the form:

U_A (Defect, Cooperate) $> U_A$ (Cooperate, Cooperate) $> U_A$ (Defect, Defect) $> U_A$ (Cooperate, Defect)

where U_A represents the *utility* gained by Competitor A. The game in the case above is *symmetrical*, that is the utilities for each player playing the same strategy combinations are equal for example:

U_A (Defect, Cooperate) $= U_B$ (Defect, Cooperate) $= 3$
U_A (Cooperate, Cooperate) $= U_B$ (Cooperate, Cooperate) $= 2$
U_A (Defect, Defect) $= U_B$ (Defect, Defect) $= 1$
U_A (Cooperate, Defect) $= U_B$ (Cooperate, Defect) $= 0$

That is to say, each player has the same utility as the other (dependent of course on their strategy). The question for both players is which strategy to play. We can consider this by investigating the payoffs for each player. If we consider Competitor A, the decision they have to make is whether to choose the Defect or the Cooperate strategy. If we look at their payoffs, we have the following:

Competitor A

Cooperate   Defect

Competitor B

	Cooperate	**2**	**3**
	Defect	**0**	**1**

(Continued)

Conceptual Box 2.2 (*Continued*)

We can then consider Competitor A's choice to be dependent upon Competitor B's actions. If B chooses to Cooperate, A will have utility of 2 if it chose the Cooperate strategy, and will have a utility of 3 if it chose the Defect strategy. Therefore, A should choose Defect, as this offers a higher payoff. Similarly, if B chooses Defect, A will have a utility of 0 if it chose the Cooperate strategy, and utility of 1 if it chose the Defect strategy. So, for each and every option played by B, Cooperate or Defect, it is in A's interest to choose Defect. We say that strategy Defect *dominates* the Cooperate strategy. (We shall see later that this is an over-simplistic view.)

The same applies to the reasoning behind B's choice. From B's point of view:

Competitor A

Cooperate Defect

		Cooperate	Defect
Competitor B	**Cooperate**	2	0
	Defect	3	1

So, if A plays Cooperate, the options to B are to play Cooperate (with a payoff of 2), or to play Defect (with a payoff of 3). So, B chooses to play Cooperate. On the other hand, if A plays Defect, B has the choice of playing Cooperate (with a payoff of 0) or Defect (with a payoff of 1). Therefore, for both plays by A (Cooperate or Defect), B should choose to play Defect (as 3 > 2 and 1 > 0). So, as discussed earlier, the strategy Defect dominates the strategy of Cooperate. Putting this together, the payoffs to A and B, once their decision has been made, is as follows:

Competitor A

Cooperate Defect

		Cooperate	Defect
	Cooperate		
Competitor B			1
	Defect	1	

Both players therefore achieve a payoff of 1. This is called the *Nash Equilibrium* of the game, defined as an equilibrium where if a player were to unilaterally change their strategy, they would not benefit. However, if we look more closely at the game, we can see (with hindsight) that if both players had played Cooperate, both players would have had payoffs of 2. This is obviously higher than the payoff of 1 from the Nash Equilibrium solution. The solution of (Cooperate, Cooperate) is the *Pareto Optimal* solution to the game, defined as the solution to the game where no alternative solution exists where neither player would suffer and at least one player would benefit.

(*Continued*)

Competitor A

Cooperate   Defect

	2	
Cooperate	**2**	
Defect		

If we consider only our strategy without consideration for the other player in such bilateral competition, we risk an outcome that is sub-optimal for the players. The Nash Equilibrium that is achieved is not necessarily the Pareto Optimal solution.

themselves in the position of their competitors; they need to take an informed view on the likely competitor actions, and choose the best course of action.

Conceptual Box 2.2 shows how if players behave rationally, by attempting to maximize their utility, they will have an outcome that is sub-optimal for each of the players.

The Prisoner's Dilemma demonstrates that strictly rational behaviour can lead individuals to payoffs that are actually *lower* than those that could have been obtained if the players did not behave rationally.

Case Box 2.1 The battle of the video consoles

In October 2000, Sony revolutionized the video consoles market by launching its PlayStation 2, a console that, in addition to allowing the user to play the latest generation of videogames, enabled them to watch DVD movies and play CDs. In this way, entertainment needs normally provided by different products could be now satisfied with a single machine. Its launch price in the United States was $299.

By the end of 2001, PlayStation 2 started to face competition from two other new video consoles. Microsoft's Xbox was launched in November 2001 at a price of $299. In addition, Sony's traditional competitor Nintendo released the GameCube, a simpler video console that did not include DVD, at the substantially lower price of $199.

The first mover status of Sony enabled it to achieve a high installed base, which enabled it to achieve important competitive advantages against its rivals due to economies of scale in manufacturing. At these prices, industry analysts estimated that Microsoft was losing around $100 per Xbox sold and Nintendo $20 for each GameCube.

Market analysts disagreed on whether there was room for three players in the industry. Some of them forecasted that the three consoles would co-exist and eventually all would compete successfully. Others thought that one player would necessarily disappear citing as an antecedent Sega's withdrawal of the console Dreamcast that left the video console market for Sony and Nintendo in 2000, before Microsoft's entry.

(Continued)

Case Box 2.1 (*Continued*)

By April 2002, Xbox was failing to achieve the expected sales volumes, leading one of the business founders to quit and causing a massive reduction of 38.5 per cent in the price of the console in Europe and Australia only six weeks after its introduction in Europe, an all-time industry record. This move was imitated by Nintendo reducing the price of the Game Cube by approximately 20 per cent in Europe.

Microsoft's announcement of a price reduction for the Xbox in the United States was expected during the Electronic Entertainment Expo in May 2002. Pre-empting Microsoft's foreseeable move, by mid-May Sony startled the market by reducing the price of the Playstation 2 from $299 to $199, starting a price war in the sector. This move from the comfortable market leader neutralized the potential impact of Microsoft's expected move and caused a shock to Nintendo as the GameCube was already selling at $199 and did not include the DVD player function. The company then denied having plans to reduce the price of the GameCube. However, only a week later Nintendo's console could be bought in the United States at $150.

In an industry in which 'content rules', the three firms focused their strategy on trying to secure the exclusive services of the best game developers. In doing so, they integrated backwards acquiring game development firms or offered better conditions to the main suppliers.

By mid 2002, sales of PlayStation 2 (available in the market one year before its competitors) reached the 30 million units versus 4 million for GameCube consoles and between 3.5 and 4 million Xboxes. However, all the firms were losing money. Industry sources estimated that if Microsoft had not entered the market, Sony still would have reduced its price, but only to $249. The big winners of this price war were the consumers and the game developers who benefited from the better conditions offered by the three console manufacturers.

Despite Game Theory's robust assumptions that are difficult to replicate in the analysis of real-life competitive interaction, its strong call for a careful analysis of our competitors' reactions constitutes an important managerial insight. Failure to do so may result in ruinous competitive wars, as the one that took place in the video consoles market between 2001 and 2002, as illustrated in Case Box 2.1.

Case Box 2.2 The market for aspartame

Aspartame was invented in 1965 by James Schlatter, a chemist working for G. D. Searle & Company. Aspartame, the methyl ester of the dipeptide L-aspartyl-L-phenylalanine, is 100–200 times sweeter, by mass, than sugar, and therefore is an attractive ingredient for low-calorie foodstuffs. In 1974, the U.S. Food & Drug Administration approved the use of Aspartame for food use.

Companies who invest in research and development are rewarded for their investment by being given a legal monopoly over the manufacture of their invented product. This protection comes in the form of a patent, and gives the inventing company a limited time in which they can exploit this monopoly. At the end of the monopoly period, so-called 'generic' products can be produced without paying a licence fee to the patent holder.

Searle, the company that owned the Aspartame patent, was facing a problem. The patent in Europe was about to expire, and there was possible entry from new entrants such as the

(Continued)

Holland Sweetener Company (HSC) into what was promising to be an attractive market. Should Searle cooperate or compete with HSC? We can consider this through a game theoretical analysis: Searle has alternative strategies which it could play: of cooperating or competing. Using a Prisoner's Dilemma payoff matrix, we can see that the Pareto Optimal solution would be to cooperate, but a Nash equilibrium (where both parties would have lower profits) would be to compete. Searle is a much larger company than HSC (as we shall see later, equality of firm size needs to be considered in game theory), and large companies are able to sustain lower profits for a longer time than small companies. HSC was unable to be profitable in the aspartame industry, and withdrew from the aspartame business in 2006 (see Figure 2.3).

Figure 2.3. Website of Holland Sweetener Company, 2007

This case study draws from material and inspiration from van Witteloostuijn (1993); Brandenburger (1993), and United States General Accounting Office (1987). NutraSweet is a registered trade mark of NutraSweet Property Holdings, Inc.

As we can see in our account of competitive rivalry in the video console industry, the interactive nature of decisions and competitive moves between these three competitors triggered a price war wherein eventually all the firms were transferring value outside the industry, to clients and suppliers. Similarly, Brandenburger and Nalebuff (1997) use the example of the aspartame (an artificial sweetener) market in order to illustrate a game theoretical analysis, as shown in Case Box 2.2.

2.3.3.2 Co-opetition

In 1997, Brandenburger and Nalebuff applied the notions of game theory to business in their book 'Co-opetition'. Rather than considering other firms in the industry as being purely competitors, they claim that if other firms are also seen as potential co-operators, this may benefit all firms. The mobile phone handsets industry is a good example of successful co-opetition. Firms such as Nokia, Samsung, Sony Eriksson, and Panasonic are fierce competitors in hardware (handsets), but, at the same time, collaborate in the Symbian OS joint venture, sharing ownership of the Symbian Operating System for mobile phones. The rationale for this collaboration initiative between competitors is that by joining forces in Symbian, manufacturers share the benefits from owning the industry's dominant operating system and thereby preventing losing value in the hands of suppliers of alternative mobile operating systems, notably Microsoft through its products Windows CE and Windows Mobile.

In game theory terms, this may result in a Pareto Optimal solution rather than a Nash Equilibrium. We saw earlier that in the Bertrand competition model, firms will charge the marginal cost (and produce zero profits). There is however an alternative outcome to the Bertrand model: the firms could *collude*

Conceptual Box 2.3 The potential problems of cooperation and co-opetition The U.S. Sherman Act (1890)

'Sec. 1. Every contract, combination in the form of trust or otherwise, or conspiracy, in restraint of trade or commerce among the several States, or with foreign nations, is hereby declared to be illegal. Every person who shall make any such contract or engage in any such combination or conspiracy, shall be deemed guilty of a misdemeanor, and, on conviction thereof, shall be punished by fine not exceeding five thousand dollars, or by imprisonment not exceeding one year, or by both said punishments, at the discretion of the court.

Sec. 2. Every person who shall monopolize, or attempt to monopolize, or combine or conspire with any other person or persons, to monopolize any part of the trade or commerce among the several States, or with foreign nations, shall be deemed guilty of a misdemeanor, and, on conviction thereof; shall be punished by fine not exceeding five thousand dollars, or by imprisonment not exceeding one year, or by both said punishments, in the discretion of the court.'

Article 81(1-2) of the Treaty Establishing the European Community

1. The following shall be prohibited as incompatible with the common market: all agreements between undertakings, decisions by associations of undertakings and concerted practices which may affect trade between Member States and which have as their object or effect the prevention, restriction or distortion of competition within the common market, and in particular those which:

   (a) directly or indirectly fix purchase or selling prices or any other trading conditions;
   (b) limit or control production, markets, technical development, or investment;
   (c) share markets or sources of supply;
   (d) apply dissimilar conditions to equivalent transactions with other trading parties, thereby placing them at a competitive disadvantage;
   (e) make the conclusion of contracts subject to acceptance by the other parties of supplementary obligations which, by their nature or according to commercial usage, have no connection with the subject of such contracts.

2. Any agreements or decisions prohibited pursuant to this article shall be automatically void.

---

and charge prices higher than the perfectly competitive price. However, when cooperating with other firms, firms should bear in mind that these actions may be illegal under anti-trust or competition laws. There can be legal problems if communication takes place between the players, as these could be seen as anti-competitive. Collusion between players has been deemed illegal for over 100 years, as the U.S. Sherman Act of 1890 (United States 1890) makes clear in the Conceptual Box 2.3. Article 81 of the European Community Treaty (1957) makes similar provisions (in the United Kingdom, the Enterprise Act has analogous requirements).

2.3.3.3 Limitations of game theory

Game theory created high expectations in the strategy field as a tool for the analysis of the dynamics of interaction between firms. However this early promise has not been entirely realized within mainstream strategy work. This is due to several reasons. First, in order to make game theory models relevant, the firms that are being analysed should be of similar size. If one firm is significantly larger than the other, as in the Aspartame case with Searle and HSC, the strategic moves of the smaller firm will not usually have a significant impact on the outcomes of the larger (as we shall see later, other approaches such as organization ecology allow these smaller firms to prosper even in the presence of the larger). Game theoretic models are also restricted in that there exist only a limited number of 'strategies' that a firm can play, the number of firms competing is small (typically two, in a duopoly), and, like many economic models described in this chapter, the focus is on the equilibrium outcome, although contemporary game theory research on repeated games addresses this problem (Mailath and Samuelson 2006). However, these recent developments of game theory have been largely contained within the economics world and not been taken up by mainstream strategy scholars.

In Porter's article 'Towards a Dynamic Theory of Strategy' (1991: 106), he notes that although game theory may be seen as dynamic, in that there is a sequence of actions made by firms, this is not a dynamic theory:

by concentrating sequentially on small numbers of variables, the models fail to capture the simultaneous choices over many variables that characterize most industries. The models force a homogeneity of strategies. Yet it is the trade-offs and interactions involved in configuring the entire set of activities in the value chain that define distinct competitive positions. Finally the models hold fixed many variables that we know are changing.

Most of the best known game theoretical models rely on the assumption that the players of a game are perfectly rational: the decisions of the other players in a game can be predicted based on one's own behaviour and therefore one can play optimal strategies. In addition, much of the research in game theory is used to define a Nash equilibrium state: where no one player has an incentive to deviate from their hypothesized equilibrium strategy. However, it is debatable whether such assumptions provide a satisfactory methodology for investigating problems in the real business world. We may ask whether this paradigm is appropriate for the business world often not in a state of equilibrium. Whilst newer approaches to game theory, such as evolutionary game theory (Hofbauer and Sigmund 1998) relax some of these assumptions, the focus remains largely on solving the game theoretical model. By focusing instead on the outcome of models that are *not* in equilibrium, we may gain more insight into strategic problems that reflect environments where there is no equilibrium. As we shall see in Chapters 3 and 7, agent-based models provide us with a modelling technique that need not rely on finding equilibrium, and therefore may be more appropriate to the business world.

2.4 **Strategic positioning of firms**

After reviewing several classic formal models of competition, we focus now on more recently developed strategy frameworks. One of the most important contributions to strategic management, certainly the most influential in the 1980s and 1990s, was the work of Porter (1979, 1980). In Porter's seminal work, rooted in the Structure-Conduct-Performance paradigm (Bain 1956), the important decision that a strategist must determine is to decide in which industry the firm should compete, and *how* to compete within that industry. The Five Forces model posits that there are five determinants that determine the level of attractiveness (or otherwise) of an industry. The Five Forces are as follows: the bargaining power of the firms supplying the industry; the bargaining power of buyers; the threat of new firms potentially entering the market; the threat of substitute products; and the intensity of competitive rivalry. Our example of the video console industry (Case Box 2.1) illustrates how whole industries can lose profitability as value is captured by other 'forces' such as customers (gamers) and suppliers (game developers).

Despite its strong merits, this model has also been criticized because of its static nature. Hamel and Prahalad (1989: 64) described this analysis as: a snapshot of a moving car. By itself, the photograph yields little information about the car's speed or direction – whether the driver is out for a quiet Sunday drive or warming up for the Grand Prix.

The fact that Porter's Five Forces model is taught in the vast majority of the world's top business schools, thirty years after its publication, lays testament to the success of this idea, and the influence that industrial organization economics has had on the field of strategic management. Porter introduced the notion of 'strategy as positioning'. Firms need to develop their strategy through a combination of competitive dimensions, such as a pricing policy, a level of customer service, brand franchise, product quality, logistics man-agement, etc., that enable it to achieve an *attractive* and *defendable* position in the industry. A position is attractive when it enables the firm to obtain a return on capital employed higher than the average returns of the industry. A defendable position is one that is 'safe' from the erosion of profitability associated to the action of the five forces discussed previously. The conception of strategy as the art of finding a *defendable position* that protects the firm's competitive advantage from the action of the five forces that shape competition in the industry has since then become widespread. Perhaps because of the tremendous importance of the work of Porter during the 1980s, the basis of economics within strategic management has appeared to be unquestioned.

Many different approaches exist for representing a firm's strategy relative to one or more strategic dimensions. The birth of the so-called positioning school can be considered to date back to the work of Porter (1979, 1980), and has to a certain extent been ignored by recent work; we emphasize that there is scope for a revival of industrial organization economics models and frameworks. How-ever, if such a revival is to take place, it is important that the limitations of such techniques are understood. The inherent lack of a dynamic approach has to be overcome, and we shall see later how we can achieve this. Furthermore, there are several similar models that can be translated from the domain of other social sciences such as economics (notably Hotelling's model), or sociology (where organizational ecology has been used to represent the location of firms in an industry). These antecedent models are coupled with more recent analyses of social space within strategic management – the location of firms within an organizational ecology space, or more recent approaches such as the Levinthal (1997)–Kauffman (1993) *NK* model, used in strategic management, that posi-tions a firm in an N-dimensional space (see Chapter 7), or the game theoretical space that defines strategies to be played by an individual firm.

Within the realm of strategic management, we are continually confronted by the reduction and subsequent representation of data from a necessarily rich, multidimensional, and complicated set of data into a lower dimensional, more easily interpretable form. Two-dimensional 'matrices' can seem ubiqui-tous within strategic management, being used to classify firms' strategies according to their location on two 'dimensions'. We are used to constructing representations in a geographical space as being a *map* of the real world, there are difficulties when we extend this process to mapping social variables: some variables are essentially qualitative in nature – how do we represent these? And how do we represent two different quantitative variables that are meas-ured on different scales, often with different dimensionality? In order to gain a better understanding of the logic and limitations of representing firm loca-tions within strategic dimensions, we can refer to the fundamental social science and statistical literature that discusses the representation of such positions within social 'property space'.

2.4.1 STRATEGIC GROUPS

One of the ways that firms are considered to inhabit 'strategy space' is in the representation of strategic groups. Porter (1980: 131) introduced the concept of strategic groups, work that followed from the work of Hunt (1972) further developed by McGee and Thomas (1986). It was noticed that firms within markets that were in seemingly oligopolistic markets could be grouped into classifications where their strategies were remarkably similar. Porter looked to the industrial organization literature to provide an explanation for this apparent grouping. Whilst the notion of strategic groups was most important from a strategic point of view in the 1980s, it is necessary to review the construction of the strategic groups model to determine what methodological considerations (particularly those that concern the dimensionality of the model) were made by Porter and others in its construction.

The industrial organization literature enabled Porter (1980: 131) to represent the location of groups of firms: 'the strategic groups in an industry can be displayed on a map... *the number of axes are obviously limited by the two-dimensional character of a printed page*, which means that the analyst must select a few particularly important *strategic dimensions* along which to construct a map' (emphasis added). Higher dimension strategic space is reflected upon by Chakravarthy and White (2002: 186): 'even though most strategy typologies have limited the strategy space only to two dimensions, any number of dimensions are strategically possible ($S_1, S_2, \ldots S_n$)'.

However, the notion of N-dimensional strategic space is an arbitrary construct – the dimensions that are used in this space may not be orthogonal nor may they be normalized (we shall consider these points later in this chapter). This is not an issue when our aim is to represent firms within this space merely as a way of representing the locations of firms: there may however be problems when there is a correlation between two of the 'dimensions': this will lead to an artificially induced grouping that will produce difficulties in interpreting whether such groupings are real or merely artefacts of the correlation between the dimensions.

An additional problem arises when we are considering *distances* between firms in such an N-dimensional strategy space. Two issues arise: firstly, if the dimensions are not normalized, there is the issue that a change of one unit in dimension x is not equivalent to a change of one unit in dimension y. Therefore, when we consider distances in such space, there is a difficulty in interpretation of movements through more than one dimension. Studies in

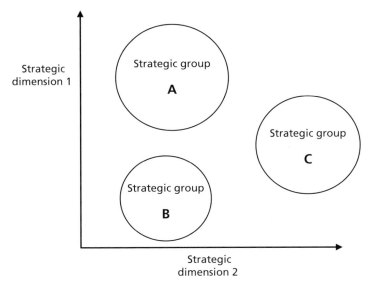

Figure 2.4. A map of strategic groups in a hypothetical industry
Source: Porter (1980: 131).

more-than-one dimensional space have been performed, but they can assume implicitly that the dimensions used are orthogonal and linear (see Figure 2.4).

[In Porter's example, vertical integration and specialization are used as two critical strategic dimensions. The notion of constructing a higher-dimensional space in order to represent the characteristics of a firm was introduced, also in the 1980s, by Spender. Spender (1989: 69) refers to his conceptualization of 'industry recipes': 'I argue that the [industry] recipe is made up from around 15 distinctions or "constructs". These are synthesized together to create a universe of discourse attached to a particular industry.' As we can see, the conceptualization of attempting to represent a firm's strategy within a higher-dimensional space is well established. One of the problems, however, is how to represent such a high dimensional space. The concept of the 'strategy hypercube' (Robertson 2003*b*) will be introduced later in the chapter, a representation that can allow such high-dimensional representations to be made.

One limitation of the strategic groups framework is that it considers the positioning of firms within this strategy space at one moment in time, and does not allow the consideration of the dynamics of the changes of position over time, changes that can be as a result of the reactions of one firm's positioning affecting the subsequent positions of firms over time. As we shall see later in the chapter, we can develop models that allow firms' strategic positions to evolve over time, allowing us to model the changes of the positioning of firms within the strategy space over time.

2.4.2 THE *NK* MODEL

One of the models that has recently been introduced into strategic management is the *NK* model, that originated in the field of evolution biology, and was conceived by Kauffman (1993) to model the 'fitness' of an organism as being dependent on the inter-relationship between the 'on' and 'off' characteristics within genes within an organism. Work based on the *NK* model has been developed and adapted by organization theorists to model organizational problem-solving processes incorporating features of 'real-life' organizations usually neglected by closed form economic models. This model conceives firms as systems that cannot optimize their performance, but just evolve solving problems under bounded rationality. This evolution is conditioned by past moves (path dependence) and by the degree of interdependence between the different parts of the firm (Levinthal 1997; Gavetti and Levinthal 2000; Siggelkow et al 2005; Caldart and Ricart 2007). This model wil be discussed in more detail in Chapter 7 where we analyse jointly how the competitive and the internal dynamics of the firm affect its performance.

2.4.3 THE STRATEGY HYPERCUBE

Porter (1980: 131) represents the location of firms within a two dimensional space where firms are located on a plane at coordinates based upon their position with respect to two strategic dimensions. Clustering of firms indicates the strategic groups within the industry. The representation of strategic dimensions is very widely accepted, as it enables an easy understanding of the strategic positioning of firms and is therefore particularly successful as a strategic tool. Later research into strategic groups extended the Porter model to use multiple strategic variables. Hatten and Hatten (1987: 336) refer to the 'strategic space' resulting from multivariate analyses of strategic groups. However, a problem remains: how do we represent *N*-dimensional space? In order to do this, we introduce the mathematical device of a 'hypercube' (Robertson 2003*b*). Whilst the positioning of firms using two strategic dimensions can be accomplished by representing the positioning on a plane, and whilst the positioning of firms using three strategic dimensions can be accomplished by representing the position of the firms within a cube, problems occur when one tries to represent firms on a space with a number of strategic dimensions exceeding three. However, using the mathematical notion of a hypercube can represent higher dimensional space: 'the analogue in a space of four or more dimensions of [a

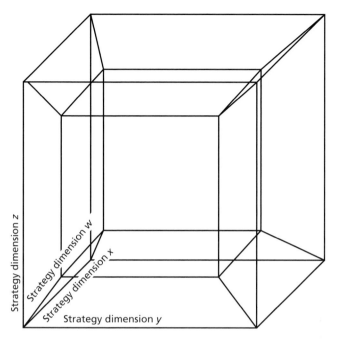

Figure 2.5. Example of a strategy hypercube with four dimensions

cube] in ordinary three-dimensional space' (*OED* 1989). We can therefore represent *N*-dimensional strategy space by using an *N*-dimensional hypercube. By extending these notions of *N*-dimensional space to the realm of strategic management, Robertson (2003*b*) envisages the strategy of a firm as being *the position and movement within the strategy hypercube*. The strategy hypercube can be represented as shown above. In one-dimensional space, we could represent the strategy of a firm as the '*x*' distance along a line as in the Hotelling or Downs models; in two-dimensional space, we could represent the strategy as (*x, y*) coordinates on a plane following Porter (1980); and in three dimensions as (*x, y, z*) coordinates in a cube. For *N*-dimensional space, we require there to be the same number of coordinates as there are dimensions in order to represent the full location of a firm (see Figure 2.5).

2.4.3.1 Orthogonality of dimensions

Dimensions being described as orthogonal are defined as 'having or of the nature of a right angle, right-angled (*obsolete*); pertaining to or involving right angles; at right angles to something else, or to each other; rectangular' (*OED* 1989). Using a statistical definition, this alters to: 'of a set of variates:

statistically independent. Of an experimental design: such that the variates under investigation can be treated as statistically independent.' (*OED* 1989). Whilst the strategic dimensions in Porter's model do not state that they are independent, this is a strong presumption by using this kind of approach. If the 'dimensions' are not independent, there may be bias in the results caused by such correlation of variables that are assumed to be independent but in actual fact are not. Whilst further research in strategic groups has emphasized the notion of factor analysis as being important, this subtle but important rigour has not fully percolated from the economics literature into the strategic management literature.

2.4.3.2 Strategic dimensions

Throughout this chapter, and indeed throughout this book, we are interested in how we construct models of the landscapes on which firms compete. It is interesting to note that very few, if any frameworks of strategic positioning consider more than two dimensions. This may be due to the difficulties involved in representing the positions of firms on a two-dimensional page. At best, we can hope to model two or three dimensions. Yet to limit our analysis to very few dimensions may mean that we risk introducing bias. Barton (1955: 40) defines the concept of 'property-space' in social research. Barton notes the difference between the dimensions used to locate objects (such as people) in 'property space' (Lazarsfeld 1937); the location in this space can be in the form of *continuous variables, unordered classes* (such as countries of birth), *rank-ordered classes* (such as ranks in the armed forces), or *dichotomous attributes* (such as male or female). Barton discusses that attributes that can be divided into classes constitute a matrix form of representation (such as the two by two matrices that are prevalent in management literature). The notion of higher dimensional property-space is mentioned (Barton 1955: 42). It is clear, therefore that the classification of properties of a firm, of customers, or other entities is important. In the example given earlier, however, it is possible that the so-called 'dimensions' actually have some correlations with each other, whereby the 'dimensions' may not be independent. Therefore, if we were to plot the locations of these 'dimensions' (which we may more accurately describe as 'variables') we may obtain clustering or linearity of results caused by their inherent relationships. If, for example, we were measuring the heights of children on one column and their ages in another, it is probable that these variables are correlated. However, if we know that the variables are independent, it is satisfactory to describe these as dimensions. It is important to make this distinction in order to provide a more rigorous approach to models that aim to classify firms with respect to strategic dimensions. Dimensions should be unrelated to each other in order for such an analysis to be rigorous. Lancaster (1966: 133) refers to a 'commodity space of dimension n, where consumers are seeking characteristics of products rather than products *per se*: there is a mapping between consumer requirements (referred to by Lancaster as 'C-space') and the space occupied by goods ('G-space'). This distinction will become important when we, in a later chapter, introduce an agent-based model of customer and firm interactions. We will assume that there is an overlap on certain dimensions of G- and C-space (in Lancaster's construction). We can therefore see that there is a corpus of methodological literature that supports the construction of such a space; we do however have to be cautious when we build models to explicitly state our assumptions (and hence the limitations) in our model, rather than making them implicit.

Higher-dimensional space (generally regarded as a space of $n > 3$ dimensions) is a widely defined and accepted construct within the natural sciences where the concepts of normality and orthogonality of dimensions are defined explicitly. However, within the social sciences, such distinctions can become blurred in the desire to classify the objects that we observe. Despite this, there have been uses of higher-dimensional space, usually Euclidean space, within the social sciences.

Within the sociological literature, McPherson (1983) refers to using population ecology to determine niches in space: 'multiple dimensions generate multiple (hyper) boxes in multidimensional (hyper) space' (McPherson 1983: 521). The notion of strategic dimensions is also important in the organizational ecology literature, and we shall review this in more detail in Chapter 3.

Of course such representations may be satisfactory where our aim is to communicate ideas to managers where the analytical rigour of the technique is not of critical importance. However, if we consider the use of 'two-by-two' matrices as popularized for instance by the BCG Matrix, there are various problems that we may have when analysing the position of firms or industries or the elements we wish to analyse within this two-dimensional dichotomous attribute space. Such representations assume that there is a clear distinction between variables that are high or low; borderline cases are not treated any differently and as such there may be misclassification of data. Spender (1989: 88) sums up this important difference in pre-structuring the dimensions in which one intends to analyse an industry: 'cluster analysis is a technique for systematically exploring similarities in a body of allegedly comparable data. It contrasts with many techniques, such as factor analysis, which explore differences. The latter are essentially positivistic in the sense that they require prior structuring in the dimensions in which differences are to be examined. While cluster analysis is not interpretative, it makes fewer logical demands on the data and can be used to examine poorly structured data, data whose meaning is uncertain'. Orthogonality (where the axis of each dimension is at right angles to each other) is an issue that needs to be considered when using such a strategic space. In Porter's discussion of strategic groups (1980: 131), there is no discussion of the orthogonality – dimensions are implicitly assumed orthogonal (one can also think of this in terms of variables; orthogonality being similar to variables being independent).

The determination as to whether different factors actually constitute *dimensions* is not a trivial problem as is sometimes assumed in management literature. For example, if we are to consider for example vertical integration and differentiation (as in Porter 1980) as being dimensions of strategic space, we are stating implicitly that these attributes are independent. If we were to be able to measure distances between points in this space, in mathematical terms we would refer to the dimensions as being orthonormal (meaning that each dimension is orthogonal and normalized enabling us to measure distances correctly). The concept of orthogonality means that each dimension is at 'right angles' to each other. Lancaster's definition of product attribute space (1966: 134) ('C-space' or characteristics space) takes this into account: 'the characteristics possessed by a good or a combination of goods are the same for all consumers and, given units of measurement, are in the same quantities'. Lancaster (1966: 134n) does however point out the units of product attribute space: 'since the units in which the characteristics are measured are arbitrary... the *relative* quantities of a particular characteristic between unit quantities of any pair of goods must be the same for all consumers' (emphasis in original). This is an important point, in that a scale can be set up that can measure the qualities of each product. These are strong assumptions, yet are ones that have been widely accepted in social science literature other than management science, Lancaster's work producing a wide range of further work, not only in economics, but also in management science. The implicit assumption of space in the management literature raises methodological problems. Firstly, the space (if it is to be treated as a Euclidean space assumes that the dimensions are orthogonal to each other. If the dimensions are *not* orthogonal, there lies a problem with the representation of data on a plane, for if the coordinates are plotted, they are not plotted on a plane but actually on a 'surface'. In order to overcome these problems, we can use factor analysis of the data (more specifically common factor analysis) whereby such data (with k variables) is reduced to n dimensions. Although we will use fitness landscapes later on in the book, we assume that the positions in which these firms reside are within the strategic dimensions of the strategic space.

If we choose arbitrary dimensions in, for example strategic groups analysis (as is supposed in much of the management literature where such methodological issues are not addressed explicitly), there is a risk that we are imposing a solution on a data set. Recent studies have used methods of *not* assuming what the dimensions are (such as factor analysis) before finding such strategic groups but using the data set to derive them. In order that research using strategy space can be treated as methodologically sound, there are several requirements of models and frameworks that make such an approach valid. At the very least, these issues should be considered when constructing such models and frameworks. The requirement of dimensional orthogonality is critical. If dimensions are not orthogonal, issues arise when we try and move in such a strategy space or attempt to measure distances in this space. In fact, if we do move in a space where dimensions are not orthogonal, we are in fact traversing a surface rather than a space where Euclidean geometry holds (and where for instance we can calculate Euclidean distances). This can be done, in the case of a theoretical model by stating this assumption explicitly; for the case of empirical data, it is important that the dimensions are constructed *from the data* in order that the multivariate technique *imposes* orthogonality on the dimensions (such as in the case of factor analysis which reduces the data to orthogonal 'principal components'). Another important issue is that of normalization of dimensions: if we are to make any meaningful measurements in strategy space, it is important that a movement of one unit in the first dimension is the same scalar value as the movement of one unit in a second or subsequent dimension. Without this requirement, measurement cannot be realistically maintained.

By considering such important points when constructing models or frameworks in strategy space, we should consider the properties of the space as a fundamental part of the methodological considerations of this approach. By explicitly considering such requirements of a 'well behaved' strategy space, we can reduce the criticisms of our models and frameworks on methodological grounds.

2.5 **Limitations of an economics-based approach**

The formalization of economic models does allow the presupposition of the model to be explicit rather than implied. The very notion of devising an economic model brings a certain amount of rigour to the formulation process, a level of formalization that cannot be overlooked. However, there are significant limitations when taking the economic paradigm for granted, particularly in the way that equilibrium is an important part of this framework, the fact that firms within industries are supposed homogeneous, and the emphasis on stasis. With the continuing emphasis on economics being a social science where models are 'solved' means that there remains a significant limitation on using such approaches within strategic management. Because of these limitations, other approaches lacking the elegance of closed form models but introducing more 'real-life' dimensions in the analysis of competition have gained ground in the last three decades.

While these models are entirely appropriate for industries where such equilibrium exists, most non-idealized industries are anything but. With industries being described as 'hypercompetitive' or 'turbulent', it is clear that most industries are not in this idealized state, and the notion of how to deal with these competitive environments is an active research area.

Economic models, such as those introduced earlier are limited in that, at their core, they assume equilibrium outcomes. This assumption that competitors will settle down into a final state, such as a fixed position or fixed level of price can be applicable in the realm of bilateral competition where there is nothing other than the competing firm to knock your firm out of this equilibrium. Rationality is also assumed in many models, in that actors (such as firms) will behave in a way that maximizes their utility function under the given constraints. The concept of maximization of expected utility is a central tenet of neoclassical economics. Real actors, such as strategists within a firm do not always behave rationally – they may follow 'boundedly rational' behaviour (Simon 1957) and not always optimize their utility functions. Indeed, Porter himself (1991: 98) notes:

it is well known that [industrial organization] models are highly sensitive to the assumptions underlying them and to the concept of equilibrium that is employed.

While game theory was seen as a potential new dawn for dynamic strategy (indeed, in the Winter 1991 special issue on *Fundamental Issues in Strategy* published in the *Strategic Management Journal*, several articles were directly or indirectly commenting on the good prospects of game theory applied to strategic management). The introduction of more than two firms into the market poses additional problems. One (of the many) firms may move, and perturb the entire system.

Finally, economic models assume that the world jumps immediately to equilibrium. All the models identified earlier show the reasoning for equilibrium, but the *path* to equilibrium is not considered explicitly. Furthermore, the *existence* of equilibrium is assumed in these economic models: firms jump to a state where there is no incentive to move locations or change strategies. These models are considered to exist in isolation, where there are no external shocks, or indeed an external environment to perturb the system out of equilibrium. Knott (2003) introduces the problem: 'the goal of strategy is persistent profits – in short, to overcome the microeconomic equilibrium of homogeneous firms with zero profits'. This emphasizes the over-reliance on microeconomic models within strategic management: such models are merely *models*; the equilibrium of zero profit homogeneous firms is the equilibrium of the *model* rather than the equilibrium (if there be one) we may (or may not) observe in the empirical world.

Microeconomic models have a twofold impact on being used in strategic management: they provide analytical solutions to problems (in that they provide mathematical solutions to problems modelled), yet this also carries with it the over-emphasis on *equilibrium* as a prerequisite of such a formulation – the existence of which may not be present within the real business world (particularly in high velocity or turbulent industries). The existence of homogeneous 'representative firms' within economic models eliminates the possibility of analyzing the impact of differences between firms on their performance. More recent theoretical approaches, such as the resource-based view of the firm (Barney 1986, 1991) and the dynamic capabilities perspective (Teece et. al 1997; Eisenhardt and Martin 2000), are specifically focused on understanding how inter-firm heterogeneity leads to differences in firm's strategies and performance.

As we will see in Chapters 3 and 7, the assumption of firm homogeneity can be removed by modelling firms and industries with the use of agent-based models. By modelling firms as individual agents, each firm in the model may possess its own profit, location, evolutionary path, and individual firm strategy. Such models can perhaps more importantly incorporate the *dynamics* of an industry – whether these are modelled as exogenous effects or as endogenous movement as a result of the reaction to the movement of firms or customers within the model. This provides a significant benefit over other modelling techniques that are primarily static in nature.

Although formal *economic* models such as the ones discussed in this chapter may be of limited value when we consider environments that are turbulent and dynamic, we should not discard the framework of modelling: such models can be of benefit in that they can simplify our understanding of the environment and thereby provide a model that, whilst not reflecting the entire idiosyncrasies of the environment, can however capture its salient features. We propose that agent-based models can if required combine the rigour of economic models but can also give rich insights from what is fundamentally a quantitative and rigorous approach.

3 Dynamics of Competition

3.1 Introduction

In this chapter, we go beyond traditional, economics-based models and review how we can use new, alternative models to study the dynamics of competition. 'Turbulence', 'high velocity environments', 'hypercompetition': these are all notions that describe environments that are not stable and do not conform to the idealized notions of equilibrium that characterize the formal models discussed in the last chapter. In this section we review several different theoretical approaches that address the dynamism of competition.

3.2 Research on strategy in dynamic environments

Whilst the most widely used strategy models are static and linear in nature, there is doubt as to whether such models are appropriate under high-velocity, turbulent conditions, characteristics of which include inherently *non*-static, *non*-linear behaviour. There exists a debate in the strategy literature as to which types of strategies are appropriate under differing levels of environmental turbulence. As we mentioned in the last chapter, the well-known Porter (1980) approach is essentially static, assuming well-defined and stable competitive landscapes. Little emphasis is placed on the *dynamics* of strategy. Chakravarthy (1997:75) notes that Porter's framework (1980) is 'useful only if the competitive forces represented by competitors, suppliers, buyers, and substitutes are relatively stable and independent'. In the forty years since the birth of Strategic Management as a discipline, several waves of research have come and gone, each with their own research emphasis. Mintzberg et al. (1998) set out ten 'Schools of Thought' for reviewing the now large literature within the strategic management field. Other authors, such as Whittington (1993:10–41) conceptualize strategy as having four approaches: the planning or 'classical' approach, the efficiency-driven 'evolutionary' approach, the craft-like 'processual approach', and the 'systemic' approach that considers strategies peculiar to their sociological context. However, although there is this apparent diversity and delineation of different strategy 'camps',

Mintzberg et al. (1998:372–3) note that such delineation may not be in the best interests of strategy research: 'it is convenient that strategic management has, for the most part, slotted so neatly into these ten categories...unfortunately, it may not have been the best thing for practice...we have to go beyond the narrowness of each school: we need to know how this beast called strategy formation, which combines all of these schools and more, really lives its life'. Other works have emphasized incremental change in strategy as an important factor in strategic management. In a response to earlier work on 'disjointed incrementalism' (Braybrooke and Lindblom 1963), Quinn (1978, 1980) introduced the concept of 'logical incrementalism' to explain why planning did not describe the actual strategies adopted by managers: 'when well-managed major organizations make significant changes in strategy, the approaches they use frequently bear little resemblance to the rational, analytical systems so often described in the planning literature' (Quinn 1980). Mintzberg (1994) differentiates between 'deliberate' strategies where 'intentions [are] fully realised' and 'emergent' strategies, 'where a realized pattern was not expressly intended'. As we saw in Chapter 2, limitations to managers' abilities are introduced by Simon's concept (1947, 1957) of 'bounded rationality' whereby agents, due to the uncertainty of the future and costs of acquiring information, act in a way that is not completely rational. Managers may also have different schemata (the organization of perceptions followed by responses), and will also have different causal maps or mental models (Huff 1990) that will influence their individual decision-making and therefore the ensuing strategy of the firm. These mental models are influenced by factors such as, for instance, the academic backgrounds or career paths experienced by the managers. Chaffee (1985) confirms that one of the objects of strategy is to deal with changing environments, and notes that strategy is 'multidimensional'. Chaffee divides strategy into three models: linear, adaptive, and interpretive. Chaffee notes that the *linear* model of strategy involves varying the organization's links with the environment (by changing their products or markets or by performing other entrepreneurial actions), noting that the problem with this approach is 'though decisions may be made on beliefs about future conditions, they may not be implemented until months, even years from now'. The *adaptive* model differs from the linear model in that monitoring the environment and making changes are simultaneous and continuous. Chaffee notes that this mode is more applicable to an environment that is less susceptible to prediction and is more dynamic.

One of the most fundamental questions to management researchers remains that of why firms are different, and why certain firms achieve and maintain competitive advantage. Chandler (1962) defines strategy as: 'the determination of the basic long-term goals and objectives of an enterprise, and the adoption of the courses of action and the allocation of resources necessary for carrying out these goals'. Despite this definition being over 40 years old, such fundamental questions remain largely unanswered.

In the next section we refer to two theoretical approaches that overcome the limitations of the formal economic models discussed in Chapter 2. We introduce the Resource-Based View and Dynamic Capabilities in order to show how current thinking within strategic management enables us to set the foundations for further work in understanding the dynamics of strategy.

3.3 **Dynamic capabilities**

The dynamic capabilities perspective is an extension of the resource-based view of the firm. One of the criticisms of the traditional resource-based view is that it largely ignores the external environment. Dynamic capabilities attempt to resolve this shortcoming: Teece et al. (1997) define dynamic capabilities as 'the firm's ability to integrate, build, and reconfigure internal and external competencies to address rapidly changing environments'. This definition brings into play both the resource-based view which we shall discuss in this section, and the notion of *rapidly changing* environments, which we shall discuss in the next section.

An attempt to explain differences between firms, their heterogeneity, came from the resource-based view of the firm. Authors such as Wernerfelt (1984) and Barney (1991) see *resources* as being the most important components of a firm. Wernerfelt (1984) developed the notion of the resource-based view of the firm, building on the work of Penrose (1959) that perceived a firm as a bundle of resources. Wernerfelt (1984:172) argues four propositions:

- 'looking at firms in terms of their resources leads to different immediate insights than the traditional product perspective. In particular, diversified firms are seen in a new light',

- 'one can identify types of resources that lead to high profits. In analogy to entry barriers, these are associated with what we call resource position barriers',

- 'strategy for a bigger firm involves striking a balance between the exploitation of existing resources and the development of new ones. In analogy to the growth-share matrix, this can be visualized in what we will call a resource-product matrix', and

- 'an acquisition can be seen as a purchase of a bundle of resources in a highly imperfect market. By basing the purcase [*sic*] on rare resource, one can *ceteris paribus* maximize this imperfection and one's chances of buying cheap and getting good returns'.

Barney (1991) builds on the notion of strategic resources: 'building on the assumptions that strategic resources are heterogeneously distributed across firms and these differences are stable over time', Barney (1991:99) examines the link between firm resources and sustained competitive advantage, firm resources being defined as 'all assets, capabilities, organizational processes, firm attributes, information, knowledge etc. controlled by a firm that enable the firm to conceive of and implement strategies that improve its efficiency and effectiveness'. However, the notion that the distribution of resources remains stable over time, whilst being convenient from the point of view of analysis, does not provide a realistic notion of inter-firm competition in times of high turbulence when such resources may be buffeted around between firms, and the resources that may have been relied upon to contribute to competitive advantage in the past may now not be of use. Therefore the resource-based view too poses limitations when we are considering such turbulent industries and situations.

There is much confusing terminology, some of it conflicting, within the realm of the resource-based view of the firm. Indeed, Teece et al. (1997) in their key work on dynamic capabilities go so far as to say 'we do not like the term "resource" and believe it is misleading'! We describe in some detail the fundamental building blocks of the Resource-Based View so that we can understand more fully the concept of *dynamic* capabilities, an active area of research whose definitions are still being fought over.

3.3.1 CAPABILITIES

Like much of the resource-based view, the terminology of these theories is difficult to define. Dosi et al. (2000) describe the 'terminological anarchy' of the resource-based view: 'the term "capabilities" floats in the literature like an iceberg in a foggy Arctic sea, one iceberg among many, not easily recognized as different from several icebergs near by'. Makadok (2001) uses the rather contrived definition of resources: 'organizationally embedded non-transferable firm-specific resource whose purpose is to improve the productivity of the other resources possessed by the firm'. He is making the point that unlike ordinary resources, capabilities are firm-specific; perhaps more eloquently, Teece argues that 'capabilities cannot easily be bought; they must be built'. Although resources can be 'picked' in order to bring them within the firm, capabilities are different: they are *built* not acquired – capabilities are embedded within the organization whereas resources are not. Collis makes a very valuable point when discussing capabilities as a source of sustainable competitive advantage. Where competitive advantage is based on organizational capabilities, such strategies are susceptible to competitors developing 'better' capabilities – higher level capabilities – that can out-perform the capabilities of the firm with the existing 'first order' capabilities. This 'infinite regress' where ever more sophisticated capabilities can be developed, *ad infinitum*, means that the basis for *sustainable* competitive advantage is eroded as competitors develop higher and higher order capabilities. Collis (1994) advocates three prescriptions for overcoming this infinite regress: firstly, firms should not forget that the basis of competitive advantage is not *only* through the resource-based view: the positioning of products, as conceptualized by Porter (1980) is also important; secondly, there is an argument that capabilities are built up in sequence, higher level capabilities being only available to firms after they have achieved capabilities at a lower level – in this way, firms cannot immediately jump to higher level capabilities; thirdly, Collis argues that the source of valuable capabilities is dependent on the context of the industry at a particular time, therefore it may be possible for a firm to identify the capability that underpins sustainable competitive advantage in a particular industry at a particular time.

Conceptual Box 3.1 Definitions from the resource-based view

Firm Resources

'. . . include all assets, capabilities, organizational processes, firm attributes, information, knowledge etc. controlled by a firm that enable the firm to conceive of and implement strategies that improve its efficiency and effectiveness' (Barney 1991, referencing Daft 1983)

Competencies

'combinations of input and knowledge-based resources that exist at higher levels in a hierarchy of integration' (Galunic and Rodan 1998)

Core Competencies

'capabilities which are fundamental to a firm's competitive advantage and which can be deployed across multiple product markets' (Grant 1996)

Capabilities

'. . . refer to a firm's capacity to deploy *Resources*, usually in combination, using organizational processes, to effect a desired end. They are information-based, tangible or intangible processes that are firm-specific and are developed over time through complex interactions among the firm's *Resources*. They can abstractly be thought of as 'intermediate goods' generated by the firm to provide enhanced productivity of its *Resources*, as well as strategic flexibility and protection for its final product or service' (Amit and Schoemaker 1993)
'an organizationally embedded non-transferable firm-specific resource whose purpose is to improve the productivity of the *other* resources possessed by the firm' (Makadok 2001)

Dynamic Capabilities

'the firm's processes that use resources – specifically the processes to integrate, reconfigure, gain and release resources – to match and even create market change. Dynamic capabilities thus are organizational and strategic routines by which firms achieve new resource configurations as markets emerge, collide, split, evolve, and die' (Eisenhardt and Martin 2000)

There is a hierarchy of definitions of terms related to the resource-based view of the firm. Competences are combinations of resources (particularly combinations that involve knowledge resources), such resources including: Knowledge-Based Resources (such as knowledge within the firm, organizational processes and information); Tangible Resources (such as assets or capital); and Firm Attributes.

Capabilities are a firm's capacity to deploy the resources that it holds. While acquiring resources may have been seen as sufficient to sustain competitive advantage during the early years of the resource-based view, more current literature has changed the focus from the acquisition of resources to the development of capabilities that allow these resources to be used. Our discussion of capabilities is to set the scene for *dynamic* capabilities.

3.3.2 DYNAMIC CAPABILITIES

Winter (2003) differentiates between 'ordinary' organizational capabilities and dynamic capabilities. Basing his definition on his earlier work with Nelson (Nelson and Winter 1982), organizational capabilities are defined as 'a high-level routine (or collection of routines) that, together with its implementing input flows, confers upon an organization's management a set of decision options for producing significant outputs of a particular type', basing the concept on routines: 'behaviour that is learned, highly patterned, repetitious, or quasi-repetitious, founded in part in tacit knowledge – and the specificity of objectives'. What makes dynamic capabilities different from ordinary capabilities is that dynamic capabilities are concerned with change and learning. The notion is that dynamic capabilities govern the rate of change of organizational capabilities.

The link to the resource-based view is clear: dynamic capabilities are the routines by which managers alter the resources within the firm – whether this is acquiring new resources, disposing of others, or combining resources. Eisenhardt and Martin (2000) suggest that dynamic capabilities are of several types: firms may use dynamic capabilities to create, integrate, recombine, and release resources from the firm. For instance, a firm's ability to make people from different departments (such as sales, operations, product development, or marketing) work together effectively in project teams for new product development is a dynamic capability. Similarly a firm's organizational ability to manage M&A integration processes or to manage the relationship with partners in joint-ventures are dynamic capabilities.

Eisenhardt and Martin (2000) distinguish between dynamic capabilities in 'high velocity' and stable markets: in high velocity environments, dynamic capabilities are experiential (i.e. not analytic), iterative (i.e. non-linear), and are inherently simple in nature. In markets that are moderately dynamic, they suggest that dynamic capabilities become efficient and robust routines become embedded in cumulative, existing knowledge within the firm.

Dynamic capabilities should be purposefully simple in order for them to be able to adapt to a changing environment. The emphasis is less on analysis, more on activities that allow knowledge to be generated rapidly, where information being acquired by the firm may change rapidly. In other words, effective dynamic capabilities enable a firm to adapt to a changing, turbulent environment.

3.4 **Environmental turbulence**

Competitive landscapes are usually characterized as stable or turbulent. In stable landscapes, actors have well defined roles and competitors' strategies rely on a similar set of competitive dimensions, making those strategies rather repetitive. These characteristics ease the analysis of the industry using traditional frameworks, such as Porter's Five Forces, and also the prediction of the possible evolution of the industry using economic models. For instance electricity transmission is a highly predictable industry. Demand from customers, that is, electricity distribution firms, evolves rather predictably. The price charged by the transmission firm is also quite stable as it is usually determined by precise and long lasting regulatory frameworks. Finally, the management of the operation and the evolution of technology offer little uncertainty.

Turbulent competitive landscapes are precisely the opposite case. In these industries, the roles of the different actors are blurred. Competitors rely on a more complex and varied combination of competitive dimensions at the time of designing their competitive strategies. This makes prediction more difficult to achieve and traditional static competitive analysis less valuable in the best case and even dangerously misleading in the worst. The mobile phone industry referred to earlier is an example of a turbulent industry. In addition to the fact that competitors cooperate by supplying themselves with the operating system for the handsets they sell (Symbian), other new developments such as Nokia's bundle of the mobile business with its music download business (Nokia Music) show clearly that traditional clear-cut definitions of competitor, supplier, substitute, etc. are less applicable. These environments demand new ways of thinking about competition and industry dynamics. The dynamic capabilities approach, discussed earlier, has been developed as an attempt to respond to the challenges posed by turbulent competitive landscapes. As we saw in Teece et al.'s (1997) seminal definition of dynamic capabilities, firms may have to deal with rapidly changing environments.

This concept has several siblings that consider very similar notions, but with different nomenclature: turbulence, high velocity environments, hypercompetitive environments (D'Aveni 1994). We will discuss these notions in order that we can understand how the dynamics of the landscape affect competition and make the environment appear unstable, dynamic, and complicated. Such dynamics may be affected either by exogenous phenomena, such as the rate of economic growth, interest rates, etc., or by endogenous phenomena such as actions from competitors, clients, etc.

Igor Ansoff is the father of the notion of environmental turbulence, even though there is an ideological divide between his views and that of Henry Mintzberg – for instance in a rather spirited exchange in the *Strategic Management Journal* where the authors *literally* attempt to score points off each other (Ansoff 1991; Mintzberg 1990, 1991). Mintzberg (1993:34) states 'the argument about escalating or endemic turbulence is as silly as are all the claims about today's turbulence'. What exactly is meant by the term turbulence? The *Oxford English Dictionary* (OED 1989) defines the phenomenon as 'violent commotion, agitation, or disturbance; disorderly or tumultuous character or conduct'. McNamara et al. (2003) describe the notion of the environment of a firm being turbulent, unstable, and fast moving. However, the sentiment of increasing turbulence within industries is not without its critics. The notion of increasingly competitive, unstable, unpredictable environments is one that can be found in several streams of literature: hypercompetition, high-velocity environments, turbulence, reviewed in the following.

Chakravarthy's introduction (1997:69) to his 'Strategy Framework for Coping with Turbulence' states: 'most of the extant frameworks in strategic management assume a benign environment that is simple and not very dynamic'. Conversely, more recent literature on the subject can be criticized for precisely the opposite reason, the criticism being that there is an a priori assumption that a highly turbulent environment exists, for example 'evidence of increasing turbulence is everywhere' (Rigby and Rogers 2000:78). Of course, by 'blaming' the environment for underperformance, executives have an excuse for underperformance, even if this underperformance has nothing to do with environmental turbulence. Few concrete definitions of 'turbulence' exist within the management literature, even though it is a term that is often cited. Chakravarthy (1997:69) notes that 'complexity is a measure of the number of competitive configurations that a firm must ideally consider in shaping its strategy. The dynamic of the environment, that is, the rate at which these configurations change over time is the other key determinant of turbulence'. Existing frameworks for analysing strategy have not proved useful at understanding why firms build competitive advantage in times of rapid change (Teece et al. 1997).

If we consider the business environment to be complicated, it is inappropriate to consider models developed under paradigms of equilibrium, stability, and linearity to produce an appropriate analysis of a turbulent environment. Just as non-linear mathematics is required when studying turbulence within engineering, we too must adopt models and tools that capture the non-linearity of a firm's environment. Chief Executive Officers have also indicated the attractiveness of a turbulent environment should their firm possess 'dynamic capabilities' (Teece et al. 1997): 'the only advantage Intel has is that we have been faster to get to some places than other people have. That implies we have places to go. If I don't have places to go, I lose time as a competitive advantage. So give me a *turbulent world as compared with a stable world* and I'll want the turbulent world' (emphasis added, Karlgaard and Gilder 1996:63, cited in Lee et al. 2002). Chakravarthy (1997) cites falling entry and mobility barriers and increasing returns to scale contributing to turbulence (1997:77–80). Furthermore, Chakravarthy suggests several strategies for coping with turbulence including: 'repeat first mover advantages', 'maintaining network effects', 'going with the flow'. The concept of there being 'turbulence' within the business environment was popularized by authors such as Ansoff (1979), hypothesizing that there has been a 'growth of environmental turbulence' (1979:35) in that: 'during the 20th Century, the key events in the environment of ESOs ["environment serving organizations", including firms] have become progressively: (1) novel; (2) costlier to deal with; (3) faster; (4) more difficult to anticipate', supplementing this implicit definition with an explicit definition: 'the *level of turbulence* in an industry is the state of knowledge at which ESOs [firms] in the industry must start responses in order to respond effectively to environmental changes'.

Ansoff (1988:173) states that environmental turbulence is determined by a combination of changeability of the market environment, speed of change, intensity of competition, fertility of technology, discrimination by customers, and pressures from governments and interest groups. Ansoff asserts that the more turbulent the environment, the more aggressive must be the firm's response. As well as citing precursors to turbulence, Ansoff (1988:174) states that the factors that contribute to differences in behaviour of firms in turbulent environment include: their past history, their size, their accumulated organizational inertia, the relevance of their skills to the environmental needs and, particularly, the ambitions, the drive, and the capabilities of management. Ansoff (1988:176) further categorizes environments into four types: stable, 'a placid, non-turbulent competitive environment'; reactive; anticipatory; and initiative, 'a highly turbulent environment'. Whilst this may be appropriate as a metaphor for instability, Ansoff may have meant it to have a more literal meaning: if one looks at Ansoff's writings (1979) on turbulence, it does appear to be slightly esoteric: Ansoff uses the metaphor of an electron's orbit, which may follow Ansoff's choice of the word 'turbulence' for this condition: the engineering definition being 'of, pertaining to, or designating flow of a fluid in which the velocity at any point fluctuates irregularly and there is continual mixing rather than a steady flow pattern' (*OED* 1989).

Boisot (1996:37) concurs with the notion of turbulence: 'the major transformation in the strategic environment which strategy must deal with has been well documented and can be summed up in a single word: *turbulence*' (emphasis in original).

The concept of environmental turbulence is therefore important in that the models that are appropriate under environments at equilibrium (as early industrial organization economists may have assumed) may not be appropriate under rapidly changing environments. While environmental turbulence may be a convenient label upon which chief executives can blame their poor performance, the continuing discussion of the concept does indicate that it is an important concept.

3.4.1 DYNAMISM

Duncan (1972:316) refers to the differences between dynamic and static environments, referring to the static ↔ dynamic measure as being the 'degree to which the factors of the decision unit's internal and external environment remain basically the same over time or are in a continual process of change'. Dess and Beard (1984:56) refer to environmental dynamism as referring to 'turnover [described as the 'rate of change' by Priem et al. 1995:914], absence of pattern, and unpredictability'. Emery and Trist (1965:26) introduced the concept of turbulent fields into the management arena to describe the most complex of environments. Emery and Trist (1965) classify a firm's environment in terms of the 'complexity' and the 'dynamic' of the firm's environment. Emery and Trist note that a 'turbulent field' exists where there are interdependencies within the environment, its 'causal texture' (in addition to interrelations between the firm and the environment).

3.4.2 HYPERCOMPETITION

D'Aveni (1994, 1995) represents the notion of 'hypercompetition' – a state that is defined (1995:46) as: '[resulting] from the dynamics of strategic manoeuvring among global and innovative combatants. It is a condition of rapidly escalating competition based on price-quality positioning, competition to create know-how and establish first-mover advantage, competition to protect or invade established product or geographic markets, and competition based on deep pockets and the creation of even deeper pocketed alliances...the frequency, boldness, and aggressiveness of dynamic movement by the players accelerates to create a condition of constant disequilibrium and change... in other words, environments escalate toward higher and higher levels of uncertainty, dynamism, heterogeneity of the players, and hostility'. D'Aveni (1994:215) suggests that there exists a new type of competition – 'hypercompetition', fundamentally different from the traditional notion: 'in the old days of stable environments, companies created fairly rigid strategies designed to fit the long-term conditions of the environment'. D'Aveni suggests that a competitive equilibrium was in the past set up whereby 'less dominant firms accepted their secondary status because they were given the opportunity to survive by a leading firm that avoided competing too aggressively'. D'Aveni also states that hypercompetition presents an entirely different system: 'in hypercompetitive environments this equilibrium is impossible to sustain. Here, successful companies rely on a different combination of strategies and actions to achieve the goal of temporary advantage and to destroy the advantages of competitors through constantly disrupting the equilibrium of the market'. 'A key insight in the study of the intensely disruptive and turbulent environment of hypercompetition is that the strategic paradigms that work well in one environment don't work at all in another'. A limitation of this approach is that D'Aveni gives no prescription as to how to determine whether a particular firm or industry lies in a hypercompetitive environment. Thus we cannot decide whether we should be using the strategy formulations that have been devised in a stable environment, or strategy formulations that are more appropriate when we are faced with a turbulent environment. The most appropriate strategy when faced with a truly turbulent situation may be to not set a detailed strategy at all: the effects of being buffeted and carried by the rapidly shifting environment can make planning and reaction impossible; the concept of strategic intent, discussed in Chapter 1, may be more useful here, without going into the specifics required to carry out the strategy. The chances of being successful or not successful may be – under a truly turbulent environment – independent of the strategy that is set. If risk-averse, managers should examine the possibility of exiting the industry entirely. Conversely, if managers are risk-seeking, a turbulent or complex environment may be attractive – but only on the understanding that profits may be higher or lower than expected.

3.4.3 STRATEGIZING IN TURBULENT ENVIRONMENTS

In the previous section, we saw how various authors had described the notion that environments are inherently unstable. Several authors have also discussed how firms should strategize in such environments, going beyond traditional strategies that are suitable only for benign, equilibrium environments.

The concept of measuring the turbulence of an industry is predicated upon the understanding that managers are able to quantify the level of turbulence within an industry. However, this approach, similar to the approach of Porter (1979) and other industry analysis techniques does not take into account the level of uncertainty as perceived by an *individual firm.* Yet the turbulence is described usually as being an industry-level phenomenon: industries such as the telecommunications industry may considered to be turbulent. The perception of the industry may vary significantly between firms in the same industry. If we are going to determine a level of industry, as we perceive the attractiveness of an industry using a Porterian analysis, one approach is to borrow from the physical sciences and engineering the methods for quantifying the level of turbulence within an industry. Management writers and scholars have similarly stated that increased turbulence – or at least trying to create turbulence for one's competitors – is an appropriate strategy when faced with turbulence or hypercompetition: 'the goal of incumbent leaders and challengers in each environment is to achieve strategic supremacy by controlling the degree and pattern of turbulence' (D'Aveni 1999:134). Yet the notion that we are able to control the degree and pattern of turbulence is a very strong claim. If a system is truly turbulent, it means that the effect that one can have on the environment is minimal, and the rapidly changing environment will overwhelm the decisions of managers. This is where strategic mistakes are most likely to be made: managers' efforts are being channelled into setting strategies that, by definition, are ineffective. The effects of managers damping the transition to turbulence is far more beneficial in this region, for if we are in a strongly turbulent region, it may be impossible, through management intervention, to bring the system back to control; instead the effects of managerial interaction may be overwhelmed by the turbulence within the industry.

We discuss in the following text some of the approaches that have been advocated for dealing with turbulent environments, namely strategic intent, imitation, incremental change, fast decision making, and the benefit of first mover advantages.

3.4.3.1 Strategic Intent

Rather than using Porter's generic strategies such as cost leadership or differentiation or focus, Hamel and Prahalad (1989) suggest that a firm should instead use 'strategic intent' to guide its strategy. Strategic intent is the overall direction of an organization that, according to Hamel and Prahalad (1989:64–6), captures the essence of winning, is stable over time, and sets a target that deserves personal effort and commitment. Examples include Komatsu's objective of 'encircling Caterpillar' or Canon's objective of 'beating Xerox'. Boisot (1996:44) notes: 'strategic intent relies on an intuitively formed pattern or *gestalt* – some would call it a vision – to give it unity and coherence . . . strategic intent yields a simple yet robust orientation, intuitively accessible to all the firm's employees, an orientation which, on account of its clarity, can be pursued with some consistency over the long term in spite of the presence of turbulence'.

3.4.3.2 Imitation

Bourgeois and Eisenhardt (1988) suggest that one of the strategies available to firms that find themselves in a high velocity environment is to imitate others. This is modelled by moving the firm's strategic position towards that of the leader. It is asserted by Brown and Eisenhardt (1998) that such changes should be made incrementally, the movement is formed by the vector of the difference between the firm's current position and the position of the lead firm in the industry.

Rivkin (2000) writes about the imitation of complex strategies. Yet, there is a difficulty for firms to imitate complicated strategies. Whilst Rivkin's assertion is that there is high interconnectedness (high K) between strategic variables, this may not be the case as in fact what appears to an observer as a complex strategy may in fact be a simple strategy that generates complex behaviour. Using this method of seeking to analyse this in terms of interconnectedness of strategies may not be appropriate in this case. This is due to the fact that the NK model used by Rivkin sees strategies as *internal*; however, this approach does not take sufficiently into account the changing environment. The NK model will be discussed in more depth in Chapter 7.

3.4.3.3 Incrementalism versus Discontinuous Change

In a response to Braybooke and Lindblom's notion (1963) of 'disjointed incrementalism', Quinn (1978, 1980) introduces the notion of 'logical incrementalism' as being the process whereby 'one proceed[s] flexibly and experimentally from broad concepts towards specific commitments, making the latter concrete as late as possible in order to narrow the bands of uncertainty and to benefit from the best available information' (1978:19). Hayes (1985:115–16) asserts that large 'strategic leaps' are favoured by U.S. firms, as opposed to small, incremental steps favoured by Japanese and German firms. Furthermore, Brown and Eisenhardt (1997:1) suggest that 'the ability to change *rapidly* and *continuously*, especially by developing new products, is not only a core competence, it is also at the heart of highly innovative firms'. Google or Apple are good examples of firms having the dynamic capability to develop breakthroughs in innovation.

3.4.3.4 Speed of Strategic Decisions

Eisenhardt (1989) suggests that the ability to take 'rapid and relentless continuous change' is a crucial capability for survival in high-velocity environments. We would therefore expect that the speed of decision should have a positive impact on the profitability of the firm. However, we expect that there are costs involved with making quick decisions (quick strategic decisions may imply that such strategic reviews are taken more often which means that the rate of decision making is higher which in turn implies that in a set period of time more strategic decisions are taken). We can therefore investigate the joint effect of the cost of decision-making and the rate at which decisions are taken.

3..4.3.5 First Mover Advantages

Lieberman and Montgomery (1988:44) mention explicitly the occupation of geographic and product characteristic space in their paper on first mover advantages: 'first-movers may also be able to deter entry through strategies of spatial pre-emption . . . the first-mover can often select the most attractive niches and may be able to take strategic actions that limit the amount of space available for subsequent entrants'. For instance, in the oil business, firms that secure the ownership or operation of central production areas, characterized by the large size of reserves and relative ease of extraction, develop a first mover advantage with respect to peers that operate in less productive marginal areas. Something similar happens in retail; firms that move first to areas of a city that eventually booms, have an advantage over late arrivers who have to pay a much higher real estate cost. Lieberman and Montgomery also note that there may be disadvantages in being a first mover, for example, where there are large costs for entering the new market and when customers do not show loyalty to the new entrant. The benefits of first mover advantages are however most beneficial when network effects can be exploited – for example eBay entering the online auction market making it more attractive for both buyers and sellers. First mover advantages are particularly relevant where there are strong network effects. This theme will be explored in more detail in Chapter 4.

3.5 Modelling competitive dynamics: organizational ecology

In Chapter 2, we discussed extensively the use of models developed in the realm of economics for the purpose of analysing competition. We also warned that those models sacrificed relevance in the pursuit of rigour and advocated richer representations of the competitive landscape. One such dynamic model, organizational ecology, interests itself with the evolution of a system of interacting firms, concentrating on how the *population* of firms changes over time.

The use of organizational ecology or population ecology models (Hannan and Freeman 1977) is a good example of how modelling techniques from other disciplines – in this case ecological and biological models – have been accepted into the strategic management community and have provided a new insight into the problem of achieving sustainable competitive advantage. Organizational ecology models propose that certain firms occupy positions that possess higher 'fitness' than others; and use a Darwinian approach to the evolution of a population of firms, modelling the evolution of the population on the premise that fitter firms will survive and less fit firms will die out. Firms differ by, for instance, the breadth over which they attempt to compete, the so called niche-width of firms, firms having large niche-width being labelled generalists, whilst firms with low niche-width are labelled specialists. Organizational ecology models also consider firms having an evolutionary advantage by being 'inert'. The evolution of an industry can be modelled by considering how different types of firms compete over time, and how certain populations of firms survive for longer than others. However, the population ecology perspective tends to consider firms as being of a certain type (e.g. specialists or generalists) and therefore true heterogeneity between firms is not modelled explicitly. Furthermore, there is a high degree of formalization of organizational ecology models whereby mathematical relationships be-tween variables are modelled. As we shall see later in this chapter, agent-based models do not rely on such macro-level interactions being defined; rather they can focus on the micro-level interactions between firms that (as a consequence) demonstrate an effect at the macro level of the industry.

The concept of fitness as used by Hannan and Freeman (1977, 1989) also borrows heavily on biological metaphor: 'fitness means the rate at which genotypes produce copies of themselves across generations'. However, fitness in an organizational ecology perspective is not defined explicitly – the bio-logical metaphor is used here (as well as in the NK literature). Therefore the problem of the translation of a natural science definition, especially one that is not well defined within biology, poses problems of misinterpretation when translated to a non-natural science discipline. The maximization of a fitness function can be viewed as an analogue of the maximization of a utility function from within economics, and common problems are therefore asso-ciated with maximization approaches within management science. Organiza-tional ecology is essentially a Darwinian approach where 'natural' selection of organisms (or in the case of organizational ecology, organizations) that adapt to their environment and thereby increase their fitness have a higher prob-ability of surviving from one generation to the next. Dawkins' definitions (1982) of fitness are not limited to one clear definition – his definitions of types of fitness include: historical, genotypic, individual, inclusive, and per-sonal. Natural selection is defined as 'survival of the fittest' (although the phrase 'survival of the fittest' is linked to Darwin's theory of natural selection, the phrase was not used in the first edition of *On The Origin of Species* (rather, the phrase was used after Alfred Russell Wallace persuaded Darwin to use Herbert Spencer's term) Smith (2009). The use of the phrase 'survival of the fittest' has been thought of as tautological: the emphasis here is on the *survival* of those individuals with the highest *fitness*. Whether this is an appropriate notion for use in management science is very much debatable: the use of *survival* is not what is (usually) required from a strategist: most traditional views of sustainable competitive advantage do not mention *survival* – rather maximizing profits and market share. And whether a strategic analogue of fitness can be quantified within management is also debatable. It may therefore be more appropriate to concentrate on a measure that is more readily quantifiable: profit within an organization or market share within an industry; we can therefore concentrate on measuring profitability of an organization (as is done in the majority of empirical studies as a proxy to sustainable competitive advantage). In this way, we can think of a more applicable management-related interpretation of the landscape approach, by using new concepts of 'profit landscapes' or 'market share landscapes' rather than fitness landscapes.

As the concept of fitness landscapes is used in the management literature mainly to discuss so-called '*NK*' landscapes, the following reviews the methodology for producing landscape.

In this chapter, we do *not* use the *NK* model in order to generate a static fitness landscape – instead we use the interaction of firms and customers to generate a dynamic fitness landscape. Unlike the *NK* framework that looks at *internal* attributes of strategy (similar to the genes of a protein, that can be turned 'on' or 'off'), the model introduced later in this chapter provides a competitive landscape for *competition* between firms. The fitness landscape provides an indication of where a firm would ideally wish to locate given the absence of other competing firms – for instance where a new entrant would like to position their firm. For example, locating at a certain position will provide increased chance of profitability. There is no notion of competition in the *NK* model, rather the model relates fitness to the internal decisions of a firm, albeit capturing the interconnectedness of decisions. There are issues with the *NK* model, a discussion we shall leave until Chapter 7.

Hannan and Freeman (1974) argue for a measurement of *organizational* fitness, which they define as the probability that a given form of organization would persist in a certain environment. However, this does not explicitly take into account a changing environment where the level of fitness is likely to change under differing environmental conditions.

Behind organizational ecology is the notion that only limited resources are available in a market. While an industry analysis would consider the level of analysis to be the industry as a whole, organizational ecology goes beyond that by realizing that certain positions *within* the industry can still be attractive even when there are dominant incumbent firms with large market share, which would mean that an initial industry analysis would make entry into such an industry unattractive. There is also a bias within strategic management in the firms that tend to be studied as exemplars tend to be biased towards large firms (where quantitative data and rich case data are more readily available), and successful firms (as the case approach sees these firms as being models for strategic action by other firms). Population ecology allows the analysis of smaller firms, and also considers the fact that some firms may fail.

3.5.1 SPECIALISTS AND GENERALISTS

Carroll (1985) considers the evolution of the brewing industry, and considers the classical, environmental view of Porter:

In the brewing industry, product differentiation is coupled with economies of scale in production, marketing and distribution to create high barriers. (Porter 1980:9)

This would, taking a Porterian approach, mean that this is a seemingly unattractive industry: surely there can be no room for entry of firms into an unattractive industry. Carroll contrasts this view:

The U.S. market appears ready for an upsurge of specialist breweries. (Carroll 1985:1280)

These appear to be contradictory statements. On one hand, the industrial organization view would predict that due to high entry barriers, firms would not be attracted to the industry. However, the organizational ecology view does not treat firms as homogeneous but instead predicts that a specific *type* of firm will enter. What is important about this statement is that there is a prediction that *specialist* firms will enter the market. And this prediction does indeed appear to have been realized: Figure 3.1 shows the *concentration* of the number of brewers in the United States over the 1940s to the 1990s, but also the rapid growth of microbreweries. If we had considered the total number of breweries instead, we would not have seen this interesting dynamic over time. This shows that the differences between firms are vitally important. Of course, microbreweries do not produce the same volume of production as the mass producers, but their 'density' (as organizational ecologists describe the number of firms in an industry as density) is significant.

The organizational ecology explanation of this phenomenon is that there are two separate types of firms operating: generalists and specialists. They use the familiar concept of fitness, as a function of the dimension of competition, to describe these two different types of organization (see Figure 3.2).

Generalists are able to attract resources or consumers from the wide range of competitive dimension whereas specialists attract only a limited range. Although competing firms operate in the same market, there can be significant differences

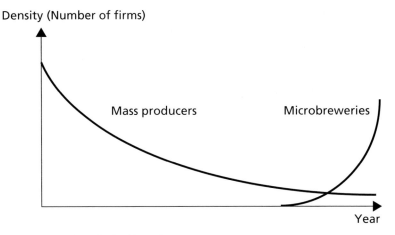

Figure 3.1. Density (number) of beer firms 1940–2000

Source: Carroll (1985).

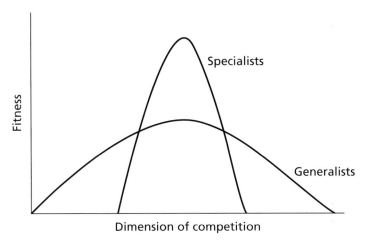

Figure 3.2. Specialists and generalists

between consumers within this market. Consider the example of the market for beer (Carroll 1985): beer drinkers are distributed amongst age and social status, with a majority of consumers being of a middle social status and are middle aged. Generalists can (and do) target this mass market. Specialists may however target a particular part of the market, for example providing products that are attractive to older or younger consumers or provide specific products that appeal to lower or higher status consumers. These differences matter, in that 'niches' emerge where there exists an opportunity for a specialist to enter the

Resource level (number of customers)

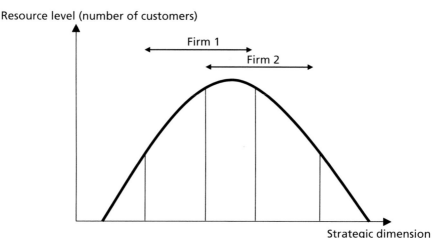

Figure 3.3. Early competition: generalists compete at the centre of the market

Source: Carroll and Hannan (2000).

market and gain market share from the incumbent firms. Organizational ecologists study the growth of these niches. Firms' success, survival, or death is strongly influenced by their positioning on this competitive landscape. Figures 3.3–3.4 (after Carroll and Hannan 2000) show how niches can form.

In early competition, generalists enter the market and tend to compete at the center of the market, without necessarily competing head-to-head. This is consistent with the Hotelling model, where competing firms tend to move towards the center of the market (see Figure 3.3).

In further competition, the market may not be able to support two generalists, and one may be selected, forming a niche where the customers of the second firm are no longer served. This periphery of the market becomes unserved and exposed meaning that specialists are able to enter the market in these locations. These niches are often 'legitimated' by the entry of more specialists, and movement barriers may persist based on the difficulty for consumers to return to a generalist product (see Figure 3.4).

Finally, these niches take away customers from the incumbents, meaning that the generalist firm has fewer customers. Since the distribution of customers moves towards the niche supplier, these niche locations become 'legitimated'.

Therefore, as concentration of the industry increases it may mean superficially that it is an unattractive industry, and that the generalist firm is not satisfying the needs of peripheral customers. Rather than considering this as an unattractive industry, this can be an ideal breeding ground for specialist firms willing to offer a product closer to the needs of these peripheral customers.

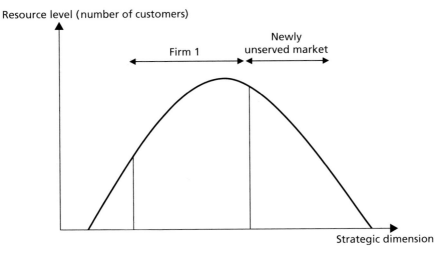

Figure 3.4. Firm 2 departs leaving an unserved market

Source: Carroll and Hannan (2000).

Organizational ecology looks not only at the initial locations of firms, but at firms' trajectories over time, modelling explicitly the birth and death of firms.

3.5.2 ORGANIZATIONAL ECOLOGY DIMENSIONS

We saw in Chapter 2 the importance of strategic dimensions: the concept of an N-dimensional space is used in the population ecology literature, particularly in niche width literature, building on a theoretical biology perspective: 'an ecological niche is defined as the N-dimensional resource space within which a population can exist' (Hutchinson 1957, cited in Carroll 1985), thereby proposing an N-dimensional resource space as an organism's ecological limits.

Organizational Ecologists such as Hannan and Freeman (1977) translate the space used in organizational population biology to space that commercial organizations inhabit. One of the premises of Hannan and Freeman's work is that organizations are either generalists or specialists, the measure of which can be defined as the width of the niches that they inhabit in this space. However, it is debatable whether a firm's strategy can be defined merely in terms of the space it inhabits – the absolute position of the firm is also important. In addition, the fact that a firm is a specialist (and therefore targets a narrow niche) surely does not define its strategy so that it will actively reject customers that are not within its niche. The argument used by Hannan and Freeman is that generalists perform better under conditions of rapid environmental change whereas specialist firms are more likely to succeed in stable environments. It should be noted that an analogue to the niche size (which has produced a large literature) could be thought of as the '*strategic domain*' that is inhabited by the firms in a general strategy space.

Péli and Nooteboom (1999) review the properties of '*n*-dimensional Euclidean space' from an organizational ecology perspective, and point to the uses of this space in other sociological and economic literature. Burt and Carlton (1989:727) building on Burt (1988:359) define a 'market topology map or market topology' that is 'a multidimensional scaling of distances between [*n* production activities]'.

Conceptual Box 3.2 Comparing research based on agent-based models with Econometric Methods

---

Although the use of an attribute space to plot firms is used both in regression analysis and in product space, there are fundamental differences between the two approaches, even though they have in common the plotting of firm locations on the *x* and *y* axes of a two-dimensional space. The concept behind regression models is to infer the relationship between an independent variable and a dependent variable. This contrasts to the plotting of firms on product space in that the aim here is to plot two variables where no one variable has been chosen in advance as the one of predominant interest. In regression models, we assume that there is a relationship between variables; this relationship is what we set out to discover by undertaking a statistical analysis. This is in contrast to the positioning of firms within two or more dimensions. This emphasizes the importance of 'dimensionality' – for a variable to be considered a dimension, it has to meet certain characteristics such as orthogonality, which we discussed in Chapter 2.

These constructions (which are merely frameworks upon which we can construct models) have indeed been converted into models that use the location with respect to one or more dimension as a strategic decision that can influence the success of the entity that determines its location. Notable examples are Hotelling's model and Downs' model that are described briefly above.

3.6 **Agent-based models**

Several methodologies are employed for this purpose within management research, some of which are discussed next. Simulation, whilst it may be a relatively new tool in the social sciences and particularly strategic management, provides a well-proven research tool in the physical sciences. The interaction of physical and social sciences is gaining momentum – first by the interaction of economics and physics ('econophysics'), latterly with 'sociophysics' providing a growing area of research (Schweitzer and Troitzsch 2002). Much of the research into agent-based modelling has been based in the trans-disciplinary work of Complexity Science of which several 'centres of excellence' have emerged. For example, the Santa Fe Institute in New Mexico, has as its aim the concentration on collaborative multi-disciplinary research in order to 'break down the barriers between traditional disciplines, to spread its ideas and methodologies to other institutions, and to encourage the practical application of its results'. Many new centres for complexity science are being set up. Later in this chapter and in Chapters 4 and 7, we will use some of the tools of complexity science (such as agent-based modelling) that are appropriate for studying dynamic environments in strategic management.

Agent-based models provide a significant potential to model and understand the dynamics of strategic management. The identification of the advantages of the agent-based approach has been highlighted within the wider social sciences literature. Gilbert and Terna (2000) describe the use of agent-based models as the 'third way' of carrying out social science (over and above augmentation and formalization). McKelvey (1997, 1999) explores the phenomenon of complexity research applied to management and includes agent-based modelling as a promising research methodology. Axelrod (1997) explains agent-based modelling as the difference between induction and deduction: induction being the discovery of patterns within empirical data; deduction being the proof of consequences that can be derived from a set of specified axioms. Not only does this methodology point to new areas of research, but potentially to a new contribution to the body of explanation with social science, and specifically strategic management.

Agent-based models grew out of the burgeoning research into complexity, with the use of agent-based models increasing in the last few years (Epstein and Axtell 1996; Gilbert and Troitzsch 1999). Most of the models used in management research are linear, non-dynamic, and almost by definition pay limited attention to complex interactions within and between agents. Such models restrict their analysis to a few key variables, under an assumption of perfect rationality, and do not investigate fully the complicated interactions between multiple variables. Agent-based modelling provides a way of overcoming the restriction imposed by mathematical modelling, that of being able to define all relationships between variables in a rigorous form, often not allowing scope for non-deterministic relationships.

One of the earliest tools used for agent-based modelling is *Swarm* (Minar et al. 1996). The rationale behind *Swarm* was to provide a framework for modelling a collection of independent agents interacting via discrete events. More recently, tools such as *RePast* (Collier 2001) and *NetLogo* (Wilensky 1999) have been developed, each with their own idiosyncratic advantages.

A review of several agent-based modelling toolkits for use in strategic management contexts is contained in Robertson (2005).

The language of agent-based modelling is rather specialized. We set out in the following some of the main components of agent-based models in order to show how we can construct an agent-based model, and how the modelling approach varies from traditional techniques.

3.6.1 THE AGENT

Agents are at the heart of an agent-based model. Whilst there is no universally accepted definition of an agent (Gilbert and Troitzsch 1999), Ferber (1989:249, cited in Bura et al. 1995) provides an appropriate conceptualization: 'a real or abstract entity that is able to act on itself and its environment; which has a partial representation of its environment; which can, in a multi-agent universe, communicate with other agents; and whose behaviour is a result of its observations, its knowledge and its interactions with the other agents'. Importantly, agents can be heterogeneous in that they all have individual characteristics, unlike other models that may as a first approximation assume that all entities are homogeneous.

Agents are assigned behaviours, rules that enable them to interact with and in their environment. For example, an agent may have a set of rules that indicate how it may respond to stimuli from its environment. It should be noted that the response need not be deterministic: a level of randomness or stochastic behaviour can be included in the agent. In addition, a cognitive element can be built into the agent – it may have a perception of the world that is different to another agent. In this way, the actions of the agent need not be restricted to behaviour that is rational.

The agents within an agent-based model interact repeatedly at different times over the course of the run of the model. An agent is an actor in a system that is capable of generating events that affect both itself and other agents. Agents can be created or destroyed as the model is run, such creation and destruction being controlled by rules defined within the model. Whilst the model is being run, it is possible to interrogate or 'probe' the properties of each agent. In this way, one can extract details of each agent rather than being restricted to the macro-parameters of the model itself.

3.6.2 THE ENVIRONMENT

Agents are populated in an environment. In the simplest form, this can be a two-dimensional square lattice (the topology familiar to cellular automata, although cellular automata models are usually restricted to homogeneous agents). However, agent-based models in toolkits such as *Swarm* and *RePast* are not restricted to such topologies. The topologies can be discrete (e.g. a lattice) or continuous (e.g. a plane). The topology can be defined by the user, although topologies such as grids and networks are available from predefined examples within the modelling package. Abstract spaces (useful, e.g., in network analysis) can also be defined and used to construct models. The space, as well as the agents that are situated within this space, comprise the model 'world'. Agents can interact with the environment thereby altering their world. This in turn changes the agent's perception of the world and offers a notion of feedback to the system. Thus, agent-based models can incorporate the feedback effects found in game theoretical models.

3.6.3 THE SCHEDULE

The organization of these discrete events takes place through a 'schedule', an ordered list of events that are triggered as the model is run. The simulation system orders these events by assigning each time step a 'tick' count. The schedule is important in an agent-based model, as it controls when the interactions between agents take place. Schedules can be created dynamically, in that when one agent triggers a response, an entry can be made to the schedule for another event to occur at a future time. Therefore, we do not have to restrict our models to pre-defining the order of events that will take place in the model. At each time step or 'tick', the events by which agents interact are assumed to take place simultaneously. This may cause problems when agents are assumed to interact with each other, but the software packages have developed ways of handling such concurrent events in order to give arbitration rules that determine the order in which the events actually occur (within the time step which is assumed to be infinitesimally small).

3.6.4 THE MODEL

The collection of all agents, the schedule that instructs these agents, and the rules of the simulation together comprise the model. This will control the initialization of the model and the progress of the model over time. The model is parameterized, in that one can change the initial conditions of the simulation without having to rewrite the simulation. In this way, param-eter spaces can be 'swept', allowing an analysis of how the interactions of parameters change the results of the model. The model itself, along with the definition of the agents, are the most important parts of the construction of an agent-based model: the model determines how agents are created and destroyed, how the agents are displayed, and how the data is exported for further analysis. It should be noted that the introduction of agent-based modelling toolkits has allowed the modeller to concentrate on the salient features from a strategic point of view, rather than spending time on the 'housekeeping' elements of the model, for example the methods used to display the agents, to export the data for later analysis, or to construct probability distributions used in the model.

3.6.5 EMERGENT BEHAVIOUR

The concept of emergence (Holland 1998) within agent-based models explains how global properties of the system can come from simple rules of agent behaviour. One of the most useful facets of using agent-based models is that, from the simple behaviour of locally-interacting agents, complex global behaviour can be exhibited by the system which is in turn observed by the researcher. This is one of the unique and interesting properties that can come from using agent-based models. The results at a global level may reveal global behaviour that is not immediately obvious given the simple interaction rules of the agents.

3.6.6 RATIONALE FOR USING AGENT-BASED MODELS

The use of simulations and agent-based models is a new field for strategic management, although agent-based models are becoming more widely used within other social sciences (Axelrod 1997, Gilbert and Troitzsch 1999, Epstein and Axtell 1996). Recent use of agent-based models within strategic management has been concentrated in the *NK* model; later in this chapter we shall see how we can construct an alternative agent-based model for studying the interaction of a competitive set of firms with customers.

Models that are developed from an economic perspective tend to focus on the *market*, rather than the individual firm. The goal of any simulation within the strategic management discipline should be to aid in understanding strategic decisions from the point of view of the *individual firm*. Although we focus on a particular set of firms (within an industry) to review some of the strategic decisions that are faced by the firms, it should be noted that the model devised is appropriate to most industries, particularly those where there are important linkages between customers and firms.

The use of computer models within social science research has long allowed higher (greater than two) dimensions to be modelled. For example, components of a firm's location may be stored using a high number of variables. Therefore, the concept of working in higher dimensions and representing the coordinates of a firm in N-dimensional space is not new to this computer-based modelling approach – high-dimensional arrays can be used to store variables of different entities. One advantage of using agent-based models over other computer-based models is that agent-based models are designed specifically to have the capability of dealing with heterogeneous agents, or firms.

It should be noted for clarification that 'agent' in agent-based models should not be confused with principal-agent theory or principal-agent models that deal with the theory of incentives intended to persuade an employee or contractor (the 'agent') to act in the best interests of the 'principal' (the employer). It would, of course, be possible to investigate such problems with the methodology of agent-based models, but this would only be a specific case of the agent-based model methodology being used.

As discussed in Chapter 2, the realization that the actions of one firm have reactions to the wider system of firms has been widely accepted within the strategic management literature, building on the work of game theorists following von Neumann and Morgenstern (1944). However, game theoretic approaches to strategy have been criticized on bases including the presumption that they assume rationality of behaviour (Camerer 1991). Further criticism can be levelled by the fact that game theoretical 'solutions' are usually in the form of Nash equilibria, and therefore are not ideally suited for a non-equilibrium system, an example of which is a turbulent industry. Agent-based models do not require equilibria to be found in order to be of use – indeed they do not require equilibrium solutions to exist. Output from the model can be used without the existence of an analytical solution, which may not be the case with mainstream game theoretical solutions.

There are several advantages of using agent-based models over 'system-wide' approaches:

- they allow for heterogeneous agents; firms with different attributes such as profit, size, strategic location, and dynamics can be modelled at the same time; in addition different types of agents, such as firms and customers can be modelled simultaneously;
- bounded rationality of agents can be incorporated: agents can be simulated whereby they have limited cognitive ability; this can be different for each agent;
- the system can be dynamic: the system need not be at equilibrium (a supposition of models such as those early strategy models whose roots are in neo-classical microeconomics); and
- emergent phenomena can be explored.

3.7 **An agent-based model of customer-firm interaction**

Robertson (2003a) modelled turbulence within an industry by modelling the changing firm–customer linkages caused by the movement of *firms*, which we shall describe as *endogenous turbulence*, as well as the turbulence caused by the movement of customers ('value-generating agents'), that we describe as *exogenous turbulence*. The value-generating agents in this model may also themselves contribute to turbulence within an industry, for example when customers switch from firm to firm.

As this agent-based simulation is interested primarily in the strategies of firms (as opposed to customers, which may be the focus of a more marketing-inspired model), most emphasis in the design of Robertson's model is placed on how firms move. It is however a trivial extension to model the behaviour of consumers as the focus of the model. Firms occupy a position within the strategy space (see the earlier discussion) and derive profitability and market share dependent upon their location in this strategy space, where the level of competitiveness is also influenced by the location of their competitors. In the model, it is assumed that the source of competitive advantage for the firm is derived from holding (and maintaining) relationships with value-generating agents (in this specific case, customers who generate profits for the firm).

Initialization of the Model
This model situates firms within a strategy space, the 'strategy hypercube' (see Chapter 2). This strategy space is an *N*-dimensional space with the firm having a set of coordinates which describe its strategy. To aid interpretation of the model, although the space is *N*-dimensional, we shall simplify its representation by showing only two of the *N* dimensions.

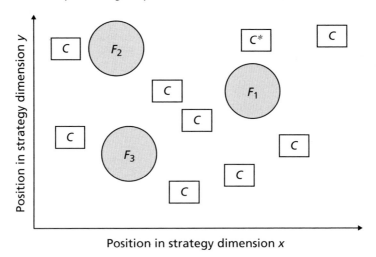

Figure 3.5. Location of firms (F) and customers (C) in strategic space

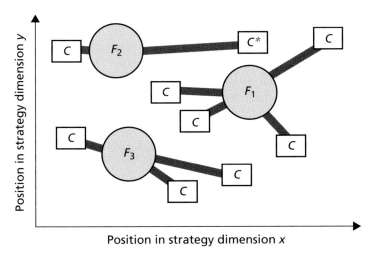

Figure 3.6. Formation of links between firms and customers

We start with a population of firms that are distributed in the strategy space. Value-generating agents (we assume these are customers) are also positioned in the same space. For the moment, we can consider customers to have a set of requirements that determine their position in the strategy space. Similarly, firms are positioned according to the strategies they adopt (although their strategy is more than their static position; it also encompasses how the firm *moves* within this space) (see Figure 3.5).

Customers set up relationships with firms according to the proximity of the firm's strategic positioning in relation to the customer's requirements (customers select firms closest to them in strategy space). Customers are initialized as perfectly rational, that is, they form a link to their nearest firm. As the model runs, however, they may decide to change to a firm that is not closest to them, as long as this meets a minimum satisfaction level. This incorporates the notion of bounded rationality and satisficing (e.g. in Figure 3.6, customer agent C^* has a relationship with firm F_2 whereas if the customer was exhibiting purely rational behaviour, they should be linked with firm F_1).

It should be noted that the decision as to which firm a customer should buy is being made by each individual customer. This of course is influenced by the position of firms and firms' competitors, which are in turn influenced by the customers, but the final decision is made by the customer, not the firm. There is continuous feedback between the movement of firms and the competitive landscape. Although this concept has been used as a metaphor in the past, this is the first time that a dynamic competitive landscape deformed by the movement of the firms has been modelled.

In Figure 3.6, we can see a representation of the model, where all customers (C) are purchasing goods from firms (F).

3.7.1 CUSTOMER/VALUE-GENERATING AGENTS

Customers may have a wide range of rules that they use to decide which firm to select to give their custom, for instance they may choose a firm randomly from the entire population; choose a firm of their nearest customer neighbour; search for firms within a certain distance and select from these firms; or if their search is unsuccessful, lower their minimum satisfaction level in order to compensate.

Value-generating agents are assumed to be located in the same space as the firm agents. For the special case of a Lancaster-type of product space, this is clear: firms produce products with certain characteristics (coordinates), and customers require products with certain characteristics. For other strategic dimensions, we can think of customers' preferences mapping onto the firms' strategic dimensions. The customers/value-generating agents are parameterized by defining the coordinates in space $(x, y, \ldots)$ located in the N strategic dimensions and the rules for the movement of these customers. The presence of the value-generating agents in the strategy space creates certain locations which are attractive (by virtue of having many customers and few competitors) and those which are superficially unattractive (where there may be few customers or many competitors). However, the actual attractiveness of every location within the strategy space is difficult to interpret. We therefore create a fitness landscape of the strategy space by calculating, for each point within the space, the number of customers who would be buying from a firm at each location. By calculating this for each position, and drawing it as the 'height' on the strategy space, we create a three-dimensional map (for a two-dimensional strategy space) that is the fitness landscape of the industry (we shall show how we construct the fitness landscape later in this chapter).

As we are primarily concerned with the behaviour of firms (and the behaviour of *customers* is only a special case of the behaviour of value-generating agents) we can assume that customers behave rationally (i.e. they will always connect to a firm and will always connect to the firm nearest to them in strategic space). If we wanted to adapt the model to investigate the behaviour of *customers* (e.g. if this were to be a marketing problem as opposed to a strategy problem), the behaviour of such customers would be modelled in more depth. We do not of course have to assume this rationality: customer inertia can also be modelled, as described in a later paragraph.

The uncertainty of position of value-generating agents is a source of turbulence within the industry. If the position of all customer agents were fixed, a firm would find it easier to locate sources of such agents (perhaps by exploring the firm's strategic environment) and therefore obtain a better mapping of the concentrations of the agents. (Of course, other firms would be doing the same, and the dynamics of what plays out, which firms attract the customers, is a non-trivial problem.) If however the location of such agents is not fixed, we introduce a level of 'turbulence' into the industry. We can think of this as being turbulence exogenous to the movement of firms within the industry, in that the movement of firms *per se* does not influence the movement of the value-generating agents. However, this is not to say that turbulence cannot exist without this exogenous effect: *endogenous* turbulence is possible by way of the reaction of firms to the position of other firms. However, the turbulence modelled by means of the movement of value-generating agents can be thought of as 'endogenous' turbulence by virtue of the changes emanating from the agents themselves.

3.7.2 INITIAL DISTRIBUTION OF VALUE-GENERATING AGENTS

In the model, a parameter is used to set the initial distribution of value-generating (customer) agents where, depending on this parameter, customers are distributed according to a statistical distribution. The distribution of both customer agents and firm agents is random; the coordinates of each firm are chosen from a uniform distribution. We could of course decide on a different distribution of customer agents, for example a normal distribution; this would have the effect of concentrating the value-generating agents in the centre of strategy space. The justification of using a uniform distribution is, in the absence of any industry-specific knowledge of the positioning of firms or customers, that the uniform distribution represents a general model of an industry. It should be noted that, at this stage, the model is intended to be able to be generalized to *any* industry and therefore industry-specific knowledge is not required (although it would of course be useful where we intend to gain insights into a particular industry). This data could, of course, be obtained, and models specific to particular industries could be obtained from marketing data.

3.7.3 'CUSTOMER' INERTIA

As an extension to the model, customers can either link to the firm that is closest to them in strategy space, or they can have a minimum satisfaction level below which they do not change the firm to which they are attached, and above which they look for the closest firm and then link to them. Figure 3.7 represents this satisfaction level below which customers do not switch.

If d, the minimum distance to invoke switching, is zero, then customers behave as in the original model, that is, they are always 'unsatisfied' and therefore behave 'rationally' by always linking to the firm agent that is closest to them in strategy space.

Formal Representation of the Model
The formal representation for the model is shown in the following equation:

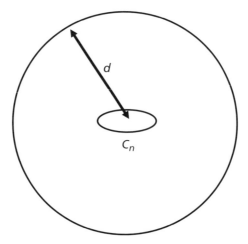

Figure 3.7. Switching boundary d for customer Cn

$$\Pi(k,\mathbf{F}_k) = \sum_{i=1}^{n} \pi(k,i) \text{ where } \pi(k,i) = \begin{cases} 1 \text{ if } d(\mathbf{F}_k,\mathbf{c}_i) = \min_{j=1}^{m} d(\mathbf{F}_k,\mathbf{c}_i) \\ 0 \text{ otherwise} \end{cases}$$

where:

Π is the profit accruing to firm k;
n is the number of customers;
m is the number of firms;
F_k and c_n are the vectors representing the position of firm k and customer n within strategy space; and
d is distance.

The equation shows that the profit of the firm depends on how many customers are acquired, where customers make the decision to buy from the closest firm.

A screenshot of the model running is shown in Figure 3.8: we can see that customers are connected (and are buying from) firms according to the position of the firms in the strategic landscape within the strategy hypercube.

We can construct a profit landscape from the position of the customer and firms. In order to do this, we can calculate, for each position in the N-dimensional space, the number of customers that a firm would obtain were it to be in that position. We can calculate the number of firms for each location in the space, and plot these values on a third dimension, thereby constructing a fitness landscape which is a landscape *generated by the model* rather than being a landscape that is set exogenously. An example of such a landscape can be seen in Figure 3.9.

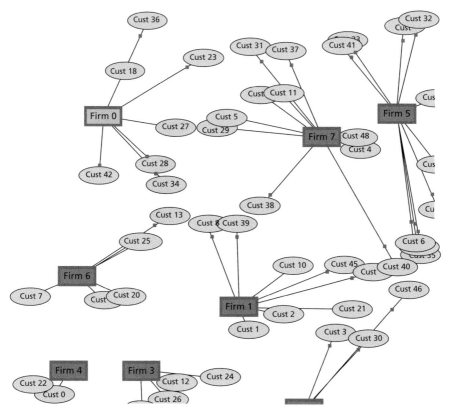

Figure 3.8. Links between firms and customers in the Robertson agent-based model

In Figure 3.9, the left-hand side of the diagram shows the positions of firms and customers, whereas the right-hand side of the diagram shows the profit landscape for the industry: higher, 'hotter' points show positions that are more attractive to firms, while lower, 'cooler' points show positions that are unattractive. The model is run, where firms move their position according to their own strategies (which can differ from firm to firm), and customers change affiliation as competitors become closer. In this way, there are a series of 'frames' of the model, which in turn create an animation and in turn a dynamic model, as shown in Fig 3.11.

The interaction between firms and customers can be summarized in the framework given in the following text. We can see that, for each movement of a firm, customers will react, in that they may switch supplier to a firm that, as a result of its movement, is now closer to that customer. However, as a result of this customer switching, competitors may now find that their customers have switched, and in turn, this may mean that they now change location in

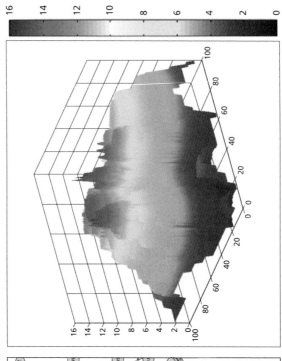
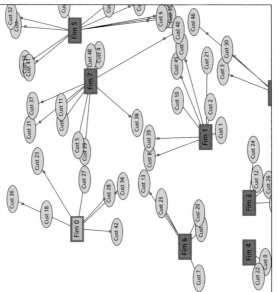

Figure 3.9. Construction of a profit landscape from the model

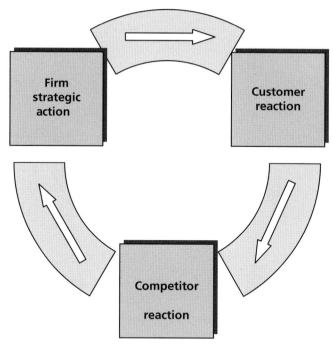

Figure 3.10. Interaction cycle between customers and firms

order to capture further customers. This cycle continues, and is the driver of the dynamics of the model (see Figure 3.10).

By allowing firms to move according to their individual strategy (which can differ between firms), we are able to model the changing landscape as a result of the interactions between firms, intermediated by customer switching. An example of the evolution of the landscape, showing the dynamic nature of the model, is shown in Figure 3.11.

One of the main advantages of this model is that it models competitive behaviour with several firms, as opposed to models that only model one firm.

Several results are seen when we model different types of firm behaviour such as comparing customer-led firm behaviour with market-oriented behaviour (Slater and Narver 1998, 1999):

- customer led strategies are beneficial when competitors are seeking customer density – that is, a good defensive strategy;
- a strategy of moving towards the peak of the profit landscape is beneficial but may not be practical when there are high numbers of agents (competitors/customers);
- if all competitors are moving towards the peak of the landscape, we can benefit from moving towards locations of highest customer density;

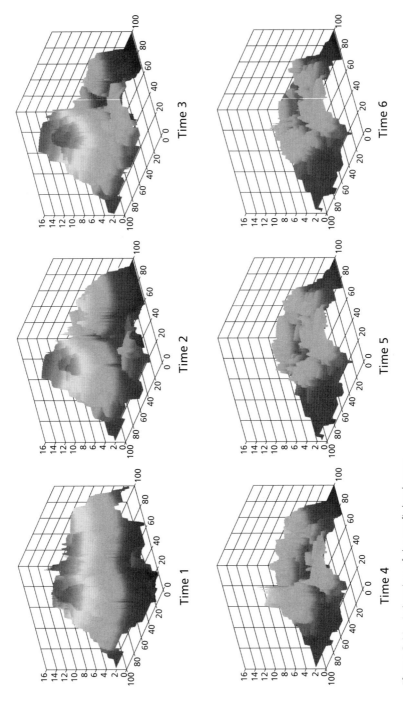

Figure 3.11. Animation of the profit landscape

- a differentiation strategy (moving to low firm density) is bad when faced with competitors who are customer-led;

- if all firms move towards the highest customer density, we benefit from following another strategy;

- if competitors are moving towards customer density, we should move towards low firm density; if competitors are moving to low firm density, we should move towards high customer density;

- market-oriented strategies can be a source of competitive advantage, as suggested by Slater and Narver, but are not always so.

This agent-based modelling approach can be extended to the economics models introduced in Chapter 2. We discussed in Chapter 2 the fact that models such as Cournot's model jump immediately to an equilibrium without the path to equilibrium being considered. The Hotelling model of spatial competition is another model where economists may be more interested in the equilibrium rather than the path to equilibrium. The work of Robertson and Siggelkow 2005 shows the path to equilibrium is of importance. A description of this work is shown in the following text.

3.8 **An agent-based model of price-location competition**

We saw in Chapter 2 that firms can compete by setting their location (the Hotelling model) or by changing their prices (directly or indirectly) as in the Cournot or Bertrand models. Robertson and Siggelkow (2005) combined

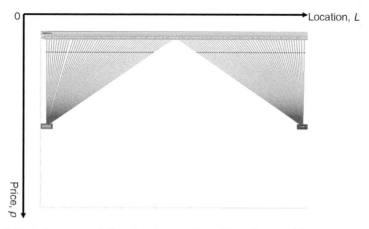

Figure 3.12. Robertson and Siggelkow's agent-based Hotelling model

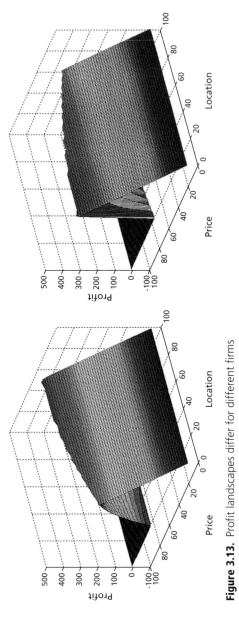

Figure 3.13. Profit landscapes differ for different firms

these approaches to model the Hotelling model dynamically, where firms are able to change their location or price in order to maximize their profits. This was undertaken by means of an agent-based model so that the individual firms (and indeed customers) could be modelled individually.

In Figure 3.12, firms are placed in location–price space, and are free to compete on these dimensions. Customers are equally spaced along the location dimension, and they form links with the firm that is 'closest' to them – by this we mean that the transportation cost (difference between their location and the location of the firm) plus the price set by the firm. The red lines show the links that are made between the firms and the customers.

Each of the firms experiences a different profit landscape, and these are shown in Figure 3.13.

Similar to the model in section 3.7, the movement of each firm causes the profit landscape to change, not only for the firm that moves, but also for the other firms in the industry. By doing this, Robertson and Siggelkow were able to turn the static Hotelling and Cournot/Bertrand-type models into *dynamic* models of inter-firm competition. It is interesting to note that the analytical equilibrium solution to the Hotelling model is also found in their agent-based model, validating the model.

4 Networks

4.1 Introduction

If the 1980s was the decade of the environmental or 'structuralist' view of strategy, the 1990s the decade of the resource-based view, then the 2000s may well be the decade of networks. Not only are firms waking up to the fact that organizing their inter-firm relations in a different way may lead to competitive advantage, customers too are realizing the power of social networks.

Networks of firms and networks of individuals can be a source of competitive advantage. Networks are of interest in a dynamic context in that network ties can be created and broken over time. From a strategic point of view, firms may wish to encourage the development of network ties that go beyond conventional relationships with other firms. We will see this in the case of Toyota discussed in the following text, where suppliers are encouraged to develop ties between themselves, rather than having a traditional contract-based tie between a supplier and a core firm. We also study the importance of social ties within the context of strategic management theory development. We also comment on the importance of firms setting themselves to be an attractive ecosystem to encourage the development of new firms in what we describe as 'mutualistic entrepreneurship' (Robertson and Fan 2008). While this can be considered to be a co-operative relationship from a game theoretical perspective, the fact that the two parties are not in the same industry (one is a supplier, the other a host) means that the anti-trust issues arising from co-operative relationships are eliminated.

4.2 Network analysis

The importance of networks as a study within the strategic management field at a firm level is well established (Gulati 1995; Gulati et al. 2000). More recent studies have identified the importance of networks as a source of knowledge sharing and generation (Dyer and Nobeoka 2000) and the importance of interpersonal networks (Westphal et al. 2005).

Recently, networks have been seen as important in the foundation of entrepreneurial firms – the first volume of the *Strategic Entrepreneurship Journal* devoted several papers to networks: Rosenkopf and Schilling (2007) examine differences in network structure across industries, while Stuart and Sorenson (2007) investigate the *social* network that determines the development of net ventures and the creation of new firms. The importance of social networks in a competitive sense should not be underestimated: social networks are at the very heart of new venture creation, and the making and breaking of network links in order to change the environmental landscape changes the nature of competitive landscapes and subsequent competition. Even though the analysis of a network shows the state of the network at a particular time, one has to remember that the network has only reached that state as a result of an evolution of network connections and network cleavages. By taking snapshots of the network structure at several times, it is possible to see the development of that network over time and thereby understand more about the dynamics of the environment.

The creation of new scholarly 'enterprises' in the form of academic collaboration and the exchange of ideas is akin to the entrepreneurial process, where opportunity scanning for new ventures plays an important part. Recent attention has turned to how different disciplines, namely psychology, sociology, and economics have influenced management, and how the field of management compares to these 'parent' disciplines.

Social network analysis has become an increasingly important tool in analysing the connections between individuals and therefore understanding the informal organization they constitute. However, in the context of this chapter, network analysis is a more general term, where we can analyse (using the tools and terminology of social network analysis, that is being constantly developed) to determine and understand the connections between firms rather than merely restricting ourselves to the connections between individuals within a *social* network.

Network analysis is a method for describing the connections between actors. These actors can take multiple forms, as networks can be created from the links between individuals or firms. Much of the recent work on network analysis has been determining the type of network that exists at a macro level.

Aldrich and Kim (2007) identify the importance of social networks in entrepreneurship. They note (2007:148) 'most strategic network research focuses on network structures and their consequences within and between established firms. There are very few papers on the genesis of ties and even fewer that consider the role of networks in the founding of new ventures'.

4.2.1 THE DYNAMIC NATURE OF NETWORK MODELS

Although network models can be criticized in that they take a snapshot of the state of a network at a particular point in time, network analysis is now taking an interest in the dynamic, longitudinal nature of networks. By investigating network properties at different times, one can construct a longitudinal analysis of the state of the network, building a series of snapshots that in conjunction make up a dynamic picture, rather as individual frames of a motion picture together make up a movie. Although this procedure is relatively new, we set out examples of research in this field.

4.2.1.1 Small world networks

In the 1960s, Stanley Milgram, a social psychologist at Harvard, conducted an experiment to determine whether people selected at random could find a path, via intermediate social acquaintances, to a seemingly unconnected individual. What Milgram (1967) found was that many individuals were indeed able to find a path to the target, a stockbroker in Boston.

The phenomenon of 'small-world' networks (Watts and Strogatz 1998; Watts 1999a, 1999b) can be traced back to Milgram's work (1967) in *Psychology Today*:

Fred Jones of Peoria, sitting in a sidewalk cafe in Tunisia, and needing a light for his cigarette, asks the man at the next table for a match. They fall into conversation; the stranger is an Englishman who, it turns out, spent several months in Detroit. 'I know it's a foolish question; says Jones, 'but do you by any chance know a fellow named Ben Arkadian? He's an old friend of mine, manages a chain of supermarkets in Detroit . . . 'Arkadian . . . Arkadian . . .' the Englishman mutters. 'Why, upon my soul, I believe I do! Small chap, very energetic, raised merry hell with the factory over a shipment of defective bottle caps'. 'No kidding!' Jones exclaims, amazed. 'Good lord, it's a small world, isn't it? (Milgram 1967:61)

Of course, the packages sent from Kansas to Boston could have taken virtually any number of routes through the social network of connections between individuals in the social network that is the American population. Studying the connections between these individuals has become increasingly an area of research, that has discovered that such 'small worlds' exist in many different situations such as the network between directors of companies (Conyon and Muldoon 2006). Conyon and Muldoon showed that both directors and boards of directors were tightly interlocked, forming a small world network of directors.

Many of the studies of social networks and inter-firm networks have studied the network statistics at a particular time. What has been neglected is how these networks evolve over time. Recent developments in network research have enabled the study of the evolution of these networks over time. Kossinets and Watts (2006) investigated the *evolution* of a social network over time.

Before going on to discuss specific networks, we will review some of the basic concepts of social network analysis in Conceptual Box 4.1.

Conceptual Box 4.1 Social network analysis concepts

Before we go into more depth in describing the different types of network, such as small world networks, we can review the definitions of networks that are used in these analyses.

Nodes and Edges

In graph theory, networks are diagrams consisting of connections (known as *edges* or *arcs* or *lines*) between points (known as *vertices* or *nodes* or *points*). These nodes may differ depending on the sort of network we are studying. For instance, in a social network diagram, the nodes represent people, and the vertices will represent social ties between these people. We can represent the connections between the six directors of a firm, for instance, as follows in Figure 4.1:

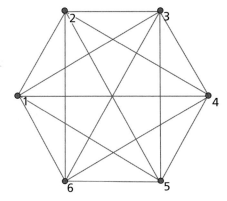

Figure 4.1. Social network diagram

Degree Centrality

Centrality of nodes can be measured in several ways. The simplest, *degree centrality*, measures the number of nodes that are connected to that node. In the example illustrated in Figure 4.1, each node has degree centrality (or just 'degree') of five, as they are each connected to five other individuals.

Cliques

Several things are apparent even from this simple network diagram. There are six nodes (representing directors), and they are each connected to every other director. For instance, Director 1 is connected to Directors 2, 3, 4, 5, and 6. This network is known as a *fully connected* network or a *clique*.

4.2.1.2 Inter-firm networks

Network analysis is not only performed at the social level: Dyer and Nobeoka (2000) look at how inter-firm networks can be a source of competitive advantage in Case Box 4.1.

Case Box 4.1 Knowledge sharing networks at Toyota

How is it that Japanese productivity per worker increases at a rate faster than at the equivalent firms within the United States? These are questions that were posed when considering the improvements in efficiency at Toyota, far after the explicit knowledge of the Toyota Production System have diffused to competitors. If we look at a graph of Toyota automotive labour productivity from the 1960s to the 1990s, we see that productivity increased steadily over this period, *and* the productivity of its suppliers increased accordingly. This can be contrasted with U.S. productivity, which *did* increase in the 1980s (after the Toyota Production System had diffused to the US), but the productivity of the suppliers to U.S. car companies did not increase. Networks have a role to play in explaining this anomaly.

Toyota is now the largest and one of the most profitable automotive manufacturers in the world. Both Toyota and General Motors produce nine million cars per year, but Toyota's valuation remains ten times that of GM. How is this possible? Even though the Toyota production system is well known, and can easily be copied by competitors, Toyota organizes its supplier relations in a different way. Dyer and Nobeoka (2000) attribute the success of Toyota to the network structures. While traditional buyer–supplier relations have the focal firm at the centre of the network, with suppliers having unilateral relationships with that firm, Toyota organizes these relationships so that, in addition to having a relationship with Toyota, its suppliers also have relationships with other suppliers. In this way, a more connected network takes form where suppliers are more able to learn from each other, enabling not only higher profits for Toyota, but also for its suppliers (see Figure 4.2).

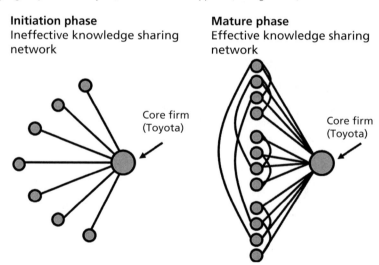

Initiation phase
Ineffective knowledge sharing network

Core firm (Toyota)

Mature phase
Effective knowledge sharing network

Core firm (Toyota)

Figure 4.2. The development of an inter-firm network

This case study draws from material and inspiration from Dyer and Nobeoka (2000), financial data from *Financial Times* (2008). Diagrams are after Dyer and Nobeoka (2000).

4.2.1.3 Academic social networks

Studies of networks between collaborators who work on the production of academic publications have been developed in various disciplines. In the specific context of academic work related to strategic management theory, Robertson and Collet (2008) used the relations between authors who had worked on papers within strategic management to determine how the network of co-authors had evolved since the early years of strategy (see Case Box 4.2).

Case Box 4.2 Social connections between academics publishing in the strategic management journal

---

Robertson and Collet (2008) investigated the connections between authors who published in the *Strategic Management Journal*. The following social network diagram, overlaid on a map of the world, shows the locations of authors (primarily academics) as indicated by the country of their institutional affiliation. This shows the strong influence of the United States, with the United States being central to the network (the width of the lines shows the number of collaborations between authors of different countries). Robertson and Collet carried out a dynamic study of the evolution of the network over time: by calculating network statistics over time, they were able to show that the network is becoming more connected, and more of a 'small world' over time (see Figure 4.3).

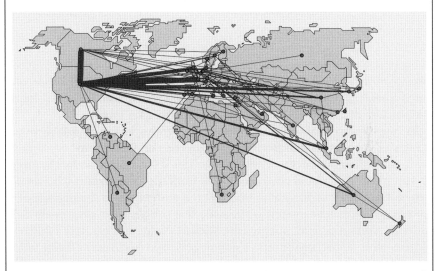

Figure 4.3. International collaboration network of Strategic Management Journal authors

World map © 2008 passportstamp.com. Used with permission.

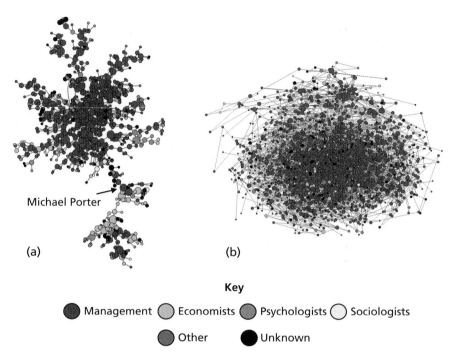

Figure 4.4. The giant component of strategic management scholars: (a) in 1987 and (b) in 1998

We can also use social network analysis to understand the dynamics of the field. In Figure 4.4. we show the giant component of authors cited from the *Strategic Management Journal* in 1987 and 1998. Each node represents an author, coloured according to the main discipline in which they publish. Figure 4.4 shows the structure of this giant component, as it changes over time.

As can be seen from the social network diagrams in Figure 4.4, there are clusters of economists and psychologists on the periphery of the network in 1987, establishing well-defined sub-groups. This is especially true for the group of economists who would remain removed from the management scholars if it were not for the bridging nodes that link the economists to the management scholars. Of particular interest is the node that bridges the management field with this economics field: it represents Michael Porter. In 1998, it is a different picture, with some economists, psychologists, and sociologists being more central to the network, representing an integration of the field.

4.2.1.4 Entrepreneur networks

Social networks exist where individuals join together to work on projects that may one day become commercialized and a new firm being created. Many entrepreneurial studies investigate the effects of management team demographics when the enterprise has grown to such a stage where the heterogeneity is increased by adding new members to the 'core' entrepreneurial team. For example, when enterprises grow, the entrepreneurial team needs to introduce team members to carry out administrative tasks such as company secretarial work or accounting. These members of the organization are vital to the success of an enterprise, but in these support roles, they do not contribute directly to the entrepreneurial task. Studying entrepreneurial organizations at this stage of their development does not truly reflect the demographics of the entrepreneurial team.

Many enterprises are formed by members of knowledge networks, networks such as universities, where their members may use time to develop ideas, tools, or products. From a corporate entrepreneurship view, this can be positively encouraged, for example Eric Schmidt of Google is reported to use the '10 per cent rule' for innovating (Schmidt 2005); 10 per cent of employees' time is spent on 'exploratory' projects to develop new products. This '10 per cent' of employees' time results in new product development. Some of the products developed from this 'non-core' time will result in the formation of entrepreneurial firms. Shah and Tripsas (2007) call this 'accidental' entrepreneurship, and cite the example of Yahoo! being formed as a student hobby:

Case Box 4.3 Facebook & the facebook platform: mutualistic entrepreneurship

---

Facebook Inc. was launched in 2004 by Mark Zuckerberg, then a student at Harvard University. It has since grown to more than 58 million active users, with an average of 250,000 new registrations per day, with active users doubling every 6 months (Facebook 2007a). It has recently been valued at $15 billion (*Times* 2007).

In May 2007, the Facebook Platform was launched (Facebook 2007b). This Platform allows any user of Facebook to develop an 'application' – in effect a software program – that is shown on a user's Facebook profile page. This allows users of Facebook to perform a wide range of activities, such as playing games or changing the look of their Facebook profile. As at the end of 2007, 11,000 such applications had been developed (Facebook 2007c). Robertson and Fan (2008) studied this interesting environment, studying the network structure of entrepreneurs.

Applications built using the Facebook Platform are valuable. Even though these applications are very new, they have been valued at many thousands of dollars. Subsequently, single applications have been developed that have over 1,000,000 active users per day, with over 10 million total users.

By developing the Platform, Facebook was able to construct an 'ecosystem' where entrepreneurs were able to access Facebook network resources and build organizations in a far shorter time period than would have been the case under traditional development. This benefits Facebook, as it introduces new members and offers new activities for those already members. In summary, both the host (Facebook) and the tenants (entrepreneurs) benefit by this mutualistic interaction.

In 1994, Ph.D. candidates in electrical engineering David Filo and Jerry Yang started a guide as a way to keep track of their personal interest on the Internet and called it 'Jerry & David's Guide to the World Wide Web.' What began as a student hobby evolved into a global brand – Yahoo! – that changed the way that people communicate and exchange information. (Shah and Tripsas 2007:123)

Robertson and Fan (2008) worked on the analysis of what is arguably a twenty-first century equivalent of these collaborations by university students – members of universities collaborating to develop software 'applications' that are used on their friends' Facebook profile pages as detailed in Case Box 4.3. They focused on the investigation of these enterprises at their genesis – when the idea has been developed into a product but *before* a corporation has been formed. We are fortunate to be able to see this entrepreneurship *in situ*, as the ideas are developed that will eventually become entrepreneurial firms, but before being 'corrupted' by non-entrepreneurs joining the organizational team and biasing their results.

4.2.1.4.1 Co-operation between the host and entrepreneur: mutualistic entrepreneurship. At first, the rationale for Facebook to open its Facebook Platform may seem weak. Technology companies such as Microsoft develop their software in a traditional software environment, using their own software engineers. This 'closed-source' development of products, where users pay for a product that evolves over time, requires the development funded by revenues generated by users updating software licences to the latest version. The Facebook Platform model works differently. While the core of the Facebook system is developed by Facebook employees, Facebook does allow users of Facebook to host their own applications on users' pages. This encourages user innovation and lock-in of the user (and the users' friends and friends-of-friends).

The Facebook Platform model is not however open-source. Facebook retains the intellectual property of the computer code for the Facebook site, and the entrepreneurs retain the right to the code for their application: they are able to use the software they develop on other sites such as Google OpenSocial (seen by many as a reaction by Google to the success of the Facebook model), and are able to use it as the code basis for their own web sites.

This is what Robertson and Fan call a 'mutualistic' interaction, a specific type of symbiotic relationship where the host organization enables entrepreneurial firms to thrive, with positive feedback to the host organization. Similar to honeybees feeding on a male flower's nectar in order to propagate the host, Facebook allows developers to propagate the Facebook utility, sharing 'rents' or benefit between the host (Facebook) and the entrepreneur. While mutualistic relationships are often seen as co-operation between the species, it is in fact exploitation of each by the other to the benefit of both parties. This mutualistic relationship is propagated through lead users of Facebook, users who are willing to develop their own applications to fill their own product needs. Von Hippel (1986:791) describes 'lead users' as being a source of product innovation:

since lead users often attempt to fill the need they experience, they can provide new product concept and design data as well.

However, what was not envisaged by von Hippel was, rather than lead users being a source of innovation and products for the host firm, the users themselves may form firms in order to react to their own needs. The rents from this mutualistic innovation are shared between the host and the entrepreneur. This is similar to what Shah and Tripsas (2007:123) describe as 'user innovation' where users 'create, evaluate, share, and commercialize their ideas'.

Developers of Facebook applications form entrepreneurial teams in a different way than in the traditional model of entrepreneurial team founding. Given the low costs of starting an enterprise – and the low risks of failure – the teams founded by Facebook entrepreneurs are more spontaneous: two individuals will discuss an idea, and then co-develop an application. Their search mechanism for 'ideal' members of the entrepreneurial team are restricted to current associates (or may be brokered by discussions via Facebook itself). The entrepreneurial teams we have studied are not as formalized in the team selection process. This is largely due to the non-profit primary motive for the enterprise.

There are low barriers to innovation: it costs only a few dollars per month to host an application built on the Facebook Platform, well within the budget of most. Shah and Tripsas also see 'collective creative activity prior to firm formation'. We see that in the Facebook model, developers engage in collective activity at all stages of the venture from inception of the idea, development through, and past, firm formation. As an example, in early 2008, over 5,000 topics have been discussed on the Facebook Developers' Forum, with over 30,000 posts by potential entrepreneurs. Shah and Tripsas note that the field of user innovation is ripe for further investigation. We use the novel dataset for entrepreneurship at its very origin for our empirical study. Aldrich and Kim (2007) promote the importance of identifying different types of social network – random, small world, and truncated scale free – and propose that the type of network is important in discovering entrepreneurial possibilities.

The introduction of social network tools such as Facebook, MySpace, Bebo, or 'professional' networking sites such as LinkedIn, vastly expands users' networks (as users are able to see friends of friends), and in some ways promote the importance of weak ties by codifying these structures and increasing the ease of identifying potential new team members who are friends of friends by displaying the information about these individuals. The information about members of 'networks' is usually visible to other

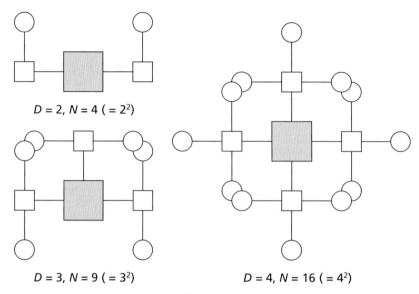

$D = 2, N = 4 (= 2^2)$

$D = 3, N = 9 (= 3^2)$ $D = 4, N = 16 (= 4^2)$

Figure 4.5. Scaling of the network as D^2

members of the network. This transforms what may be a loosely connected network into a fully connected network. This vastly eases the identification of new individuals who may in turn add to a project and eventually form part of an entrepreneurial team. They reduce the ability of friends or colleagues to act as information brokers, as connections can be made directly without the need to use the connecting individual as an intermediary. We can demonstrate the ability of this connectivity in terms of the number of friends, N, as this scales as D^2 where D is the degree (number of connections) of the members of the network, as shown in Figure 4.5.

Developer Social Network. The social network of developers is constructed by forming links between developers who had been joint-developers on a specific application. For single-entrepreneur applications, this meant that they were not part of the network (as they had no connections with other entrepreneurs). For two-entrepreneur applications, we constructed a dyad between these entrepreneurs, and for a three-or-more entrepreneur application, we constructed a triad between the first three named developers. Examples of the building blocks of the network, dyads and triads, are shown in Figure 4.6.

From these individual connections, we were able to construct a social network of all entrepreneurs, as shown in Figure 4.7. In the social network diagram shown in Figure 4.4, each circle represents an entrepreneur. The

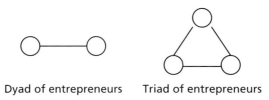

Dyad of entrepreneurs   Triad of entrepreneurs

Figure 4.6. Dyads and triads

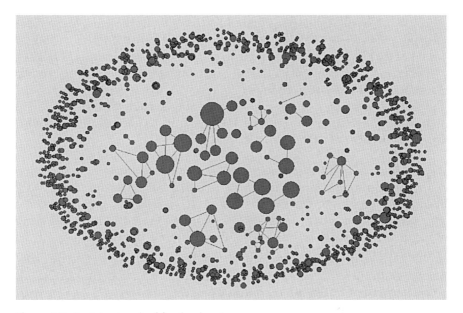

Figure 4.7. Social network of facebook entrepreneurs

size of the circle indicates the number of enterprises on which that entrepreneur has collaborated. Links between the developers are shown as lines between entrepreneurs. We can see that there are a few developers who have collaborated extensively. However, the network is disperse: there are few developers who collaborate extensively in order to produce many applications, and there are many developers who collaborate only on one project. Furthermore, there are certain developers who bridge several projects as presumably a source of technical knowledge central to the development of the enterprise.

Due to the low connectivity in the network (it is impossible to get from any one developer to all other developers), this does not qualify as a small world network. We have to consider the *network of networks* in order to understand how a small world of inter-university collaboration exists (where universities are connected by collaborations between members of those universities).

Network of University Developers. If we turn our attention to the connections between universities to which the entrepreneurs are affiliated, we get a much more interesting result. Rather than making links between individual developers, we instead make links between universities where members affiliated to those universities have collaborated to develop an application. We can plot these links on a network graph to determine the most important universities for the innovation and development of applications (Figure 4.8). The network graph is shown in Figure 4.8; sizes of nodes represent the number of applications developed by entrepreneurs affiliated to that institution, and the layout of the graph follows Fruchterman and Reingold's algorithm (1991).

Robertson and Fan calculate the 'centrality' of the universities to the entrepreneurial ecosystem, as shown in Table 4.1. What is interesting is that this reflects what may be expected: universities such as Stanford (with its reputation for starting Google) and MIT (with its technological reputation) are all highly central to the network.

Type of Network. Aldrich and Kim (2007) make an important characterization when considering entrepreneurial social networks. We can analyse the network mentioned earlier to determine – formally – whether the network of entrepreneurs is a 'small world' or otherwise. We extend Aldrich and Kim's work in the following in order to test formally the characterization of the network of entrepreneurs in Conceptual Box 4.2.

Conceptual Box 4.2 Formal test for small world networks

Watts and Strogatz's seminal paper (1998) on Small World Networks sets out tests for determining whether a network is a Small World. Formally, a network is said to be 'small' when the dual properties of greater or approximately equal to average path length, and much greater clustering coefficient, $L \gtrsim L_{random}$, $C \gg C_{random}$ (Watts and Strogatz 1998:441). We set out in the following text the methods to calculate these two network statistics, and compare them to a random network with similar properties.

Giant Component

In order to determine whether a network is indeed 'small', we need to determine network statistics. The convention among network researchers is to use the 'giant component' of the network, that is the set of nodes and vertices such that one can trace a path from all nodes to all other nodes – there are no outlying sub-graphs that are disconnected to the rest of the network. This enables us to determine statistics such as average path length for all nodes within the giant component. If we were not to restrict ourselves to this giant component, we would find that we are left with impossible measures of path length from unconnected nodes.

(Continued)

Conceptual Box 4.2 (Continued)

Characteristic Path Length, L

In order to calculate the average path length statistic, L, for the network, we calculate the number of connections that must be traversed in the shortest path length ('geodesic') between two nodes in the network. This value is averaged over all authors to give an average shortest path length, or 'characteristic path length', L, a property of the overall network.

Clustering Measures, C

The clustering coefficient of the network, C, is defined as the average value of the clustering coefficient: $C = \frac{1}{n} \sum_{i=1}^{n} C_i$

Although the networks studied are bipartite, in that all co-entrepreneurs for one enterprise form a fully-linked clique (Uzzi and Spiro 2005:453), we can use the method of Watts and Strogatz (1998) for calculating small-worldness of networks, as the degree of all edges is 3 or fewer, and therefore the differences between treating the network as a bipartite network and a simple network are minimal.

For each node in a network, we compute C_i as follows: $C_i = \dfrac{2|E(G^1(v))|}{\deg(v).(\deg(v)-1))}$

Where $\deg(v)$ is the degree of vertex v, and $2|E(G^1(v))|$ is the number of lines in the 1-neighbourhood (immediate neighbourhood) of this vertex. We can show the degree distribution of our data, below (removing instances where there is only one node with a specific degree distribution), where k is the degree of each node (university), and $P(k)$ is the proportion of nodes with degree k. Barábasi (1999) demonstrates that most small world networks follow the form of a power law, $P(k) \sim k^{-r}$.

Table 4.1. High degree centrality universities in the entrepreneurial network

University
Stanford
Berkeley
MIT
Washington
Harvard
University of Toronto
Michigan
Cambridge
Babson
Yale

The data for the university small world network follows $P(k) \sim k^{-r}$ as shown in the graph in Figure 4.9. We can also compute the formal network statistics to test whether the network tested is a small world.

Comparison with a Random Network. In order to determine the characteristics of the empirical network we are testing, we construct a random network with

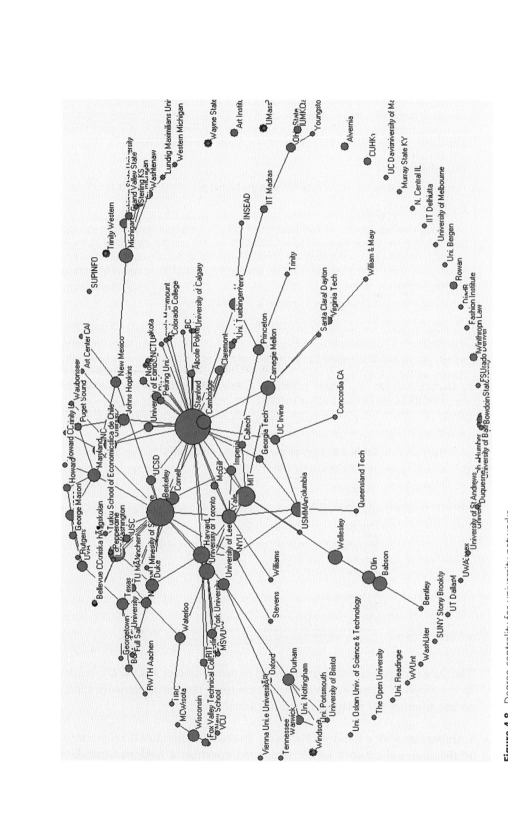

Figure 4.8. Degree centrality for university networks

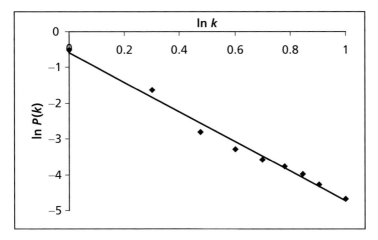

Figure 4.9. Empirical representation of a power law relationship

similar characteristics to the data. We compare network statistics, particularly the ratio of path length and clustering statistics between the empirical network and the random network. Firstly, we remove multiple lines between nodes. We then recursively remove lines in the network of degree 0 or 1 in order to remove isolated pairs and to reduce the network to the 'giant component'.

As discussed earlier, a network is said to be 'small' when the properties of greater or approximately equal average path length, and much greater clustering coefficient, $L \gtrsim L_{\text{random}}$, $C \gg C_{\text{random}}$ (Watts and Strogatz 1998: 441). The network for universities to which entrepreneurs belong meets the dual criteria mentioned previously, and we therefore can conclude that it is indeed a Small World.

4.2.1.5 Standards wars

Technology standards wars such as that between VHS (Matsushita) and Betamax (Sony) standards in the VCR market were repeated in the war between HD-DVD (Toshiba) and Blu-Ray (Sony) in high definition DVDs (Case Box 4.4). It appears that Sony was not prepared to lose the network standards war for a second time, after learning from its Betamax experience. These examples show network effects in practice. In these cases as one standard becomes rapidly embraced as the favourite by customers, the rival standard loses market share with similar (and potentially frightening) speed.

Case Box 4.4 Positive feedbacks in a standards war: HD-DVD vs. Blu-Ray

---

With the emergence of HDTV (High Definition TV), first generation DVDs are no longer useful as storage devices for movies as their limited storage capacity (4.7 gigabytes) cannot cope with the higher storage requirements of the new TV standard. Two new DVD formats emerged as a response for this need for increased storage capacity: HD-DVD, mainly backed by Toshiba, and Blu-Ray, backed by Sony. Using dual layer techniques, HD-DVD can store up to 30 gigabytes while Blu-Ray can hold up to 50 gigabytes. Both systems have backward compatibility, enabling users to play their old DVDs, but because of the vastly different physical attributes of HD-DVD and Blu-Ray discs, it was prohibitively expensive for manufacturers to produce players that could handle both formats in one machine. This forced manufacturers to take sides.

As the manufacturing technology of HD-DVD is similar to that of normal DVDs, the format was launched in 2005, before Blu-Ray was launched in 2006 at a higher price. Despite HD-DVD's first mover advantage, it was Blu-Ray that secured the support of a large number of manufacturers such as Dell, HP, Hitachi, LG, Panasonic, Pioneer, Phillips, Samsung, Sharp, and Sony as well as content providers such as Sony Pictures Entertainment, Metro-Goldwyn-Mayer, and the Walt Disney Company who offered also a non-exclusive endorsement. HD-DVD was actually backed only by Toshiba and small players such as NEC and Sanyo.

In June 2007, rental giant Blockbuster gave a strong boost to Blu-Ray by announcing its decision to stock only Blu-Ray discs in the vast majority of its locations. The decision was based on customer preferences, as Blu-Ray accounted for 70 per cent of all the HD discs rented, with exclusive Blu-Ray hits such as Spiderman and Pirates of the Caribbean beating HD-DVD exclusives.

Blu-Ray continued receiving support from key players such as Warner Bros (January 2008) and retailers such as Walmart who announced in February 2008 its decision to sell only Blu-Ray HD discs. These decisions reinforcing the positive feedbacks favouring the Blu-Ray system (discs, players, content) and harming HD-DVD.

In February 2008, while still having the commitment from Universal, Paramount, and DreamWorks studios to produce movies in HD-DVD, Toshiba announced its decision to give up in the standards fight and stop production of HD-DVD players and recorders. Of the HD-DVD format, a Tokyo salesman said 'only maniacs will buy one now'.[1]

[1] Los Angeles Times Online, 'Blu-Ray Winner by KO in High-Definition War'

4.3 Agent-based models as network models

In Chapter 3, we used agent-based models to model individual agents. In Chapter 4, we have used social network analysis techniques to describe the structure of various connections between individuals. However, there are tremendous opportunities to combine these techniques, so that we can model the heterogeneity of individuals in a dynamic manner, examining the network as it evolves by social interaction. We can also include firms as additional agents in order to understand more fully how these social interactions affect firm profitability.

4.3.1 THE FOREST FIRE MODEL

We introduce a model from physical science that is less developed compared with the NK model, but is one that has significant potential for transfer to the domain of management science.

The Forest Fire model (Bak et al. 1990) is a model where trees exist on a square lattice, with $L \times L = L^2$ cells (we can also model an N-dimensional hypercube, with L^N sites, but in this example, we shall restrict the lattice to being a square with two dimensions and L^2 sites). Each site can be in one of three states:

- the site may be empty;
- the site may be occupied by a tree that is not on fire; or
- the site may be occupied by a tree that is on fire.

The transition between these states is defined by the simple rules that govern the model (Bak et al. 1990:297):

- 'trees grow with a small probability p from empty sites at each time step;
- trees on fire will burn down at the next time step;
- the fire on a site will spread to trees at its nearest neighbour sites at the next time step'.

The model is thus specified. We are interested in the behaviour of the system over time, a system that evolves as a result of these rules being applied over many iterations. However, several variations of the 'Forest Fire' model exist, so it is important to specify the exact model that is being used. Even the simple rules of the Forest Fire model are ambiguous: what do we mean by 'nearest neighbours'? And what happens at the edges of the lattice? We assume that a von Neumann neighbourhood is used (where the four cardinal – north, south, east, west – neighbours are included), rather than a Moore neighbourhood (where, in addition to the cardinal points, ordinal points, e.g. northeast, are included in the neighbourhood). We also assume that the lattice is bounded rather than being doughnut shaped ('toroidal') (where there is no boundary). Is the behaviour of the system similar when we substitute a triangular lattice for the square lattice? These may seem trivial specifications, however specifying these attributes is important.

Later models (Drossel and Schwabl 1992:47) have included a further rule:

'a tree becomes a burning tree during one time step with probability f if no neighbour is burning'.

Table 4.2. Transition matrix for the Forest Fire model

		New State		
		Empty	Burning	Tree
Former State	Empty	$1-p$	0	p
	Burning	1	0	0
	Tree	0	α (=1 if neighbour burning; f if neighbour not burning)	$1-\alpha$

This corresponds to 'lightning strikes', which start a fire in a particular location that, if appropriate conditions exist, will spread to other trees. We can summarize these rules in a stochastic transition matrix, the parameters being the probability of a state transition for any point in the lattice during an iteration of the model (see Table 4.2).

The model, as specified within the physics domain, was seen as an example of 'self-organized criticality' (self-similar fractal structures that exhibit '1/f' noise (power laws), see Bak et al. 1987:381), although this has been debated (for a review see for example Clar et al. 1994).

For the purposes of our initial exploration of this model and its transfer to the management domain, we can investigate a system that has evolved over time, but for which there has been no fire (whether caused by lightning strike or otherwise). We can then initiate a fire and investigate how the tree density has an effect on how the fire propagates. Consider the system in Figure 4.10 where, at the initialization of the system, the trees on the extreme left-hand side of the forest are lit (lit trees are shown darker than non-lit trees). After a number of iterations, following the rules of the model, the fire starts to propagate from left to right, with the cells following the transition rules (in this case, we set $p = f = 0$, and allow the fire to transit without new tree growth). The figure shows the state of the system, with the fire front dissipating, and a fire shadow of burnt cells.[2]

We can investigate the proportion of trees burned as a function of the number of trees in the lattice (the tree density). In this particular (NetLogo) operationalization of the model, we see the following behaviour (statistics generated from several runs of the model[3]) in Figure 4.11.

---

[2] For more details of the software toolkit used to generate this model, and the relative strengths and weaknesses of such toolkits, see Robertson (2005).

[3] Simulation results are for a 101 × 101 unit grid.

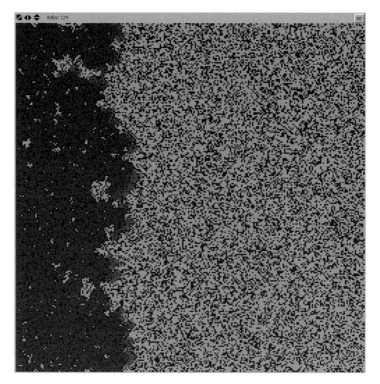

Figure 4.10. Forest Fire model with fire propagation (NetLogo)

As can be seen, there is a rapid transition from a very low percentage of trees burned to a very high percentage of trees burned. There is a critical point with a tree density of *ca.* 58 per cent. The macro-level behaviour of the system, that is the proportion of trees burnt as a function of tree density, changes abruptly. What differs from other models of propagation, is that we are modelling the individual agents (trees) that comprise the system, we are *not* explicitly model-ling the system as a whole. This is generally described as a 'tipping point', where the behaviour of the system changes dramatically from one state (very low spread of the fire) to another state (very high spread of the fire).

4.3.1.1 The Link to Analytical Models of Innovation

This sigmoidal result obtained earlier is reminiscent of the s-shaped curves that represent the effect of advertising, or the diffusion of innovation. The corresponding models in marketing science are however generally closed-form models, which are analytically tractable. For instance, diffusion models may take the form of analytical models, such as the logistic equation:

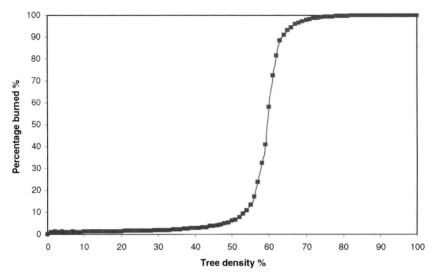

Figure 4.11. Forest Fire model results

$$\frac{\partial N}{\partial t} = \frac{rn(K - N)}{K}$$

where *r* is the rate of maximum population growth, and *K* is the carrying capacity (the maximum sustainable population). The solution to this equation gives the following sigmoidal curve, similar to the results from our agent-based forest-fire model.

While the spread of innovation, and the diffusion of ideas are well modelled using analytical methods such as the Bass diffusion model (Bass 1969) and other s-curve population growth models based on Verhulst (1845, 1847), these models ignore individual actors within the population, and report only the population statistic.

4.3.1.2 A Derived Social Network

Although the Forest Fire model is one of trees that are arranged in a lattice, we have to change our perception of this model and apply it to the management situation that we are interested in. As we shall see in the following text, we are in fact generalizing a system that has already been simplified by turning a physical phenomenon into a 'toy model'.

When we investigate the forest lattice in Figure 4.12, we can see that, rather than modelling trees on a square lattice, we can reconfigure the lattice to be a social network construction.

1	8	9	15		22		32
2		10	16	19		27	
3			17	20	23	28	33
4		11			24	29	34
5		12	18	21		30	35
		13				31	36
6					25		37
7		14			26		38

Figure 4.12. Random tree network in lattice form (probability of a tree, $p = .57$)

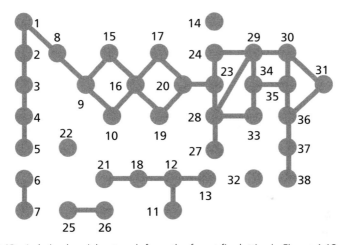

Figure 4.13. A derived social network from the forest fire lattice in Figure 4.12

If we look at the *links* between the trees within the lattice, we reconfigure this problem as one of a *network*. We can provide an alternative representation of the system in the form of a network, as shown in Figure 4.13.

The network derived in Figure 4.13 may appear restricted, in that a social actor may have a maximum degree, or number of links to other actors, of four. This however need not be a constraint: we can either change the definition of a neighbourhood, or change the dimensionality of the lattice: in a two-dimensional lattice, we have a maximum number of neighbours of 4, whereas in an N-dimensional lattice, we have a maximum degree of $2N$.

While the forest fire may be described in terms of trees in a square lattice forest, we have to realize that this is in fact a metaphor for the actual system that we are considering. As can be seen previously, the agents we consider can change from trees to people forming a social network, and the lattice changes to an unstructured linkage of people within that network.

4.3.1.3 Towards an Organizational Model

We can see that the model has now been reformulated in terms of a social network construction. However, we can use the lattice construction to obtain the same results. We can see the propagation of an idea throughout the population, and can trace the route of this propagation, by investigating the state of the system at each point in time. The model as it exists places agents randomly on the lattice. We can change this initial setup to specify the links between people, if these are known. The main result from the model is that the density of population is important, as this forces links to be made between different people. For instance, we may decide, on the basis of this model, that the best propagation of ideas takes place when many people are in the same domain. It is the *spatial* element that is important.

There exist a number of potential avenues for such a model: we can investigate how ideas or product adoption diffuses through a population by means of interpersonal contact, modelled by proximity on the lattice (and hence proximity in a social network). By taking this approach, use of this model allows us to investigate the *micro-level* behaviour which can be lost when investigating a macro-level property such as percentage of a population to which the idea or product has spread.

4.3.2 SEGREGATION MODEL

Schelling's segregation model (1978) is an early example of an agent-type model that was introduced before the introduction of computers. Consequently, this model was first introduced as a 'chess board' model, where the agents are able to compete with each other, and the agents are chess pieces on a chess board. The model is described in Conceptual Box 4.3

Similar to the Forest Fire model, we also see in the segregation model a tipping point where, above a certain threshold, the behaviour of the system as a whole changes to segregation.

We can extend this model to a grid of an arbitrary number of locations (and indeed an arbitrary number of dimensions), as shown in Figure 4.14.

Figure 4.14 shows the eventual evolution of a firm with two firm types, light grey and dark grey, each having a level of tolerance of the other colour.

Conceptual Box 4.3 Agent movement in the segregation model: the chess board approach

The decision of agents to move can be shown in the following.

Figure 4.13.a-d

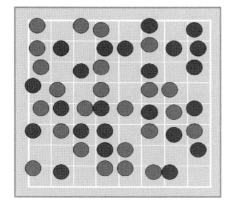

Unhappy agents can move to vacant spaces

Happiness defined in terms of two-dimensional neighbourhood

Random initial distribution

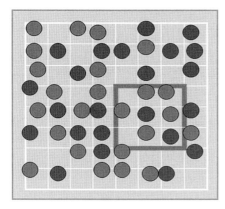

Neighbourhood defined as eight squares surrounding each agent

If agent is not happy, it moves to the nearest vacant square where it will be happy

'Happy' defined as per cent of neighbours of same colour $\geq$ 50 per cent

The yellow agent highlighted is 'unhappy' as a minority (1/6 = 17 per cent < 50 per cent) of neighbours are of a different colour

Agent therefore moves to a vacant space

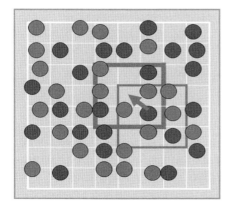

If the agent moves here, 1/5 neighbours will be of a different colour. 1/5 = 20 per cent < 50 per cent therefore the agent will still be unhappy

We need to keep searching

(Continued)

Figure 4.13. a–d (*Continued*)

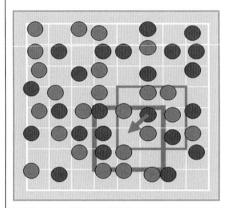

If the agent moves here, 3/6 neighbours will be of a different colour. 3/6 = 50 per cent ≥ 50 per cent therefore the agent will be happy

Therefore the agent moves here

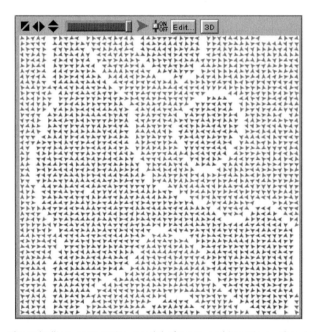

Figure 4.14. The Schelling segregation model after several iterations, showing patches of colour (NetLogo)

As in the Forest Fire model, we are actually investigating a network model, where information is gained by an agent from their neighbours. In this simple version of the model, neighbours of a particular firm may change from period

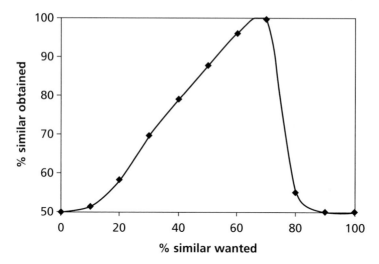

Figure 4.15. Catastrophic failure to segregate with high desired segregation

to period; we could extend this to include agents gaining information about the wider environment from their previous neighbours.

There is another phenomenon that is exhibited by this model: when the percentage of similar neighbours required reaches another, higher threshold, the model exhibits a behaviour whereby the agents, due to no overall coordination, are unable to go to a location where they are all happy; all the agents then move, causing a continual cycling of locations, with all agents continually choosing a new location: an equilibrium does not exist, and there is no segregation of the agents, as shown in Figure 4.15.

4.4 **From natural science to strategic management**

While models from natural science may be developed with specific applications in mind, the systematic reduction of a system to its elemental parts and interactions is a skill that is useful in itself. We see two distinct methods for applying natural science models to social science. We can change the agents of the model but keep the fundamental model unchanged (e.g. interpreting the Forest Fire model as a model of propagation of ideas through a social network). An alternative to this is, as discussed previously for the *NK* model, to amend the interactions of the agents from interactions that are oversimplified for a social science to incorporate behavioural assumptions and extend and develop a natural science model.

4.4.1 TOY MODELS

Many of the models of natural science are termed 'toy models' (Bak et al. 1988). Toy models are designed so that the mechanisms of the interactions can be examined, not by modelling the exact system that we are interested in, but by changing the unit of analysis to something more easily understood. An example of this occurs in the Forest Fire model: we are not actually interested in modelling trees, rather a physical system that exhibits this behaviour. We are therefore able, with some degree of ease, to apply the model to another domain, specifically management, where we understand similar behaviour exists.

4.4.2 MICRO–MACRO SCALES

Analytical models tend to look at the behaviour of the system as a whole, modelling the percentage of the system that is affected by the innovation. What is not modelled, explicitly, is the micro-level actions and interactions that comprise the system. The emergent properties of this micro-macro level interaction can be seen by the agent-based model: the macro-level system variable of interest is replicated, yet we can see the behaviour of every actor who makes up the system.

In analytical models, we may not model the connections between actors, seeing these as being trivial. However, by using an agent-based model, we can control these connections. While replicating the analytical result is possible, we can go beyond these results and alter the initial system: what is the initial state of the actors? Who is connected to whom? All these assumptions of analytical models can be made explicit by altering the initial setup (which could be chosen randomly or may be imposed) of the simulation.

Analytical models can be 'solved' by finding an equilibrium solution. Agent-based models (in Conceptual Box 4.4) such as those introduced in this note are not hampered by this restriction: we can track agent movement *out of equilibrium*. This feature permits, in the case of the *NK* model, that we analyse extensively in Chapter 7, to deal with questions on dynamic issues characterized by non-linear behaviour, such as the impact of organizational forms and/or cognitive representations of the environment on the ability of the firm to adapt (Gavetti and Levinthal 2000). In a social network context, the spread of the 'fire' actually shows the places where agent to agent, social, communication is taking place: the fire envelope actually shows where the interaction is taking place at any moment in time. We can therefore track the propagation through the network (the fire front being the envelope of propagation at a certain time).

Conceptual Box 4.4 Summary of agent-based model characteristics

	Schelling	Forest Fire	*NK*	Spatial Competition
Environment / Landscape	Grid	Grid	Boolean Hypercube	2-D space
Birth & Death of Agents	None	Death	None	None
Agents' 'Vision'	Moore Neighbourhood	Von Neumann Neighbourhood	Moore neighbourhood (one each time)	Global or Current Customers
Emergent / Interesting Behaviour	Segregation	Critical Point	Peak Finding on Landscape	Profit Heterogeneity
'Energy'	Reduce Unhappiness No Movement Cost	Trees Grow	None	Constant

4.5 **Summary**

In this chapter, we have shown how we can use social network representations to study how the structure of populations changes over time, and how this structure evolves. We have also seen how firms can use inter-firm networks to allow learning in the organizational network. Customer–customer, customer–firm, and firm–firm networks are likely to be of great interest in the coming years, as there is great potential for competitive advantage by understanding not only the structure of these networks, but how they can be influenced to attain competitive advantage. We also see great potential for adapting agent-based models from natural science with their interesting properties to models of firm–firm or customer–customer network interaction.

PART II
THE ORGANIZATIONAL LANDSCAPE

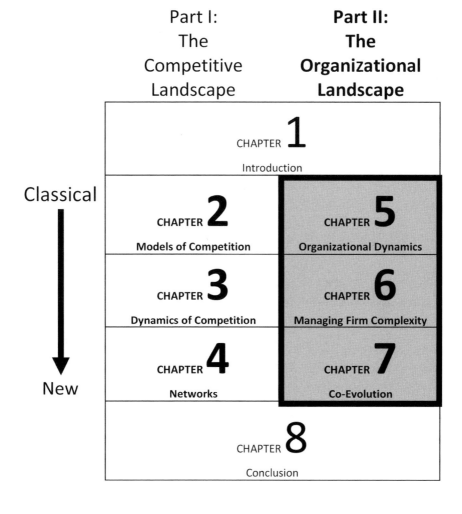

Introduction to Part II

Part I of the book focused on understanding the competitive environment of firms through the discussion of traditional and new theoretical approaches.

The second part of the book focuses on understanding how the firm's behavior in the competitive environment affects and is, in turn affected by, the way the firm is organized.

In order to be successful in their competitive domain, firms benefit from the capability of performing their business processes in a continuous, efficient, and reliable way. At the same time, organizations need to release the creative forces of their members in order to develop innovation. The problem that has attracted the attention of many scholars and managers during the last four decades is that highly rational organizational processes that help in developing efficiency and reliability are typically poor vehicles for the generation of innovation. In turn, organizational arrangements that promote the behaviours that catalyse innovation and strategic change are typically not strong drivers of reliable highly coordinated behaviour. Managing the organizational tensions created by this trade-off has foremost importance at the time of implementing the firm's strategy.

In this section, and throughout the book, we define organization design as explicit efforts to improve organizations.[1] Most of the accepted academic work on organizational structures and design was elaborated more than thirty years ago. Since then the revolutionary advances in information technology has enabled firms to develop many new ways of organizing that should be understood under new theoretical lenses or, at least, through adaptation of the classic theories. The purpose of Part II of this book is to review the main theoretical perspectives for the study of organizations and to understand how such theories can help us to understand the dynamics associated to the process of organizing.

Throughout Chapters 5 and 6, we assume a systemic view of organizations. Chapter 5 starts with an analysis of theoretical perspectives to organization design that emphasize the mechanistic aspects of such systems, referred to frequently as the rational approach to organization design. We analyse the assumptions of the rational paradigm in terms of how organizational dynamics evolve, and we discuss their merits and limitations. Then, we analyse how such limitations can be overcome by approaches that focus on the behavioural aspects associated with designing organizations, usually referred to as the natural systems approach to organizational design. Later, we will review the theoretical perspectives that reconcile and integrate these two different

---

[1] Dunbar and Starbuck (2006).

ontological perspectives of organizations and analyse how their relative importance varies at different stages of the firm's development. Finally, we discuss recent empirical work focused on understanding the dynamics of the organizing process.

Later, in Chapter 6, we focus on the analysis of three analytical perspectives that have become relevant in the study of organizational dynamics during the last years. We refer to system dynamics, social network analysis, and agent-based modelling. We will review the main features of each of these approaches and will review the main contributions to our understanding of organizations and organizing derived from each of them.

The diagram shows the area that we concentrate on in Chapters 5 and 6 of Part II, that of intra-firm connections.

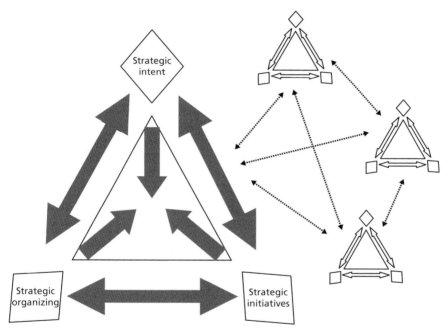

The Organizational Landscape (adapted from Figure 1.1)

The final chapter of Part II, Chapter 7, builds on the analysis of the dynamics of organizing from a complexity perspective developed in Chapter 6 and integrates it with the analysis of the dynamics of competition from a complexity perspective (Section 7.4 onwards). In this way, the second part of Chapter 7 integrates Parts I and II of the book by addressing simultaneously the intra-organizational and the inter-organizational aspects characterizing the dynamics of strategy.

5 Organizational Dynamics

5.1 **Organizations as systems**

Many of the definitions of organization developed during the last sixty years assume, explicitly or implicitly, that organizations can be deemed as 'systems'. We can define a system as a group of independent but interrelated elements (in our context, departments, divisions, functional areas or teams) comprising a unified whole (the organization). It is worth at this point remarking that our understanding of the dynamics of organizations varies significantly according to whether we consider them to be as closed or open systems.

5.1.1 CLOSED AND OPEN SYSTEMS

The key issue around this matter is the extent to which we can understand the behaviour of a system and, consequently, the degree of precision of our forecasts about such a system's future state. A system is *deterministic* if our understanding of the variables and relationships involved in it is so complete that we can predict the future states of such system with precision (Thompson 1967). Determinateness is possible in a system that either is *closed* or immunized to the action of exogenous forces, or is one that is exposed to external forces that produce perfectly predictable effects. In either case, we should be able to analyse the behaviour of a system without being concerned by the effects of any exogenous source of uncertainty.

Assuming the closure of a system can ease the theoretical analysis of the behaviour of such system. However, in practice no system is completely closed.

In the context of organization studies, a closed system perspective implies the assumption that the organization's environment does not pose any relevant uncertainty and that only the internal – organizational – environment of the firm should be considered at the time of setting its goals and developing its formal structure. The closed system model of the organization was characteristic of management studies since the infancy of the field, notably the 'Scientific Management' tradition in the United States in the 1910s–1930s. It has also been prominent in recent research based on the agent-based models that we discuss extensively in chapter 7.

In the real world, however, organizations are hardly autonomous entities. In practice, the firm's strategic decisions are made in the context of a dynamic external environment, where the firm interacts with other actors, such as competitors, regulators, partners, or customers. This interdependence links the strategies of the different actors and can make it very difficult or even impossible for the firm to forecast the future beyond a short period of time.[2] The system created by the interaction of all the actors in a specific business landscape is *indeterminate*. While firms need a long-term broad conception of their strategic direction, or 'strategic intent' (Prahalad and Hamel 1989), specific strategic initiatives cannot be based on forecasts based on deductive reasoning but instead on trial and error based on hypotheses about the possible change of the environment that need to be continually contrasted with the reality of facts. The complexity of this dialectic process increases with the number of actors and the intensity of their interactions.[3]

Acknowledging that firms operate in environments of varying degrees of uncertainty and the fact that firms need to engage in exchanges of resources with their environment in order to survive and develop leads to a characterization of firms as *open* systems. An *open* systems view of organizations stresses the fact that the external environment influences the organization in ways that – beyond a short time frame – are difficult or even impossible to predict. This requires firms to develop specific organizational arrangements in order to cope with such uncertainty and its possible outcomes. Thompson (1967) goes beyond this idea and even advises that an open systems perspective of organizations is necessary to deal with systems that could be assumed to be determinate but incompletely understood due to their complexity, therefore exposing us to uncertainty.

The open system model of organizations started to gain prominence in management theory in the early 1960s and since then has become the dominant view in the integrative approaches to organizations and organizing.

5.1.2 RATIONAL AND NATURAL SYSTEMS

When we study the dynamics of organizing, both in the closed and open systems perspectives, we mentioned that there is a major divide at the time of describing how such systems behave, change, and evolve. Following the conceptualization developed by Gouldner (1959), we will say that there are a group of works on organizations that deem them as *rational systems*. Such perspectives emphasize the existence of specific organizational goals that

---

[2] As the Prussian General Von Moltke 'the Elder' (1800–91) famously said 'No battle plan survives contact with the enemy'.

[3] We will analyse and discuss this idea extensively in Chapter 7.

provide clear criteria for decision making, and the high degree of formalization of the organization's structure.

Alternatively, we have another equally important set of contributions that deem organizations as *natural systems*. This stream of work puts the stress on the behavioural structure of the firm, rather than the formal one. Within this perspective, members of organizations are not deemed as means to an overall organizational end, but as members of communities where both consensus and conflict may arise.

Next, we review and discuss the main contributions from the rational and the natural system perspectives and also the theoretical efforts developed with the aim of reconciling and integrating the two approaches.

5.2 **Organizations as artefacts: the rational systems perspective**

The rational systems perspective considers organizations as mere instruments whose existence is only justified if they can attain a specific set of goals. The idea of rationality refers to the link between the task at hand and the purpose of such task. The more efficient the way a task aimed at a certain objective is performed, the more rational the organization. As Scott (1998) conveniently emphasizes, rationality understood in this way refers *not to the selection of the goals of the organisation but to their implementation.*

In order to achieve high degrees of rationality, the organization requires specific, unambiguous goals, and formalized processes that make people behave predictably towards the attainment of such goals. As Dunban and Starbuck (2006) suggest, attention is focused on choosing which components to include in designs and how to evaluate design performance. The assumption is that if the relationships between the different design parameters are logically consistent and if they are aligned with the firm's goals, the design will perform well. For instance, the rational perspective understands that strategy is articulated through the design of carefully crafted Strategic Plans, as tools that formally coordinate the behaviour of the firm through a cascade of operational sub-objectives and sub-plans. Rational approaches to organization design emphasize the ideas of alignment with clear goals, fitness with the environment, and congruence between the different design parameters.

The enormous diffusion of management tools inspired in the rational tradition such as Strategic Planning, Scenario Planning, Balanced Scorecards, Total Quality Management, Six Sigma, or the widespread adoption of Enterprise Resource Planning (ERP) systems such as SAP in the last decade reflects not only the theoretical prevalence but also the practical importance that the rational systems approach has when managing firms.

The rational systems perspective has been a characteristic of organization studies since the early days of the field. The initial developments within the field were introduced by the 'grandfathers' of organization studies. In the United States, Frederick Taylor, the Gilbreths, Gantt, and others developed what is today known as the Scientific Management perspective (Taylor 1911; Gilbreth and Gilbreth 1924) that viewed firms as rational systems. These experienced practitioners focused specifically on optimizing production processes through standardization of tasks. Taylor's aim was to reduce the clashes between management and labour related to the distribution of the value added by 'increasing the size of the pie' through the application of the scientific method to manufacturing processes. In this way, idiosyncratic decisions made by workers would be replaced by objectively superior, scientifically developed, production processes. In Europe, Henri Fayol developed the first attempt to rationalize not only the production processes, but the organization as a whole, developing his famous 14 principles of administration (Fayol 1916).

Early work within the rational perspective was characterized by the implicit representation of the firm as a rather closed system. In Taylor's work, the analysis is focused on the optimization of production processes. The processes through which input of the necessary quality arrives at the production line were neglected. Similarly, output 'disappears' at the end of the production process. Fayol is characterized by a far more comprehensive analysis of the organization than that of the exponents of 'Taylorism'. However, he also neglects the external environment as an important influence in the behaviour of the firm.

The rational perspective was refined and developed by the work of Herbert Simon. In his book *Administrative Behavior,* Simon (1946) criticized the anthropology embedded in the Scientific Management perspective, based on a view of human beings as selfish and self-interested agents who act rationally, in the strict sense of the word. He developed the notion of 'administrative man'. This anthropology deems people as rational 'but only boundedly so'. According to Simon, individuals try to pursue their self interest, but their decision-making skills are restricted by cognitive limitations. These cognitive limitations are manifest at the three stages of the decision-making process: the selection of alternatives, the appreciation of consequences of such alternatives, and the evaluation of the desirability of those consequences. Simon states that at the time of making decisions, we can only comprehend a subset of all the alternative courses of action available. Moreover, we can only foresee a portion of the consequences associated to such an imperfect set of alternatives. Finally, our 'ex ante' evaluation of the desirability of certain consequences versus others is also imperfect, as only experience can provide precise judgements on the value of the different consequences. In short, decision making in organizational contexts is rational but, aimed at 'good enough' outcomes rather than at optimization as the neoclassical economists assumed.

By the end of the 1950s, and thanks to work developed by the 'Carnegie School' (March and Simon 1958; Cyert and March 1963), the rational perspective evolved gradually towards an open systems model. March & Simon (1958) and Cyert and March (1963) relied on Simon's idea of bounded rationality to develop what we currently label as the Behavioural Theory of the Firm. This perspective is focused on the development of organizational processes aimed at dealing with uncertainty. Behavioural Theory conceives firms as entities that engage in problem-solving through processes of search and discovery. It assumes that, while searching for solutions to their problems, firms follow some form of adaptive behaviour, considering only a limited number of decision alternatives due to the bounded rationality of decision makers. As managers are unable to write an algorithm that will enable them to locate the optimal set of choices in reasonable time, they instead make decisions trying to satisfy a limited number of criteria they judge as relevant.

Using the intellectual tradition of the behavioural theory as a point of departure, Richard Nelson and Sidney Winter (1982) developed another seminal contribution within the rational/open systems view of firms. They reacted against ideas prevailing in mainstream neoclassical economics, in particular to the assumption of rationality of the agents and the related notion of system-level equilibrium. Working on issues related to technical change, Nelson and Winter highlighted the gap between the image of the firm represented in the neoclassical theory of the firm and the enormous and persistent heterogeneity observed in real firms' capabilities.

Behavioural theory has since been one of the most influential theoretical approaches to organizational theory. In recent years, it received a new boost due to the publication of many prestigious studies based on the use of agent-based simulations that are rooted in this theoretical tradition and contribute towards its development. (Levinthal 1997; Rivkin 2000). We will refer more extensively to those studies in Chapter 6 in our discussion on organizational complexity.

The rational systems perspective undoubtedly constitutes a major contribution towards our understanding of the dynamics of organizations. The need for consistency, efficiency, reliability, and certainty embedded in its message has been and will always be central for a certain type of organizational process. Many current business practices such as automated production, franchising, the use of computer algorithms for consumer lending decisions and online shopping represent examples of this.

The main assumptions of the rational systems approach to the study of organizations are summarized in the following:

- The determination of the system's goals – to which the organization must show congruence – results from a process that is exogenous to the system being designed; the rational perspective starts its analysis taking the objectives as a given.
- The process of design is concerned with:

  a) decomposing the 'big design problem' in order to reduce its complexity,

  b) finding partial solutions to these partial problems, and

  c) arriving at the 'grand' convergent solution to the big design problem just by aggregating such partial solutions.

5.3 Limitations of the rational approach

While powerful and influential in management practice, the rational approach is not free from serious limitations. First, by definition, a system that aims at improving and even optimizing the performance of existing processes is ill equipped as a source of 'out of the box', radical, and creative initiatives that challenge the very status quo that we are trying to optimize. These initiatives come to life through trial and error, informal collaboration, duplication of tasks, political conflict, and tolerance to ambiguity. All these phenomena are deemed as sources of inefficiency and lack of rationality under the rational approach.

Second, the assumption that the design problem can be simplified by decomposition and that we can then find a convergent solution by aggregation of the partial ones neglects the fact that organizational activities are interdependent. Perfect decomposition and adoption of local 'best practices' would only be possible if the different activities of the firm were independent. By definition, as the firm is a collection of sequential operational activities (logistics, operations, sales), local effectiveness is always interdependent with the effectiveness of other activities.

Third, the prescription to match an organization to its environment is quite a narrow one. It does not give any indication of whether it would be better to try to do so by changing the organization, or better to try to change the environment, or both (Dunbar and Starbuck 2006). As managers are able to try to alter properties of both the organization and the environment, they have vast numbers of degrees of freedom. This situation makes the problem of designing a firm a highly complex one where the designer does not have complete information 'ex ante'.

Fourth, the rational approach assumes that managers making organizational design decisions understand their contexts accurately and that no disagreement or differences in perceptions affects decision makers at the time of pursuing a design initiative. These assumptions rarely hold in real organizations as organization design initiatives generally bring changes in the balance of power of the firm, leading to debate and conflict. These reactions oblige the designer to explore different potential solutions in an iterative way before choosing the one that achieves the objectives within what is politically possible.

These limitations oblige managers to complement the rational approach with a perspective that addresses the behavioural complexity of the firm and its influence at the time of designing organizations. These approaches are, as we will see, better equipped to deal with the dynamics of creativity and innovation than the rational perspectives.

5.4 Organizations as communities: the natural systems approach

One of the main contributions of the open systems perspective is the acknowledgement that in social systems many elements are only weakly connected to others and that such elements are capable of fairly autonomous actions. In this way, the normative structure of the organization is only loosely coupled with its behavioural structure. This leads to the emergence of an informal organization that complements and sometimes contradicts the formal organization rationally designed. In other words, changes of policy do not imply instant changes in behaviour. And, in turn, changes in behaviour may 'emerge' independently from the officially enforced policies.

The rational systems view of the organization concentrates on its normative structure, assuming it is tightly coupled, therefore neglecting almost entirely its behavioural structure. As Scott remarks, under the rational view 'structure is celebrated; action is ignored' (Scott 1998).

Advocates of the natural systems perspective question the extent of the impact of the formal systems of the firm over the behaviour of people working in them. Formal structures are complemented, and many times contradicted, by the informal structure based on the personal characteristics and relations of the organization's members. Under the natural systems perspective, organizations are not instrumental entities aimed at certain specific pre-defined goals, but communities. These communities are, like any social group, mostly interested in adapting and surviving in their particular circumstances. In short, organizations are then not means to an end but ends in themselves.

Thompson (1967) explains:

Approached as a natural system, the complex organization is a set of interdependent parts which together make up a whole because each contributes something and receives something from the whole, which in turn is dependent on a larger environment. Survival of the system is taken to be the goal, and the parts and their relationships are determined through evolutionary processes.[4]

Early contributions emphasizing the importance of the behavioural aspects of organizing resulted from the work of researchers concerned by the human aspects of industry. Pioneers of this approach were the Industrial Fatigue Research Board and the National Institute of Industrial Psychology, both created in the United Kingdom in 1917 and 1921, respectively. These institutions held together groups of skilled researchers focused on certain human problems derived from the industrial society. A few years later, Elton Mayo, a Professor of Industrial Research at Harvard University, published *The Human Problems of an Industrial Civilization* (Mayo 1933), probably the best known work of what we now label as the Human Relations School. This School focused on issues neglected by the advocates of Scientific Management, such as the nature of fatigue and the impact of boredom and monotony on the worker's productivity. The best known contribution from Mayo's work was his description and interpretation of the series of experiments conducted at the Hawthorne plant of Western Electric between 1927 and 1932 (Mayo 1933). This investigation concluded that the existence of motivational problems was centred in the lack of an effective relationship between the worker and their work. Mayo interpreted that the insistence in a merely economic production logic interferes in the development of a social 'non logical' code of behaviour regulating human relationships. In the absence of this code, a continuous experience of lack of understanding and futility arises, generating a feeling of human defeat. Mayo linked this dissatisfaction also to the personal lives workers were living in big cities, characterized by *anomie*, a life without a planned self-development and without a clear sense of achievement.

The approach of these first contributions focused, as with the case of Scientific Management, on the manufacturing processes of the firm. They did not consider interdependencies across the organization's functions or its external environment. Firms were deemed as basically closed systems. Indeed, Mayo does not even refer to organizations, but about problems of the industrial society.

Another early example of the development of the natural systems perspective is Chester Barnard's *The Functions of the Executive* (Barnard 1938). This work constituted one of the first systematic attempts towards the development of a theory of organization as a whole in the United States. While

---

[4] (1967: 6–7)

containing many of the elements of the rational systems perspective, Barnard, who wrote from his experience as a senior manager, was also sensitive to the behavioural aspects of organizing. He emphasized the importance of the informal organization as a vehicle that facilitates communication and maintains the cohesiveness of the organization. He also stated that top managers are responsible for creating and nurturing the culture ('morale' in his words) of the organization. However, despite his approach he did not neglect the existence of an environment where the organization operates, his focus was mostly on the inner working of the organization as a 'cooperative system'.

By the end of the 1950s, Philip Selznick built on the ideas of Barnard and developed his own perspective that has been developed since then and is currently known as Institutional Theory (Selznick 1957). Selznick deemed organizations as 'tools that, nevertheless, have a life of their own'. He stressed the importance of institutionalization as a process by which the organization develops its character (similar to the views of Barnard). Institutionalization infuses activities with values that transcend technical requirements (Selznick 1957:179). In this way, for the committed person the organization acquires an intrinsic value, ceasing to be an expendable artefact as in the rational approach. Belonging to such a firm becomes then a source of personal satisfaction. Selznick works under an open systems perspective, emphasizing the relevance of the organization's external environment as an influence that makes the organizational structure adapt and evolve.

Social Network Analysis. From a methodological point of view, the study of firm as communities of social relationships received a boost with the development of the social network analysis techniques in the 1960s and 1970s. Sociologists such as Rappaport and the group of researchers at Harvard led by Harrison White – Mark Granovetter among others – developed a quantitative methodology currently known as social network analysis or structural analysis. This methodology, already introduced in Chapter 4, enables us to track systematically networks of relationships between people in organizations. Social network analysis views social relationships in terms of *nodes* and *edges*. *Nodes* represent the individual actors within the networks – individuals, teams, or departments in an organizational context – and *edges* represent the relationships between the actors. This approach assumes that structured social relationships are a more powerful source of sociological explanation than the personal attributes of the organization's members. Social network theorists interpret behaviour in terms of structural constraints on activity instead of assuming that the members of an organization act teleologically, that is, designing plans related to clearly defined goals. In this way, the norms affecting the individual within the firm do not determine their location, but become effects of their location (Wellman 1988). Individuals are then *embedded* in their social context. To analyse their behaviour in isolation from such context would constitute a poor picture of how they really behave (Granovetter 1985). We provide an example on the importance of understanding the evolution of different types of embeddedness when we analyse behaviour within organizations in Case Box 5.1.

Krackhardt and Hanson (1993) state that in the 'informal network' of the firm there are three types of relationships that managers should take into account. The *advice network* is constituted by the organization's members on

---

Case Box 5.1 Social network analysis in practice: how corporate strategy decisions affect the behaviour of subsidiaries

---

García-Pont, Canales and Noboa (2009) provides a very innovative and interesting application of social network analysis. His research setting was the Spanish subsidiary ('Frenos España') of a multinational car component firm headquartered in Britain ('División Frenos'). In 2002, División Frenos decided to centralize several activities such as Sourcing, New Product development, and Marketing in order to respond to the recent organizational changes from its customers (car manufacturers).

Garcí-Pont, Canales and Noboa looked at how the behaviour of the subsidiary changed as a consequence of the centralization policy and the associated loss of control over some key business activities. For that purpose he analysed the social network of the work relationships, inside and outside the subsidiary, between the key members of the subsidiary at two different moments in time, 1998 and 2003, before and after the policy change. In the following Figures we visualize both social networks.

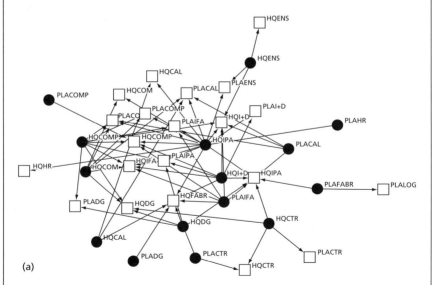

(a)

Figure 5.1. (a) Social network in 1998

Note: Circles represent functions at Frenos España (the subsidiary) and squares represent functions at División Frenos (headquarters).

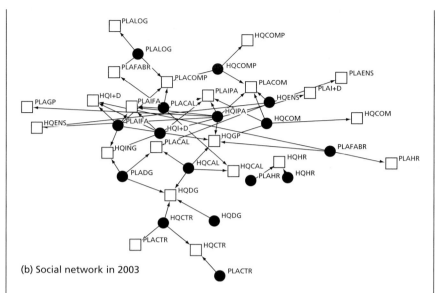

(b) Social network in 2003

The analysis of the change in these networks showed that the headquarters of Frenos España reduced its corporate embededdness as a result of the centralization of key processes – weakening the subsidiary's link with strategic issues. However the *corporate embededdness* of the subsidiary's plants increased as they integrated those of other units of the multinational corporation.

The analysis also revealed a decrease in its *external embededdness*, as the headquarters took over strategic customer relationships leaving only operational links to the subsidiary. Conversely, the *internal embededdness* increased as a result of an increase in the integration between the subsidiaries' plants.

Noboa concluded that the corporate embededdness between an MNC and its subsidiaries can be of three different types:

Operational embeddedness (OE): refers to links related to day to day activities. OE increases with centralization.

Capability embededdness (CE): refers to links related to the development of relevant capabilities for the MNC. CE decreases with centralization.

Strategic embededdness (SE): refers to links related with the subsidiary's participation in the formulation and implementation of the MNC's strategy. SE decreases with centralization.

whom a manager depends to solve problems and get access to information. Second, the *trust network* shows the members of the organization who share sensitive information and back each other in political issues. Finally, the *communications network* explains who communicates frequently with each other in the workplace.

Case Box 5.1 illustrates how the analysis of the informal links between organization's members can lead to a better understanding of how the firm really works and of the impact of changes in policy on such work.

5.5 **Reconciling and integrating the rational and the natural perspectives**

Since the late 1960s, distinguished scholars have tried to develop new perspectives aimed at acknowledging the fact that the objectives pursued by both the rational and the natural views of organizations, while contradictory, are necessary in any organization. The rational system view assumes certainty to achieve determinateness, while the natural system view emphasizes the existence of uncertainty and emergent behaviour that eliminates the possibility of determinateness. In this section we revisit different theoretical perspectives that reconcile both approaches and we discuss how the importance of these perspectives varies across the different stages of development of the firm.

The first two attempts were developed in 1967 in the work of Thompson, Lawrence, and Lorsch. Thompson stated that supporters of each perspective have different objectives in mind. Advocates of the rational paradigm are interested in optimizing – or at least improving – the behaviour of the organization as a vehicle useful for the pursuit of a certain goal or goals. This instrumental perspective characterizes managers, naturally interested in the 'for what?' of organizational initiatives and also scholars working under highly formalized approaches to organizational studies, based on precise – and frequently 'heroic' – assumptions about organizations' behaviour. Natural system researchers, instead, aim at understanding organizations per se – emphasizing the analysis of its social aspects – in order to develop more realistic pictures of organizational life that will lead to more effective action. In an attempt to give room to both perspectives, Thompson conceives complex organizations as:

'*open systems, hence indeterminate and faced with uncertainty, but at the same time as subject to criteria of rationality and, hence, needing determinatedness and certainty*'.[5]

Thompson follows Parsons (1960) in the idea that organizations have three distinct levels of responsibility and control: technical, managerial, and institutional.

The technical level is a 'suborganization' focused on the effective performance of the technical function. For instance, traders in an investment bank, members of finance departments within organizations, employees serving customers in a fast food restaurant constitute this technical core that is expected to perform efficiently and effectively on tasks and procedures that have been formulated at the managerial level.

The managerial level controls or administers the technical suborganization by deciding on policy matters related to it. Managers making decisions on

---

[5] (1967: 10)

matters such as technical tasks to be performed, scale of operations, IT strategy, sourcing, or logistics polices populate this level of control.

Finally, the institutional level is a consequence of the fact that the organization is an open system, a part of a wider social system or external environment. This social system provides meaning, legitimation, and support making the accomplishment of its goals possible. Organization members acting at this level – senior managers, board members, owner–managers relate the organization to the larger society. They formulate the policies referred to in the 'big' lines of action – or strategy – to be followed by the firm in its interface with the environment. The decisions described by Parsons as characteristic of the institutional level correspond to our characterization of Strategic Decisions (Chapter 1).

Parsons emphasizes that at each of the two points of articulation between the levels, there is a qualitative break in the simple continuity of line authority because the functions at each level are qualitatively different. This qualitative difference is related to the type of information processed at each level. Newell (1990) distinguishes between three levels of knowledge that correspond to three forms of processing information: algorithmic – corresponding to Parsons' technical level, heuristic – characterizing the managerial level, and dialectic – at the institutional level.

Thompson (1967) states that at the technical level – as described by Parsons – organizations can benefit from the closed system approach. By removing the few 'problematic' variables partially affected by environmental elements, they can eliminate uncertainty and therefore increase the rationality of the organizational design. These 'problematic' variables are the problems of resource acquisition – for instance, buying the right raw materials, hiring competent engineers, etc. – and the removal of output – selling the stock of products. Removing these variables would not compromise the realism of the representation of the technical problem and will certainly reduce its complexity substantially, enabling a highly rational design. The *databases* of information relevant at the technical level are typically highly structured and can be codified without major difficulty.

At the institutional/strategic level of the firm, where the organization deals with many elements of the environment, uncertainty is very high, therefore precluding the use of the closed system logic. Communication is mostly the way to process information.[6] The databases of information relevant at the strategic level cannot be structured and the knowledge resulting from this information cannot be codified effectively.[7]

What about the managerial level? Their task is, as suggested in the case of biotechnology start-ups (Case Box 5.2), to 'talk rationally and act flexibly',

[6] Good top managers spend a considerable amount of time socializing with key interlocutors such as clients, competitors, regulators, government officers, representatives of shareholders, etc.

[7] This is the reason why we cannot learn how to create a winning strategy in a specific context just by reading a strategy book!

Case Box 5.2 Mechanistic vs. behavioural rationales of organizing in a biotechnology start-up

---

Biotechnology start-ups reflect very well how the rational and the natural approaches to organizing need to be reconciled in order to make the organization work effectively.

A biotechnology start-up is, mostly, a research centre where a group of scientists work on different lines of inquiry that may potentially have commercial appeal. The success related to these efforts depends on scientific creativity and, to some extent, on sheer luck. There is no such thing as a 'planned discovery'. Discovery just happens (sometimes) in ways that are not clear. Because of the great uncertainty surrounding individual research projects, biotechnology companies hardly 'kill' apparently non-promising projects but just reduce the political backing to the project by cutting its budget. In this way, interested scientists still have the chance to continue working on them in 'bootleg time' apart from their official responsibilities.

Does it make sense to develop rational management tools such as strategic plans in such an uncertain environment? What is the worth of planning when the core activity of the firm cannot be planned? The answer to the first question is actually yes. 'Rational' Planning can play a major role at the time of helping a biotechnology start-up in developing its business in two ways (second question). First, a biotechnology start-up can only function if it is successful in securing funds to operate from venture capitalists that agree to commit resources to a company that, basically, does not have a product. Securing those funds involves the preparation of long-term plans detailing not only the main lines of research to be followed but also the potential products to be developed, as well as their sales potential and estimation of profits. In short, top managers are telling investors that 'my business is risky but we have a clear sense of direction and the resources and capabilities to move it forward successfully'. Investors would never bet on a venture if they do not perceive that sense of control from its promoters, no matter how uncertain is the environment. And this can only be done through the rhetoric of rationality.

Second, planning also helps for the management of the firm. The planning process triggers an in-depth discussion of the situation of the company and leads to the selection of its main lines of action in the short and long term. Once the plan is enforced, it becomes a tool to allocate resources, communicate direction, share information, and coordinate action.

Can the rationality of plans be reconciled with the flexibility of the lab environment? Good managers are specialists in managing the tension between the mechanistic rhetoric of plans as a framework that communicates a broad and robust sense of direction to the organization's stakeholders without falling into the mistake of adhering to such plans rigorously but only according to the pragmatic needs of managerial action. For instance, Amgen Inc., one of the few biotechnology start-ups that eventually evolved into a major pharmaceutical company, grants their scientists a time allowance equivalent to one day a week as 'bootleg time', in which they can engage in any project they like independently from their formal project assignments.[8, 9] In this way, scientists passionate about a project outside the priority of the firm can devote time and effort to it. Indeed, the firm's first product Epogen was the result of the resilient persistence of a team of scientists that overcame management's impatience and increasing lack of support.

In short, managers get alignment, coordination, and support by talking rationally (encompassing a rational systems approach) and get things done in practice by being sensitive to the behavioural context of the firm acting pragmatically (a natural systems approach).

[8] Interestingly, Google also encourages its engineers to spend 20 per cent of their work time on projects of their interest (see Schmidt, E. [2005]). Some of Google's well known services such as GMail, Google News, and AdSense emerged from these independent initiatives. A similar practice of granting employees 'bootleg time' is followed at 3M, a company legendary for its notable track record on innovation.

[9] Nohria and Berkley (1992).

mediating between the open dialectical logic of the institutional level and the closed logic of the technical level.

As illustrated by the example of Case Box 5.2, both the rational and the natural approaches contribute towards our better understanding of organizational contexts. In the next few paragraphs, we review some of the classic theoretical contributions that aimed precisely at reconciling these two perspectives.

Lawrence and Lorsch (1967) used the conceptual approach of open systems to research the functioning of a group of large organizations, developing a theoretical approach known as contingency theory. They found that as organizations increase in size they increase the degree of differentiation between their activities. In other words, as firms grow, their environments get more complex obliging the firm to develop new capabilities to address such complexity. For instance, as a firm expands internationally, its marketing activities need to adapt to the peculiarities of different national and regional markets. However, the more firms differentiate, the more difficult is the consequent task of achieving the integration of those parts, thereby increasing the cost of coordination. For instance, multi-business firms tend to be organized in a multidivisional form (M-form). This organizational form enables the decentralization of the management of each business in a specific business unit, increasing the responsiveness and the market orientation of the firm as a whole. It is also useful to develop a cadre of general managers at the divisional level. However, this organizational form demands the creation of coordination devices – such as a corporate centre, a corporate planning process, cross divisional committees – in order to secure the coordination of the business units.[10]

Lawrence and Lorsch also found a relationship between variables external to the organization and the states of differentiation and integration within that organization. Organizations become more differentiated as their environments become more diverse. In addition, they emphasize that the degree of environmental dynamism varies across different units within the same firm. In our example of the biotechnology firm, the R&D department faces an extraordinarily dynamic and complex environment while the accounting department probably has a highly stable one.

We can clearly see in the contingency model some paradoxes of organizing: the need simultaneously to divide tasks up and to integrate them; the need for control systems for stability but the inevitable drift from the demands of the environment as such control systems are applied.

---

[10] The intensity of the coordination will depend on the corporate strategy of the firm, with some corporate strategies being highly coordinated while others grant a high strategic autonomy to the divisions and only exercise financial control. For a discussion on models of corporate strategy see Collis and Montgomery (1998).

In Lawrence and Lorsch's contingency model of organizations, the rational approach predominates in organizations exposed to stable environments. In these firms the pressures for differentiation are lower, making integration easier through central coordination around clearly specified goals. Conversely, as environments become more 'turbulent', in the way described in Chapter 3, the firms need to increase their differentiation, through a more organic design that decentralizes decision making, and relies more strongly on the initiative of its middle managers. In Case box 5.3, this divide between the rational and the organic within the same firm is observed in the case of IBM. The simultaneous need for high integration and efficiency – essential in a firm with 320,000 employees operating all over the world – and the need of creativity and innovation in the highly dynamic IT sector led the firm to decide to run its business following two management systems, a rational one for 'business as usual' and an organic one for new business ventures.

Buckley (1967) distinguished two basic sets of systems processes: morphostasis and morphogenesis. Morphostasis refers to those processes that tend to preserve or maintain a system's given form or structure. In social systems, it refers to socialization and control activities. IBM's management system responded to this description. Morphogenesis refers to those processes that elaborate or change the system, for example, growth, learning, and differentiation. EBOs were IBM's response to this need that, by definition, could not be addressed by the 'mainstream' management system.

More recently, several authors focused on the need to reconcile the simultaneous need of organizational processes designed for the reliable and efficient execution of the ongoing operational practices, and others aimed at going beyond the status quo.

Among all these approaches, March's conceptual distinction between exploration and exploitation has emerged as a widely used analytical construct at the time of addressing issues related to continuity and change in organization studies (March 1991). Exploration and exploitation have been proposed in the literature as two qualitatively different learning activities between which firms divide attention and resources and develop competences. Exploration is concerned with creating variety in experience, and implies firm behaviour characterized by discovery, risk taking, variation, experimentation, and innovation (March 1991). In general, it is associated with organic structures, loosely coupled systems, path breaking, and emergence. Exploitation is about creating reliability in experience and implies firm behaviour characterized by refinement, efficiency, selection, and implementation, (March 1991). It is associated with mechanistic structures, path dependence, routinization, bureaucracy, and stability. Returns associated with exploration are riskier and more distant in time, while those associated with exploitation are more certain and closer in time. By generating larger variation, explorative firms are

---

Case box 5.3 Organizing for Innovation at IBM

In 1999, the then CEO of IBM, Lou Gerstner, asked a group of senior executives to find the roots of the problem behind IBM's inability to spot the emergence of new technology-related business opportunities at a time when innovations were flourishing across the industry. The study team arrived at the conclusion that IBM's organization design and processes, including the control system and management compensation, were at the heart of the problem of lack of innovation. The business system was focused on the reinforcement and incremental improvement of the current portfolio of business, but was dysfunctional for the exploration of riskier opportunities. The planning system was focused on short term and mostly 'hard' indicators of performance and penalized new initiatives that demanded a few years of erratic and uncertain performance before becoming established. As a consequence of this, middle managers' prevailing culture was developed in response to these imperatives and there was an evident lack of skills in new business building within the firm.[11]

IBM tried to resolve this problem by establishing a management system specifically designed to identify and nurture the development of radical business innovations. In 2000, IBM established its Emerging Business Opportunities ('EBO') programme. According to the company,[12] 'an EBO is a "white space" business opportunity that can become profitable, billion-dollar businesses within five to seven years'. EBOs were assigned an experienced IBM executive 'champion' to manage the venture during its start-up phase. Pilot projects, almost always involving clients, validated and refined initial ideas for the EBO's products or services. Unlike the case of established businesses, the control system of EBOs emphasized the achievement of milestones, such as the completion of a pilot project or the establishment of a strategic alliance in order to acquire a new capability. Control meetings were based on in-depth analyses of the progress where the top executive leading the project asks 'tough' questions of top management, who mainly tried to assess whether the project had a reasonable focus and 'strategic clarity'. Once an EBO has grown to sufficient size, it usually becomes part of an existing IBM business unit. Of the 25 EBOs that were launched since 2000, by 2004 twenty-two ventures were in various stages of maturation and growth. Four EBOs – Digital Media, Life Sciences, Linux, and Pervasive Computing each achieved more than $1 billion in revenue in 2003 and again in 2004. Three additional EBOs – Blade Servers, Flexible Hosting Services, and Storage Software – doubled their revenue in 2004.

Equally importantly, IBM has developed in its EBO leaders the capability for business building and management under high levels of uncertainty and ambiguity. A career path has been created around EBOs, attracting middle managers who, at the launch of the programme, were reluctant to move away from 'business as usual' to EBOs in a company with little reputation of recent success in innovation in high risk ventures.

[11] © Garvin and Levesque (2004).
[12] IBM 2004 Annual Report.

---

expected to experience substantial success as well as failure, while exploitative firms are likely to generate more stable performance.

The importance of maintaining an appropriate balance between exploration and exploitation has been deemed as a primary factor in firm's survival and prosperity (March 1991). This need of a balance has been labelled in recent work as the need to create *organisational ambidexterity* (Tushman and O'Reilly 1996) understood as the simultaneous balance between exploitation and exploration.

Ambidextrous organisation designs are composed of highly differentiated but weakly integrated subunits. While the exploratory units are small and decentralized, with loose cultures and processes, the exploitation units are larger and more centralized with tight cultures and processes (Benner and Tushman 2003:252).

In contrast to this, the *punctuated equilibrium* paradigm refers to temporal rather than organizational differentiation (Gupta et al. 2006). This approach suggests that cycling through periods of exploration and exploitation is a more viable approach than the simultaneous pursuit of both as suggested by the ambidexterity hypothesis.

   This apparent contradiction can be solved when we clarify the level of analysis. When we analyse a firm as a whole, the punctuated equilibrium makes more sense. Firms tend to show an overall dynamics characterized either by a reinforcement and refining of its ongoing activities (exploitation) or by a rupture with the past in order to pursue a new direction (exploration). Instead, if we focus our analysis at a micro level of the firm (departments within a firm, teams within a department, etc.) it is easier to see exploitation in one area while we observe exploration in another, as suggested by Lawrence and Lorsch.

5.6 **From design as a noun to design as a verb**

After reviewing and categorizing the different theoretical approaches to the study of organizational dynamics, we focus on the very process of designing a firm. In other words, we move from a scientific approach to organizational design, focused on understanding existing firms and discovering cause and effect relationships among their variables, to a focus on designing, aimed at creating new organizations or modifying current organizations from their current situation towards more desired ones.

   Due to the relevance of the behavioural aspects of organizing, organizational designers often need to devote effort to educating participants on what a design requires. A lack of shared understanding among organization's members can escalate to serious resistance that might threaten a project's success (Dunbar and Starbuck 2006). The natural systems approach assumes that designers usually misunderstand to some extent the complexity of the organizational context. Therefore, they should view their design initiatives as experiments that may not turn out as predicted. In fact, even successful design initiatives hardly achieve all the initial objectives as originally intended.

   The practical aspects of organization design received the attention of organizational researchers since Simon (1968) made a call to create a 'science of design', that is, the development of a robust body of 'teachable' doctrine, partly formalizable, partly empirical, about the design process. Simon argues that, as Romme (2003) suggests, the main question about the creation of systems that do not exist, or that are being subject to major change becomes, 'will it work?' rather than 'is it valid or true?'

Romme summarizes the normative ideas and values characterized by good practice in organizational development as well as other disciplines as architecture and community development. He expresses the pragmatic nature of research on designing. These values can be divided in those related to the *content* of design and those related to its *process*:

5.6.1 CONTENT OF DESIGN

Three ideas (Romme 2003) have to be taken into account regarding the content of any design initiative:

1. *Each situation is unique.* Each design situation is characterized by a singular set of related problems. Therefore, it is impossible for the designer to approach a design problem applying generic criteria.
2. *Focus on purposes and ideal solutions.* Focusing on purposes helps to discard secondary aspects of the situation. An agreed target solution puts a time frame on the system to be developed and guides near term solutions in the light of the larger purposes.
3. *Apply Systems Thinking.* Every problem is embedded in a larger system of problems. For instance, the success of the operations, human resources, and R&D budgets depend to a great extent on the sales budget (and the cash flow it brings), but the success of the sales budget depends on the appropriate performance of operations, human resources, and R&D, for which they need the adequate budgets. This circularity of causation in the performance of the different departments of the firm is reflective of its systemic nature. A systems perspective, as the one followed throughout this chapter, enables the designer to focus on these non-linear interdependencies between partial solutions to design problems. A non systemic design approach, based on assuming that the 'big problem' is solved through the aggregation of local solutions to 'small problems' is destined to failure due to political backfire coming from those who have been affected by the interdependencies associated with the small solution without being taken into account in the design.[13]

---

[13] The usual political "battles" between the Marketing/Sales and the Operations departments or the "unpopular" reputation of Finance within the firm are reflective of the systemic interdependencies.

The example in Case Box 5.4 illustrates how designers, consultants in this case, make decisions on the content of the design problem. We can see through the case account how the three ideas explained previously inform the work of organization design consultants.

Case Box 5.4 Organizational design practices in management consulting

---

Based on interviews with 24 expert management consultants, Visscher (2005) provides an interesting account on how expert consultants deal with their organization design projects.

The design process starts with an exploration of the questions formulated by the client. None of the consultants responded to their client's questions right away but took them as points of departure for further exploration. Typically the problem espoused by the client is not the real problem as the real problem might be one the client does not dare to talk about at that moment. Defining what is the 'core problem' can sometimes be a complex process that demands consultants to map the perspectives of the key figures within the firm and link them with the political map of the firm. This map helps in creating order in the analysis and creates conditions for an open dialogue between the key figures, facilitated by the consultant, where they can make progress towards a consensus – or at least a manageable dissent – about what is the main problem to be tackled in the design process.

Consultants then explore whether there is consensus among the key figures of the firm on what organizational form should be implemented. If there is consensus the consultant analyses the trade-off between the convenience of shortening the design project capitalizing and the risk that better possible and feasible forms that they are familiar with are neglected. The decision will depend on the judgement of the consultant in the specific situation. If there is no consensus, the consultants will use the ideas exposed by the key figures to sense the political situation, trying to steer and manipulate the debate asking extra attention in favour of their preferred forms and discouraging unfavourable ones, for instance, by asking for further analyses.

These alternative forms are assessed not only from the point of view of their functionality. Other criteria such as 'doability', strength and commitment of the client, and complexity of the design situation are also considered.

Doability refers to the difficulty associated with the implementation of a certain form and whether the resources to do so are available in the firm. This is related to the *strength and commitment of the client*. A strong and committed client makes difficult ambitious designs doable. A weak management, instead, obliges the consultant to follow a more collaborative approach, as a straightforward 'top-down' implementation would be probably resisted. The *complexity* of the project is assessed under two different categories. *Cognitive complexity* refers to the uniqueness of the situation, the number of dimensions of the problem, or the size and diversity of the firm. *Socio-political complexity* has to do with the number of stakeholders involved and their differences in opinions and interests.

5.6.2 PROCESS OF DESIGN

In addition to the three ideas referred to earlier on the content of design initiatives, Romme (2003) also proposes to take into account three ideas related to the process of design itself:

1. *Participation and Involvement in Decision Making and Implementation.* Involvement of those who carry out the solutions in making decisions about design solutions and their implementation leads to acceptance and commitment. Romme (1995) remarks that, in some cases, the benefits of participation can be even more important than the solution itself. The discussion itself can help those involved to challenge their assumptions and to engage in an honest exchange where the ideas and positions of others are better understood, leading to an increasing empathy across different areas of the firm. However, this dialogue must not result in unfruitful debate leading to lack of progress and loss of credibility of the design initiative. The organization designer has to master the art of choosing whether to keep options open in order to explore further design alternatives through debate or to 'anchor' certain aspects of the problem making the decision to adopt a particular design alternative. These points are referred to sometimes as 'design nodes' and have the implication of conditioning further design choices in a direction desired by the designer. By anchoring parts of the problem, not following a predetermined order but one suitable with the specific situation, the designer decreases the 'degrees of freedom' of the problem creating path dependence.

2. *Discourse as Medium for Intervention.* Argyris et al. (1985) suggest that for design professionals, language is not a medium for representing the world, but for intervening in it. The design process should initiate and involve dialogue and discourse aimed at defining and assessing changes in organizational systems and practices (Checkland and Scholes 1990). For instance, Gehry Partners, the firm led by the legendary contemporary architect Frank O. Gehry, conceives as a key step in its design practices the development of a collaborative network for design and construction with its customers, users, and partners. They actively involve them to inform the design process. When explaining his design approach for the Weatherhead School of Management, Frank Gehry remarked,

Some architects sell buildings that are irrational and irreverent about how people use a building. That wouldn't happen to me. I do listen. I compromise. . . . I spent time listening to the people on campus. I worry about the neighborhood. . . . I spent a lot of time worrying about the law school. I listened to their objections and made the building as a result more interesting. (Yoo, Boland, and Lyytinen 2006)

3. *Pragmatic Experimentation.* These are action experiments, attempts to explore new ways of organizing, led by the need to challenge conventional wisdom and ask questions about 'what if?' but it is tempered by the designer's own commitment to finding alternatives which are useful (Wicks and Freeman 1998). For instance, in the IBM case reported earlier, the firm started with a small number of EBOs that were quite likely to succeed in order to create a fast 'track record' and gain political momentum.

This early success increased the number of middle managers willing to engage in the EBOs in opposition to a traditional career.

The ideas on the design process are illustrated in Case box 5.5.

In Case Box 5.5 we see an example of how the path dependence of the organization design initiative can be secured by the designers. By committing to the project-based organization, under the leadership of marketing, they created a 'design node' that conditioned the rest of the design process in a way that secured the key objectives of the design initiative against political opposition that would have stalled the initiative, making it lose its strength and credibility.

Case Box 5.5 Organization redesign in Allentown Materials Corp.[14]

By 1992, The Electronic Products Division (EPD) of Allentown Materials Corp., had been failing to generate the innovative products that the markets were asking for. This led the firm to lose market share and incur multi-year financial losses.

A group of organizational development specialists working at the corporate level analysed how the EPD was organized and detected three major sources of dysfunctional behaviour. First, that the only integrating mechanism where projects were assessed by representatives of all the key activities (manufacturing, marketing, sales, and product development) were monthly meetings attended by more than twenty people where all projects were discussed sequentially. This format not only led to superficial analyses but also to the conflict avoidance culture of the division when the committee was unable to make decisions and to enforce commitments to action. Second, despite that the firm required a strong marketing leadership, due to historical reasons, the 'centre of gravity' of the organization was at the production plants. All the former managing directors of the EPD developed a career in manufacturing. Marketing was a poorly resourced department, filled with junior executives and unable to hire 'heavyweights' due to its budgetary constraints. Third, there was low trust between the different departments, engaged in a 'blame game' that led to very poor coordination and predisposition to collaborate. This low-trust environment also conspired against the cross-departmental project meetings.

The organizational development specialists decided that the EPD required a complete change in its management system around four axes:

a) Marketing had to be empowered to become the new 'centre of gravity' of the firm.
b) The division required urgent improvement in the interdepartmental relationships, a key feature in a firm urged to develop cross-departmental collaboration as a prerequisite for innovation.
c) Project management needed to be reorganized to improve its efficiency

The incentive system needed to be redesigned in order to be aligned with the new strategic priorities of the division.

The priority of the design process involved securing the achievement of the two main objectives of the redesign initiative:

[14] Beer (1997).

a) To improve the way innovation-related processes were managed within the EPD.

b) To help the division increase its market orientation by empowering the Marketing department.

The initial discussions were well received by most departments of the division, except for the strong opposition from the manufacturing plants, who were unwilling to support plans that threatened their political leadership within the division. Facing the risk of losing the momentum and support for the design project due to the lack of progress, the development specialists, with the backing of the corporate management and the commitment from the division's managing director, decided to make a decision on the organizational form for project management. Project teams working on individual projects would replace the mass project management meeting. Each team would be composed by members of each department and would be coordinated by marketing.

Later, the design process explored, in collaboration with the EPD's departments, other areas such as how to develop and coach project managers, how to adapt incentives to the new situation, the development of initiatives to increase interdepartmental trust and empathy, and the creation of a mechanism to allocate resources among the different projects.

5.7 **Summary**

This chapter analyses the internal, or organizational, landscape of the firm under a systemic perspective. The adoption of a systemic view enables us to focus on the internal dynamics of the firm. We reviewed the concepts of closed and open systems as well as the nature and evolution of the rational and natural approaches to organization studies. We also discussed theoretical approaches that reconcile these two approaches showing that each of them contributes to our better understanding of how organizations behave.

In the last part of the chapter, we focused on the dynamics of organizational design as a practice. We reviewed contributions and examples that show the pragmatic nature of organization designing and the difference between the logic of the organization analyst and that of the organization design practitioner.

6 Managing Firm Complexity

6.1 Introduction

In Chapter 5, we adopted a systemic view of organizations and discussed several classical and contemporary theoretical approaches to the study of organizations and organizing. In Chapter 6, we focus specifically on complexity as a central characteristic of organizational dynamics. In doing so, we review and discuss theoretical approaches that put complexity at the centre of their analysis of organizations and organizing. Our goal is to help the reader understand the roots and characteristics of organizational complexity in a way that will help them to manage such complexity effectively.

In doing so, first we review two concepts that constitute cornerstones of any dynamic approach to the study of organizations. These concepts are feedback loops and non-linear dynamics. We then discuss systems dynamics, a theoretical and methodological approach that emphasizes the complex, non-linear nature of relationships between a firm's decisions and the outcomes of such decisions. Finally, we discuss recent work associated to the complexity paradigm, referred by some scholars as 'complexity theory', a rather novel and increasingly influential approach to the study of organizations.

6.2 The concept of the feedback loop in management

The feedback loop concept underlying feedback and circular causality is at the heart of any dynamic approach to the study of organizations and social science in general. Feedback loops are set up whenever one action, event, or piece of information determines some other action, event, or piece of information which in turn affects the first action, event, or piece of information (Richardson 1994).

In a unidirectional view of causality, a set of independent variables X_1, $X_2, \ldots, X_n$ cause a determinate impact on the state of a dependent variable Y. The assumption of a neatly unidirectional relationship between cause and

Conceptual Box 6.1 The relationship between diversification and performance

The study of the relationship between a firm's decision to diversify its portfolio of business and the performance of such firm is arguably one of the most developed areas of enquiry within the academic debate on strategic management. Yet, this area of inquiry falls far short of consensus. After thirty years of research there is still considerable disagreement about how and when diversification can be used to build long-run competitive advantage (Markides and Williamson 1994).

The seminal quantitative study on the issue is Richard Rumelt's doctoral dissertation. Rumelt (1974) used objective and subjective criteria to classify firms into four major categories (Single Business, Dominant Business, Related Business, and Unrelated Business) further divided into nine subcategories, making a critical distinction between 'constrained' and 'linked' diversification. For constrained diversifiers the majority of a firm's businesses share a set of specialized resources. Linked diversifiers also have connections across their businesses, but of a different kind. New businesses are added to old ones by building on a variety of connections, such that each new business is related to at least one other business, but the collection as a whole is virtually unrelated.

Rumelt found persistent differences in performance across diversification categories. Dominant Constrained and Related Constrained diversifiers consistently outperformed other categories in the sample. Single businesses and linked diversifiers were average performers. Unrelated diversifiers and vertically integrated business were among the worst.

Several studies from the Financial Economics field (Morck et al. 1990; Bethel and Liebeskind 1993; Lang and Stulz 1994; Denis et al. 1997) studied the relationship between diversification and performance from different viewpoints concluding that diversification affects performance negatively.

These results were challenged by a highly influential work from Campa and Kedia (2002) published in the *Journal of Finance*. These authors argued that while there is plenty of work documenting that diversified firms' shares trade at a discount, that discount does not necessarily mean that diversification destroys value. Campa and Kedia argue that firms may choose to diversify because they already experience poor performance. Therefore, not taking into account past performance and its effect on a decision to diversify will result in (wrongly) attributing the discount to diversification activity rather than to the overall poor performance of the firm. Their analysis confirmed the existence of a discount in the value of diversified firms of roughly 11 per cent in line with previous work. However, this discount is explained by the overall performance of the firm and not just for the diversification decision. Furthermore, they found that actually the diversification discount drops and sometimes turns into a premium, when the study controls for the endogeneity of the diversification decision. In short, the value of the diversification decision depends on the firm. It can be value enhancing many times. Work from Vilallonga (2004) confirmed these results.

The debate summarized above represents clearly the risks of confusing correlation with causation. Early works assumed that the correlation between poor firm performance and diversification was explained by a neat unidirectional link between a decision to diversify (independent variable) and performance (dependent variable). Campa and Kedia and Vilallonga's work showed the existence of *causal ambiguity* in the relationship between these variables. While firms might experience performance problems due to bad diversification, they can also engage in diversification in order to remedy poor performance caused by other decisions. In this case the direction of causality would be the opposite.

effect characterizes most of the strategy-related studies based on econometric analysis. In Conceptual Box 6.1, we can find an example of work within this research tradition, mostly developed in American universities, referred to as the debate between a firm's decision to diversify its businesses and the impact of such decision on performance.

Unfortunately for us, in the realm of management and in the social sciences in general, not all the cause and effect links are neatly unidirectional as in the previous example. One of the strengths of dynamic approaches to organizing such as cybernetics, systems dynamics, or complexity theory, to be discussed later in this chapter, is the acknowledgement that causality can actually be circular.

In the circular view of causality embedded in the feedback loop concept, there are no such things as independent and dependent variables, but just variables that are both cause and effect to each other. For instance, during a price war, a price cut by competitor A leads to a price cut by competitor B that leads to a new price cut in competitor A and so on. Similarly, a firm's decision to change the price and features of a product leads to changes in customer demand that might trigger new decisions from the firm regarding the price and features of such product, restarting the cycle again.

In order to release all the predictive power of the feedback loop concept we need to rely on an additional idea, referred to by some researchers as the *polarity* of the loop. The polarity of a loop reflects the loop's tendency either to counteract a change in any of its elements creating *negative* feedback loops or to reinforce it giving rise to *positive* feedback loops.

6.2.1 NEGATIVE FEEDBACK LOOPS

A causal loop that tends to diminish or counteract a change in any one of its elements is called a negative feedback loop.[1] Negative feedback simply means that the outcome of a previous action is compared to some desired outcome and the discrepancy between the two is fed back as information that guides the next action in such a way that the discrepancy is reduced until it disappears. A very simple and classic example of negative feedback loop is a domestic heating system. It consists of an appliance and a regulator. The regulator contains a device that senses room temperature connected to a device that turns the heating appliance on and off. A desired temperature is set in the regulator. When the room temperature falls below this desired level, the control sensor detects the discrepancy between actual and desired states. The regulator responds to the negative discrepancy with a positive action, it turns the heat on. When the temperature rises above the desired level the

---

[1] In this book we use the terms negative feedback and counteractive feedback as synonyms.

opposite happens. By responding to the deviation of actual from desired levels in an opposite or negative way, the control system dampens any movement from desired levels, keeping the temperature close to a stable level over time. Similar negative feedback logic is observed when a Central Bank increases interest rates in order to keep inflation under control or, in economists' jargon, to prevent the economy's 'overheating'.[2] In this way, the Bank's monetary policy acts as a 'thermostat' or control sensor of the economy that aims at keeping the level of economic activity and the level of inflation within a desirable range.

Self-regulatory systems of this kind have been labelled as cybernetic systems (Boulding 1956). The cybernetic tradition of feedback thought postulates that two main forces drive an organization over time. The first force is the drive to achieve some purpose: organizations are goal-seeking systems and these goals drive their actions. The second force arises because organizations are connected through feedback links to their environment: they are subsystems of an even larger environmental system. Reaching the goal requires being adapted to those environments. Thus, in the cybernetics tradition, organizations are driven by attraction to a predetermined desired state which is in equilibrium adaptation to the environment. Such equilibrium adaptation enables the firm to survive in such an environment. According to cybernetics theory, organizations deploy regulators or control systems that utilize negative feedback in order to reach their goals and the desired states of adaptation to their environments. The problem is how to keep an organization at, or near to, some desired state: this is achieved through the design of a suitable *regulator*. Management is seen by the cybernetic tradition as the profession of control. Managers exercise such control through the design of management planning and control systems that work as regulators of the firm's dynamics. The purpose of management planning and control systems is to lead the organization towards a desired state of stability, harmony, and consistency.

As the reader can easily realize, this tradition of feedback thought is in line with work described in Chapter 5 based on the combination of a rational/ open systems view of firms. Not surprisingly, the cybernetic model places great emphasis on the operational level of the firm, where its assumptions hold more robustly than on the administrative or strategic levels. Control over the operation of the system involves dealing with disturbances *in degree* (e.g. a bottleneck in manufacturing leading to a reduction in output and increase in unit fixed costs, a stock shortage due to an unexpected increase in sales, etc.). These disturbances can be solved just by adjusting behaviour within the existing set of policies. For instance, the firm would deal with the restriction in capacity through capital investment, by working extra time

---

[2] Note the analogy with the functioning of a heating system.

in the process creating the bottleneck, etc. The cybernetics tradition, however, fails to address that sometimes disturbances may be caused by more fundamental causes, not related to problems in the implementation of policies but in the policies themselves. For instance, during the last five years, several car manufacturing firms have been closing plants in Western Europe due to their high cost structure and relocating production in Eastern Europe. This lack of cost competitiveness of western plants did not result from poor management but from structural factors making production in countries like the United Kingdom, Germany, or Spain inevitably higher than manufacturing in Hungary, Romania, or Slovakia. These second sources of disturbances are called disturbances *in kind* and demand to redefine the policies controlling the operational levels, in this case, the location of the plants. The existence of two natures of disturbances, in degree and in kind, or *double loop feedback* has been described by Ashby (1952) and Argyris (1982, 2004) who labelled adaptive behaviour leading to changes in the rules of choice as *double-loop learning* (see Case Box 6.1 and Conceptual Box 6.2).

Case Box 6.1 Double-loop learning at Nokia: introducing clamshell handsets

---

Since 2002, Nokia has been the comfortable market leader in the mobile phones market, usually having sales double that of its closest competitors namely Motorola and Samsung.

Its business model was based on the production of a relatively narrow range of products that appealed to the mass market. The firm was reluctant to focus on mid-to-high-end models – notably refusing to produce clamshell designs – and also refused to customize its models, in order to keep its huge manufacturing economies of scale based in producing mostly cosmetic variations of its well-known 'candy bar' design with no lid, and a rectangular shape. Its large manufacturing volume, around 60,000 phones a day, coupled with high standardization of models, enabled the firm to enjoy important cost advantages derived from economies of scale with respect to its main competitors. By early 2003, Nokia's global market share was almost 35 per cent.

However, one year later, Nokia's celebrated business model started to show some signs of exhaustion. The firm's global market share shrank to 28.9 per cent in less than a year. In Western Europe the loss was particularly sharp with a fall of 10 per cent in market share from 38 per cent to 28 per cent in only one year. This loss questioned the validity of Nokia's competitive strategy and weakened the firm's position in the high and mid-range of its handset selection against Motorola and Samsung. These two firms provided the popular clamshell models and managed to increase their share at Nokia's expense. By early 2004, Nokia addressed this problem by changing its long-term policy of high standardization (*adjustment in kind*) by launching several new handsets in order to restore its quality image, including clamshell phones and increasingly customized models. In early 2005, Nokia's market share was up again reaching 32 per cent globally.[3]

[3] Caldart (2006).

Conceptual Box 6.2 Lack of double-loop learning as the cause of failure: the Icarus paradox

---

A good example of how firms may fail due to their attempt to deal with disturbances in kind – requiring double-loop dynamics – applying only changes of degree – single-loop response – can be found in the work of Miller (1990). Miller researched the phenomenon of highly successful firms that eventually 'fall from grace' showing poor performance. He found that outstanding companies face a phenomenon that he referred to as the 'Icarus paradox':[4] their victories and their strengths often seduce them into excesses that cause their downfall. He detected four trajectories, patterns of action through which organizations extend and amplify their strategies, policies, attitudes, and events that led to their success in the first place:

- The focusing trajectory that takes *Craftsmen* organizations, those with a strong engineering and tight operational controls as their major sources of competitive advantage, and turns them to *Tinkerers*, insular firms whose technocratic structure alienates customers with perfect but irrelevant offerings. They focus excessively on engineering and forget customers.

- The venturing trajectory converts *Entrepreneurial Builders*, high growth companies managed by imaginative leaders and creative planning staffs, into *Imperialists*, companies overtaxing their resources by expanding too rapidly into businesses they know little about.

- The inventing trajectories makes *Pioneers*, companies with excellent R&D departments and state of art products move to become *Escapists*, run by scientists who squander resources in the pursuit of grandiose futuristic inventions.

- The decoupling trajectory which transforms *Salesmen*, companies with developed marketing skills, broad markets, and prominent brand names, into *Drifters*, companies whose sales emphasis obscures design issues and who become aimless and bureaucratic producing me-too offerings.

Miller makes the point that successful organizations are characterized by consistency and harmony. Being comfortable and confident of their long lasting business models, they keep reinforcing them and treat every disturbance as ones of degree. They keep building upon, reinforcing, and modifying what has made them successful. The result is a momentum for the organization that suppresses their ability to address disturbances in kind pushing it down certain typical trajectories that lead to disaster.

[4] The fabled Icarus of Greek mythology is said to have flown so high, so close to the sun, that his artificial wax wings melted and he plunged into the Aegean sea. The power of Icarus' wings gave rise to the abandon that doomed him. The paradox, of course, is that his greatest assets led to his demise.

Cybernetics sees as the main cause of the difficulty in designing regulators the variety or complexity of the environment. Variety is defined as the number of discernibly different states the environment can present to the organization and the number of discernibly different responses the organization can make to the environment. In order to be effective, the complexity and speed of the firm's response must match the complexity and speed of change of the environment. This influential idea is known as Ashby's Law of Requisite Variety (Ashby 1952). One example of how companies try to develop diverse responses to diverse environments are the new models of innovation that multinational firms have been developing during the last decade. The days when innovation was led by a centralized R&D department, typically located at the headquarters of the firm have long gone. Firms increasingly increased the variety of their sources of ideas and capabilities for innovation by running several R&D departments around the world, benefiting from contextual specialized knowledge not available at headquarters. For instance, Procter & Gamble relies strongly on its Japanese subsidiary for the purposes of developing innovation in cosmetics, as the sophistication of the Japanese customer made this subsidiary very proficient in developing high end cosmetics. One example of this is the SK II line of products developed in Japan and successfully rolled out by P&G throughout Asia, United Kingdom, Spain, United States, Canada, and Australia.

As mentioned in the previous text, a central tool used by organizations as a regulator of its dynamics is the planning system. Through it, the organization forecasts the changes that will occur and prepares a plan to deal with them over a given time period. The more complex the environment, the more difficult it will be to use that single forecast as an effective regulator which is able to respond to the many unforeseen events that are occurring. Then the regulator must be given a greater variety by preparing a number of different forecast scenarios and putting together contingency plans for each scenario. Additionally the plans will be reviewed and changed with greater frequency. The use of econometric models as a tool that enables them to predict the value of variables or techniques such as sensitivity or simulation analyses of the key variables affecting a business are examples of how planners try to understand how future events might alter the firm's plans obliging it to modify its policies.

Another, more complex way to deal with long-term uncertainty is the use of scenario planning. Scenarios are narratives containing vivid images of what some future state of the firm's environment looks like. The narrative corresponding to each scenario portrays a sequence of believable, interrelated events. Scenarios are usually presented in groups of between two and four *qualitatively different* futures that the firm may face. Quantitative techniques such as econometrics, sensitivity analysis, or the simulation of key variables do not provide this comprehensive view of the future, but just focus on one possible scenario, computing the quantitative impact of deviations in the values of key variables (prices, interest rates, inflation, taxation, etc.) from such a basis case. Scenario analysis goes further by providing distinct possible futures, allowing companies to develop strategies for different situations, and to plan for these strategies long before they are actually needed.

More importantly, scenarios follow the progression of the present into the future. That is to say, scenarios do not simply describe distinct futures, but they also demonstrate how these futures came to pass. This allows managers and strategists to watch for signs that will indicate which, if any, of the presented scenarios is most likely to come to pass. Case Box 6.2 summarizes the three main scenarios envisaged by Shell for 2025.

Case Box 6.2 Shell's Global Scenarios to 2025

Shell is arguably the leader among the private firms in the use of scenario planning as a strategic planning method. They have been using this technique since 1971, and by 2005 they engaged in a major scenario planning exercise. Among the outputs of this analysis was the development of the three 'Global Scenarios for 2025'. These scenarios differ on how 'fluid' the international business environment will be. The more optimistic scenario, labelled as 'Open Doors' describes a world of high levels of cross border integration supported by harmonizing forces such as high security, regulatory harmonization, mutual recognition between countries, voluntary best-practice codes, and close links between investors and the civil society. They see networking skills and superior reputation management as key success factors in this environment. The second scenario, called 'Low Trust Globalization', foresees a world of limited cross-border economic integration due to lack of solutions to the crisis of security and trust (e.g. Enron), rapid regulatory change and conflicting laws and overlapping jurisdictions leading to excessive controls. These factors would encourage short-term portfolio optimization and vertical integration. In this world of institutional discontinuities, complying with fast evolving rules and managing complex risks would become key challenges.

Finally, Shell identifies a pessimistic scenario, named as 'Flags' in which dogmatic political approaches, national preferences, regulatory fragmentation, and conflicts over values and religion give market insiders an advantage and put globalization on hold. In this scenario fragmentation would be exacerbated by calling for a careful country risk management.

Source: Shell (2005).

6.2.2 POSITIVE FEEDBACK LOOPS

A causal loop that typically tends to reinforce or amplify a change in any of its elements is called a *positive* feedback loop.[5] For instance, providers of software solutions are subject to a critical 'make or break' positive feedback loop where the prestige of its list of past and current customers plays a central role in acquiring new customers (this may be associated with the network effects, as discussed in Chapter 4). The trajectory of these companies typically starts with very tough times, when contracts from important firms have to be secured from a position of no 'track record'. Only the personal reputation of the partners and the quality of their contact networks can help the company to gain its first contracts. However, once the firm has successfully developed a few high profile projects, the 'bandwagon' effect starts as the track record attracts new deals at a multiplied basis. The extraordinary

---

[5] In this book we use the expressions positive feedback, reinforcing feedback and amplifying feedback as synonyms.

development of firms such as SAP AG is explained by this amplifying of reputation effects. The firm has in fact reflected its concern for its 'reputation-building machine' in its long lasting graphic advertising campaign based on communicating the names of high profile firms that 'run SAP'.

Case Box 6.3 provides an example of how positive feedbacks can also go wrong, in this case, in the form of a free fall of trust between partners in a joint-venture.

Case Box 6.3 Positive feedback in the dynamics of relational quality among partners in a joint venture: The Coca Cola and Nestlé joint venture to produce coffee-based drinks

---

A usual source of failure in joint ventures relies on how the partners manage the *relational quality* within the alliance (Ariño et al. (2002)). The case of the Coca Cola – Nestlé joint-venture ('CCNR Refreshments Company') shows that, despite the partnership making strategic sense due to the complementary nature of the partners, the relationship can end in a massive failure if poor management of relational quality leads to a sharp and accelerated reduction in mutual trust.

The joint venture was launched in 1991 in order to exploit Coca Cola's global distribution capabilities and Nestlé's brand and coffee-related formulas to create a new coffee-based drink to be sold in purpose-built vending machines. While the coffee-based drink failed to impress the market, the Joint Venture ('JV') managers took advantage that the JV also comprehended – quite loosely – the potential development of tea-based drinks, and Nestea was launched. This initiative led the JV to a fast breakthrough in key markets such as the United States, Korea, Germany, Italy, and Canada. However, as each of Nestea's cans were sold in the regular network of Coca Cola vending machines, this situation created a 'cannibalization' for Coca Cola. For each can of Nestea for which Coca Cola received 50 per cent of the total margin, it stopped selling a can of 'fully owned' Coca Cola product. Hence, Coca Cola asked Nestlé to re-balance the way profits were distributed in the JV. Nestle's refusal to compensate Coca Cola for the unexpected cannibalization of its products resulting from selling Nestea in its network of vending machines resulted in a unilateral re-balance of the joint venture by Coca Cola, by 'encouraging' the JV to accept to give up 50 per cent of its profits from sales in Coca Cola's fountain channel to Coca Cola. Nestlé reacted by withdrawing its commitment to transfer to the JV the chocolate business it committed originally and Coca Cola retaliated again by refusing to support one of Nestlé's product's distribution in Asia through its distribution network. Nestlé escalated the conflict further threatening to negotiate with Coca Cola's local competitors in Asia to handle such distribution. Later, in May 1994, as Nestea started to perform poorly in North America against competitors Snapple and Lipton, Nestlé suggested Coca Cola's lack of commitment in distribution as a probable cause of such failure.

This chain of mutual retaliation led to a complete lack of mutual trust and the dissolution of the JV.

Ariño et al. (2002) state that external events altering the partners' perceptions of efficiency and equity within the joint venture cause them either to engage in the renegotiation of the terms of the contract, or to modify behaviour unilaterally (as in the case of Coca Cola) in an attempt to restore balance to the alliance. The process feeds back until a new mutual agreement is restored – leading to increases in the 'stock' of trust between partners – or else the relationship deteriorates gradually until a point when the alliance is dissolved due to a complete loss of mutual trust.

(Continued)

Case Box 6.3 (*Continued*)

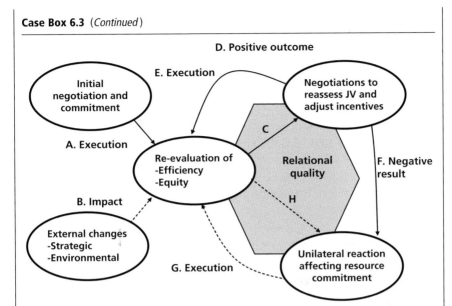

Figure 6.1. The dynamics of relational quality among partners in a joint venture

Source: Ariño et al. (2002).

As Ariño et al. illustrate in Figure 6.1, relational quality is both an input to the success of the alliance (an initial degree of goodwill) and an output of the interactions between the partners, accounting for actual observations of behaviour over time in the context of the venture.

A successful reassessment of the parties' contributions with a related adjustment in the set of incentives will reinforce trust between the parties and increase the parties' ability to solve future controversies successfully (the cycle A-B-C-D-E). Conversely, failure to rebalance the JV successfully leading to unilateral measures from the partners decreases the 'stock' of trust, thereby reducing the ability of partners to solve future controversies positively (the cycle A-B-C-F-G-H).

Positive feedback loops have the potential of escalating small changes generating amplified fluctuations of a very unstable kind. This behaviour generates different patterns of 'explosive' dynamics that social scientists have described metaphorically as 'Icarus paradoxes', 'virtuous or vicious circles', 'network effects', or 'self-fulfilling prophecies'. Such dynamics can have beneficial effects for the firm or harmful ones.

A virtuous circle is a situation of a positive feedback loop in which positive outcomes reinforce each other. For instance, corporate profits bring market growth leading to increased economies of scale and market power leading to increasing corporate profits. Conversely, vicious circles are situations of positive feedback when bad outcomes reinforce each other. A company's weak position and perspectives makes talented people leave the company generating further weaknesses due to the loss of managerial talent. Network effects describe the positive feedback loops that describe the tendency of a product, idea, or project to gain supporters at an increasingly high rate and the simultaneous rapid fall in the support for its rival's product, idea, or project. In Chapter 4, we discussed this idea in the context of competitive strategy by illustrating technology standard wars such as that of between VHS and Beta standards in the VCR market or the war between HD-DVD (Toshiba) and Blu-Ray (Sony) in high definition DVDs. Case Box 4.4 shows the network effects in practice. In these cases, as one standard becomes rapidly embraced as the favourite by customers, the rival standard(s) lose market share with similar speed. Similarly, the ability of an American presidential pre-candidate to raise funds for their campaign shows network effects based on the unfolding of the results of the first rounds of caucuses. This is the reason why many runners give up their ambitions at a rather early stage of the race while only a relatively low number of delegates have been elected. As they fail to get early victories, their funding sources shrink while the ones of the initial victors are boosted very fast.

The self-fulfilling prophecy is a positive feedback loop triggered by expectations about the future situation leading to system behaviour that eventually makes such expectations materialize. For instance, a manager assumes that one of his associates will leave the firm soon. Therefore, he does not consider this associate for promotion, training, or interesting work assignments as he considers that it would be pointless to spend resources on an employee who will leave soon. The associate, disappointed by his lack of progression in the firm, eventually quits. The manager thinks '*I was right*' while actually the associate's decision to leave was only a response to the manager's behaviour led by a mistaken 'prophecy'. Self-fulfilling prophecies also explain to a great extent the evolution of the process leading to a massive loss in confidence in the western banking system during the autumn of 2008, resulting in unprecedented government intervention in the European and American banking systems. The original problem – for example, a bank's poor results due to losses in subprime loans – creates doubts about the solvency of the institution. The shares and debt of this institution lose value in the markets triggering credit downgrades. These downgrades fuel further deterioration of value and customers lose confidence in the bank, leading to withdrawals of funds (commercial banking) or refusal to have counterparty exposure to that bank (investment banking). This reinforces the loss of confidence until the solvency crisis is real, due to the loss of funding and customers.

6.2.3 NON-LINEARITY AND FEEDBACK SYSTEMS

In addition to their positive and negative properties, feedback systems may be either linear or non-linear. Non-linearity occurs when some condition or some action has a varying effect on an outcome, depending on the level of the condition or the intensity of the action. One example of non-linearity is the law of decreasing returns of microeconomics. Extra labour added to a fixed installed capacity will increase output at varying rates till a point where extra labour leads output to decline as large numbers of people interfere with efficient operation. The dynamics of a market's supply and demand show the same non-linear characteristic, leading to frequent abrupt expansions (market 'bubbles') or brutal contractions ('bursts of bubbles') of production and drastic movement in prices of many goods.

An organization can be deemed as a complex system constituted by a web of non-linear feedback loops operating as part of a larger system or environment that is also by itself a web of non-linear feedback loops. We can say then that strategic management is concerned with dealing with the complex dynamics linking exogenous influences within the firm, policy level decisions made by the firm, and the outcomes of these decisions inside and outside the firm. We can also say that the patterns of change that the system displays over time depend entirely on the nature of the feedback interaction of that system. It is the nature of feedback that determines the dynamics of the firm as a system and therefore the nature of the change it has to cope with. Systems with positive feedback and non-linear behaviour are systems in which the potential for over or under reaction, the potential for the escalation of little changes are inbuilt characteristics of how the system behaves. These features usually characterize strategic decisions, making them 'wicked' (Wilson 2003). The complexity of the problems strategic management has to deal with, associated to the non-linear positive feedback that characterizes many of them, reduces the firm's ability to design long-term regulators such as strategic plans and makes more difficult to codify its strategic knowledge. Then, as discussed in Chapter 5, at the strategic level, communication replaces forecasting as the most important way to process information.

The main insights derived from a systemic perspective that acknowledges the existence of positive or reinforcing feedback loops and non-linear dynamics are the following:

- The patterns of behaviour of a firm as a system derive from its feedback structure;
- Such feedback structure may comprehend negative and positive feedback loops;
- Non-linearity characterizes socioeconomic feedback systems;
- Positive feedback and non-linearity may sometimes, as we will see in detail in our discussion of system dynamics, make a decision have counterintuitive outcomes that far from solving the problems they try to address, exacerbate them.

6.3 **System dynamics**

System dynamics is a methodology for studying and managing complex feedback systems. It aims at solving problems in business in general by following these steps:

1. Identification of a problem
2. Development of a hypothesis of the cause–effect relationships between the variables that comprehend the problem
3. Creation of a computer simulation model of the problem based on the hypothesis developed in 2, that reproduces the behaviour of the system in the real world
4. Test in the model alternative policies that may lead to a solution or reduction of the problem
5. Implement the solution identified through the model in the real world

The origins of system dynamics as a field can be traced back to 1958, when Jay Forrester published the article 'Industrial Dynamics: A Major Breakthrough to Decision Makers' in the *Harvard Business Review* and in his book *Industrial Dynamics* (1961). Forrester pioneered the use of computer simulations to create models of the dynamics of organizations based on the feedback concept.

Forrester illustrated his novel approach to problem-solving in complex systems by creating a simulation model of a production–distribution chain. This simulation was used as a game with thousands of participants and the pattern of shortage or oversupply is repeated time and again. Forrester's point is that the sources of the problem are not the behaviours of the decision makers involved in the situation (who typically act quite reasonably at a local level) but the structure of the system.

This methodology originated in Forrester's work (1958, 1961) eventually evolved to become the well-developed field of study known as System Dynamics. Next we review the main principles and insights associated to Systems Dynamics and later we review applications in the field of Strategic Management.

6.3.1 PRINCIPLES OF SYSTEMS STRUCTURE

A first important aspect to remark upon in our discussion of system dynamics is that the modeller takes an endogenous point of view. In other words, it is assumed that all significant dynamic variation in the behaviour of the system comes from the interaction of variables internal to it. The influences of exogenous variables are not of interest for the purposes of the model. This does not mean these 'closed boundary' systems (Forrester 1968) are closed systems but systems that endogenize all the variables, internal or external to the firm, deemed to be critical at the time of understanding the problem.

Forrester (1968) listed the characteristics of dynamic social systems that he deems as principles of system structure:

1. A feedback loop consists of two different types of variables, levels (states) and rates (actions). Except for constants, both are necessary and sufficient to represent the feedback loop.
2. Levels integrate (or accumulate) the results of actions in a system.
3. Levels are changed only by rates.
4. We need to identify in the model the difference between level variables and rate variables.
5. No rate can, in principle, control another rate without an intervening level variable.
6. Rates depend only on levels and constants.
7. In feedback loops, level and rate variables should alternate.
8. Levels completely describe the system's condition.

6.3.2 INSIGHTS FROM SYSTEM DYNAMICS

In general, system dynamics shows that our inherent difficulty in understanding and managing the behaviour of complex systems derives from their multi-loop nature. This makes such behaviour counterintuitive in many cases as it is hard for human beings to appreciate properly the multidimensional dynamics that characterize the system. Building on the work of Forrester, Senge (1990) states that managers need to adopt systemic thinking in order to understand the way their organizations work. The lack of a systemic vision of the firm leads managers to make typical serious mistakes derived from framing problems in a simplistic or non-systemic way. Those mistakes are illustrated in the well known 'beer game' illustrated in Conceptual Box 6.3.

6.3.3 USING SYSTEM DYNAMICS IN STRATEGY

System dynamics models can and have been applied to the study of business strategy. This methodology is widely used in business to help managers understand how strategies will behave over time, what might go wrong, and how to make changes that will lead to better implementation (Kunc and Morecroft 2007). In this way system dynamics helps for the purposes of 'strategic rehearsal'.

Conceptual Box 6.3 The Beer Game

The Beer Game, or Beer Distribution Game was pioneered at the Massachusetts Institute of Technology, in order to show the feedback effects of what appears to be a trivial problem: how members of a supply chain should determine the quantity of goods ordered from the member immediately higher in the supply chain. There are four members of the supply chain: a factory, a distributor, a wholesaler, and a retailer. The rules of the game are that there are costs: inventory holding cost of £1 per barrel per period, and back order costs of £2 per barrel per period. This means that each player in the game has an incentive to lower their stock holding costs and their back order costs. It is this interplay that gives rise, in practice, to surprisingly volatile dynamics. In a steady state, the system should look similar to the supply chain in Figure 6.2a.

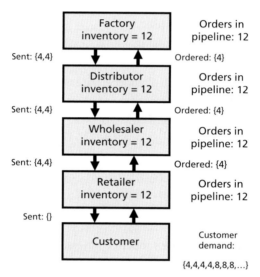

Figure 6.2.a Beer Game

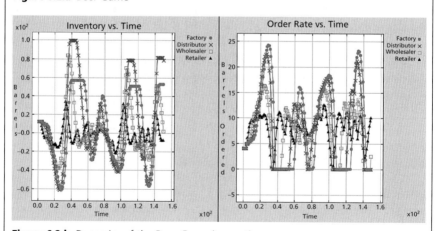

Figure 6.2.b Dynamics of the Beer Game in practice

When the game is played with real people, or modelled in RePast, very different dynamics are exhibited, as shown in Figure 6.2b.

It can easily be noticed that, despite the apparent simplicity of the problem, dynamics go out of control with inventory and order rates varying substantially across time.

Strategic decisions are characterized by their complexity and 'collateral effects' and by the time lag existing between the timing of the decision and its outcome. Then, strategic decision makers can benefit by an analysis based on a simulation of the feedback processes embedded in a strategic decision as it compresses such time lag enabling managers to experiment and learn. For instance, system dynamics has been applied to the study of strategy problems such as portfolio diversification (Gary 2005), growth and rivalry in a low-cost airline, and the launch of a new product in the consumer goods (Kunc and Morecroft 2007).

6.3.4 CHAOS THEORY

Chaos Theory is arguably one of the best known extensions of systems dynamics. It focuses on the behaviour of deterministic non-linear systems showing dynamics that are highly sensitive to the initial conditions of the system (Richardson 1994). This sensitivity is popularly referred to as the 'butterfly effect'.[6]

Chaos theory states that the values of exogenous control parameters of the system can cause its behaviour to move towards a particular state space or 'attractor'. Attractors describe global patterns of behaviour displayed by the system. Depending on the values of the control parameter, a feedback system can operate in three different modes: (1) a negative feedback manner to produce stable equilibrium behaviour; (2) it can be driven by positive feed-back to generate explosively unstable equilibrium behaviour; or (3) it can operate in a mode in which feedback autonomously flips between positive and negative feedback to produce behaviour that is both stable and unstable ('strange attractors'). When a non-linear feedback system is driven away from the peaceful state of stable equilibrium towards the hectic equilibrium of explosive instability, it passes through a phase of bounded instability in which it displays a highly complex behaviour, in effect the result of the system flipping randomly between positive and negative feedback (Stacey 1993). We might think of this phase as a state of paradox in which two contradictory forces, stability and instability, are operating simultaneously, pulling the system in opposing directions. When the system is in the border area it never behaves in a regular way that leads to equilibrium. Instead, it generates patterns of behaviour that are not only irregular but also unpredictable. Nonetheless, such behaviour has an overall, deterministic, hidden qualitative

---

[6] The expression 'butterfly' effect derives from the idea that a butterfly's wings may create tiny changes in the atmosphere that ultimately might cause (or prevent) a tornado. The flapping wing of the butterfly represents a small change in the initial conditions of the system, triggering a chain of events leading to large-scale phenomena.

pattern. Once revealed, these changes are predictable in the short term. However, they are quantitatively unpredictable in the long term.

Chaos exists, for instance, in the earth's weather system. The weather consists of patterns in interdependent forces such as pressure, temperature, humidity, and wind speed which feed into each other and thence back into themselves. It is generated by a non-linear feedback system.

The weather can follow recognizably similar patterns, but those patterns are never exactly the same as those at any previous point in time. The system is highly sensitive to some small changes and blows them up into major alterations in weather patterns. Chaotic dynamics are the reason that meteorologists are unable to forecast the weather for more than a few days ahead.

The existence of dynamics of 'bounded instability' is a key insight about the operation of non-linear feedback loops. Stable equilibrium and explosively unstable equilibrium are not then the only *attractors* or endpoints of behaviour open to such systems. Non-linear systems have a third choice: a state of bounded or limited instability far from equilibrium in which behaviour has a pattern, but it is irregular. The behaviour of the system unfolds in such a complex manner, so dependent upon the details of what is happening that the links between cause and effect are very difficult to track. We can no longer count on certain input leading to certain output.

The conclusion is that dynamic non-linear feedback systems, even deterministic ones, may generate completely unpredictable behaviour at a specific level over the long term. At that level, the state of bounded instability, the long-term future is not simply difficult to see. It is inherently unknowable. And it is so because of the feedback structure of the system itself, not simply because of changes going on outside it and impacting upon it.

In short, chaos theory works with the same kind of models of system dynamics, but leads to different conclusions. System dynamics acknowledges the lack of equilibrium but associates success to attraction to a state as close as possible to equilibrium. Chaos theory, instead, associates success to dynamics around strange attractors, 'the edge of chaos' (Brown and Eisenhardt 1998). This notion of the edge of chaos as a desirable dynamic condition, between order and randomness, in which the firm becomes able to innovate and adapt to novel challenges has been picked by strategy scholars working from a complex adaptive systems perspective such as Brown and Eisenhardt (1998) and Pascale (1999). We will refer to this work in Section 6.4.

6.3.5 INSIGHTS FROM CHAOS THEORY FOR MANAGEMENT PRACTICE

The main insight derived from chaos theory is the inherent difficulty to manage a firm led by our faith in our long-term plans. If the behaviour of simple deterministic non-linear systems is impossible to predict in the long term, it is hardly feasible to make long-term forecasts in a much more complex system such as a business firm. In a business setting, this third area of limited instability has been described as that inhabited by companies dealing with markets distinguished by turbulence and discontinuity. Leaders and employees in these organizations are obliged by necessity to develop a high tolerance to ambiguity and uncertainty. All decision-making techniques that involve step-by-step reasoning from assumptions about the future lose effectiveness and need to be complemented by other ways of making sense of reality, such as intuition or reason by analogy as suggested by Gavetti and Rivkin (2005). These techniques become effective as, despite that we cannot identify specific causes that yield specific outcomes, we do know the boundaries within which those systems move and the qualitative nature of the patterns it displays.[7] We cannot be in control of such a system in the way we would traditionally think about control.

There are strong indications that chaos theory explanations apply to the functioning of foreign exchange, stock, and oil markets. And some authors such as Nonaka (1988), Pascale (1990), and Stacey (1993) have applied these ideas to theories of managing and organizing. Richard Pascale (1990) stated that successful organizations are characterized by a paradox. On the one hand they have to achieve *fit*, meaning a state of coherence, centralization, tight central control, synergy and fit between the key aspects of the organization or '7S's':[8] strategy, structure, systems, style, shared values, skills, and staff. On the other hand, organizations need *split*, meaning breaking apart, decentralizing, differentiating, variety, and rivalry. Split allows the organization to develop new perspectives and innovative actions.

This simultaneous need of fit and split raises a creative tension that provokes inquiring and questioning. It is this tension that leads to the learning organization, with its continual dialogue between contradicting points of view. Through this clash of opposites the organization transcends to a new 'constellation' of fit and split (Pascale 1990). This is a dialectical view of organizational development, similar to that of Argyris and Schon (1978), in which opposites produce, through learning, a new synthesis consistent with more complex forms of strategy and structure. When a system operates far from equilibrium, it never follows exactly the same pattern of behaviour. It follows complex patterns that are not regular and predictable. Instead, behaviour patterns exhibit features of stability and instability, but not in a

---

[7] For instance, we know that the irregularity of the weather will itself be regular because it is constrained to some usual patterns. It cannot just do anything.

[8] The 7S's Framework was developed by Mc Kinsey & Co and highlights the importance to acknowledge the interdependence of these seven variables when studying organizations. An alternative 7S's framework for hypercompetitive environments was proposed by D'Aveni (1994).

predictable manner. Such systems generate new perspectives and new forms of behaviour. Such systems have the potential for innovation not possessed by equilibrium systems.

6.4 Complexity: firms as complex systems

Strategic decisions are frequently characterized as complex ones. Such complexity derives from the multiple dimensions of strategic problems and by the existence of interdependences between decisions and outcomes made regarding such dimensions. In this section, we focus on the problem of complexity itself and we discuss current work that puts the stress on understanding how complexity affects organizational decision making.

As Simon (1996) remarks, complexity as a key characteristic of the world we live in has been studied for centuries in many sciences. Actually, the literature discussed in the last chapter on organizations as rational systems has an omnipresent implicit focus on the behavioural and structural sources of complexity within firms. However, the novelty is the recent interest not on specific complex systems but on the phenomenon of complexity in its own right (Simon 1996). Interest in complexity and, particularly, on understanding the distinctive features that characterize complex systems has increased dramatically during the last quarter of a century across many scientific disciplines. Work on complexity originated during the mid-1980s at the Santa Fe Institute in New Mexico when a highly distinguished group of scientists working in particle physics, archaeology, microbiology, astrophysics, zoology, botany, and economics were drawn together by similar questions (Waldrop 1992, Robertson 2004). All these disciplines shared, at their core, building blocks composed by many agents. These agents – molecules, neurons, a species, customers, networks of firms – were continually organizing and reorganizing themselves and occasionally forming larger structures through natural accommodation and competition. The study of complex systems focuses on understanding how parts of these systems give rise to their collective behaviour, how such collective behaviour affects such parts and how systems interact with their environment (Bar-Yam 1998). This focus on questions about parts, wholes, and relationships explains the relevance of the study of complex systems in the agenda of all these scientific disciplines.

6.4.1 CHARACTERIZING COMPLEX SYSTEMS

Most of this chapter has focused on the idea that the firm is a complex system and analysed different theoretical approaches such as cybernetics, system dynamics, and its extension chaos theory. Now we will characterize complex systems more precisely as a way to understand complexity theory's novel approach to the topic.

Despite not being a universal notion of what a complex system is, we can characterize these systems by enumerating their key properties:

1. *A complex system contains many constituents interacting non-linearly.* As explained in the previous text, non-linearity occurs when a certain condition or action has a varying effect on an outcome, depending on the level of the condition or the intensity of the action.

2. *The constituents of a complex system are interdependent.* We cannot optimize the performance of a complex system just by optimizing the performance of its subparts and 'aggregating' them. Interdependencies create conflicting constraints between different organizational designs. This is the reason why management change processes based on the development of 'best practices' only in a part of the firm frequently fail, as they frequently neglect the systemic implications of such local changes.

3. *A complex system possesses a structure spanning several scales.* In a firm, scales can be translated as hierarchical levels: headquarters, the division, the business unit, and the different functions within each unit, such as sales or operations and the departments within each function.

4. *A complex system is capable of emergent behaviour.* A behaviour is said to be emergent, at a certain scale, if it cannot be understood when you study, separately, every constituent of this scale. Much has been written about Dell's original direct-sales business model, Toyota's production system or Zara's inbound logistics. However, despite being familiar with these accounts of how excellent firms achieve sustainable competitive advantage, competitors still struggle in their attempt to match these firms' excellence in the execution of these processes. The secret of success is not in the generic patterns that we can grasp by reading a book or attending to a business conference, but in the blend of resources and capabilities embedded in the inner workings of these complex systems, sometimes referred to as tacit knowledge in the management literature (Nonaka and Takeuchi 1995).

5. *The combination of structure and emergence in a complex system leads to self-organization.* Self-organization takes place when an emergent behaviour had the effect of changing the structure or creating a new one. Through self-organization, the behaviour of the group emerges from the collective interactions of all the individuals. Even if they follow simple rules of action, the resulting group behaviour can be surprisingly complex and remarkably effective or destructive.

As the reader can note, the three first properties mentioned earlier have also been studied by system dynamics. Complexity theory's original contribution is it specific focus on the two last properties: emergence and self-organization.

6.4.2 COMPLEXITY AND STRATEGIC MANAGEMENT

In this section, we focus on recent work in the sphere of strategic management that addresses the current interest in complexity. Contributions focused on approaching organization studies from a complexity perspective can be divided as two sets of work. The first stream is characterized by in-depth studies of organizations or groups of organizations with a focus on understanding how emergence and self-organization happen in practice and how can managers take advantage of these processes. The second stream is constituted by formal studies based on the development of agent-based simulations. In this section, we focus on the first set – qualitative contributions – and we will discuss agent-based models in the next chapter, when we explore the link between the internal and the external dynamics of firms.

6.4.2.1 Emergence and self-organization in an organizational context

In responding to their own particular local contexts, the individual parts of a complex system can, despite acting in parallel without explicit inter-part coordination or communication, cause the system as a whole to display emergent patterns, orderly phenomena, and properties at the global or collective level.

Self-organization happens when an emergent behaviour has the effect of changing the structure or creating a new one in the absence of formal authority. Self-organization is a process in which components of a system in effect spontaneously communicate with each other and abruptly cooperate in coordinated and concerted common behaviour. The development of black markets in economies with centrally planned price controls is a clear example of how self-organization works.

We can interpret self-organization in a business firm as the process of political interaction and group learning from which innovation and new strategic directions for the organization may emerge. A well known example of self-organized behaviour with major strategic implications is the change that took place in the strategic focus of Intel from focusing on the computer DRAM memory business to becoming a microprocessor company (Burgelman 1994). As we explain in detail in Case Box 6.4, this change was not enforced vertically by senior management, but as a result of a myriad of initiatives led by middle managers of the firm who challenged and eventually changed top managers' dominant logic and 'emotional attachment' to the DRAM business.

Senior management creates the context in which collaboration can happen through the development of a few guidelines or simple rules (Sull and Eisenhardt 2001). These guidelines were not initiatives fostered by the corporation, but just

---

Case Box 6.4 Emergent strategic innovation at Intel

Burgelman (1994, 2002) provides an account of how major strategic changes leading to a shift in its core business emerged at Intel during the late 1980s. Burgelman (1994) explains that 'by 1972, Intel's DRAM was the world's largest selling semiconductor product, accounting for over 90 percent of Intel's sales revenues. DRAMs remained Intel's core business throughout the 1970s and early 1980s (. . .). As the largest volume product, DRAMs were viewed as the 'technology driver' on which Intel's learning curve depended, and the company routinely allocated resources to its successful and fast growing DRAM business.' However, personnel migration between semiconductor companies led to diffusion of the DRAM technology. This situation increased competition and Intel found it more difficult to profit from the intellectual value added in DRAMs. Moreover, as the DRAM industry matured, customers moved to demanding high quantities of DRAMs with guaranteed performance, reliability, and price. This situation shifted the basis of competition towards the large-scale, precision manufacturing competence. This shift favoured tightly managed manufacturing oriented firms such as Texas Instruments and Japanese firms, over the more innovative but less disciplined technology developer Intel.

Struggling to maintain its competitive advantage, Intel continued to rely on technology development efforts through successive DRAM generations. However, these efforts failed to produce competitive advantage and eventually the firm lost its strategic position in DRAMs. Its once 82.9 per cent market share (1974) shrank to 16 per cent in 1984. In parallel to this decline, microprocessors were developed at Intel as an unplanned new technology, as a development resulting from a request from Japanese calculator manufacturer Busicom.

Eventually, by the mid-1980s microprocessors contributed an important amount to Intel's revenues. Despite this, due to emotional attachment and inertia, Intel's corporate strategy continued to support DRAM even in 1985, when the decline of this business was more than evident. Managers considered that exiting from DRAMs would have been 'kind of Ford deciding to get out of cars'. Burgelman adds that, however, 'while top management continued to view DRAMs as a strategic business, some middle managers made decisions that capitalized the rapid growth of the microprocessor business and further dissolved the strategic context of DRAMs'. Notably, middle managers made manufacturing capacity allocations that boosted the microprocessor business. Eventually, these 'silent revolutions' aggregated creating a de facto change in Intel's strategy that was eventually made official as the new corporate strategy.

---

big definitions that bounded what constituted a corporate priority and what was out of such priority. They act as 'tags', that is, as ways of labelling and giving significance to something, linking it to action. Tags are used by corporate management to define the boundaries of the firm and spreading 'the virus of the vision' in such a way that middle managers within the business units, acting independently, self-organize to achieve a common goal (Clippinger 1999; Caldart and Canales 2008). This self-organizing can also be fostered through organizational arrangements that enable managers to exchange ideas and perhaps find collaborative opportunities. Examples of such vehicles are a structure promoting interdependence, systems and processes that disseminate information across units (e.g. a firm-wide intranet), the participation of managers from one business unit in the strategic review of another, high mobility of executives across divisions, and opportunities for staff to meet informally (Chackravarthy et al. 2001). Caldart and Canales (2008) studied cross-business collaboration initiatives in three multi-business firms headquartered in Spain. They found that, while most of these initiatives were the result of corporate level policy decisions, a few of them emerged from self-organized collaboration initiatives between the business units. They identified some organizational characteristics across all the firms that provided a fertile ground for self-organized initiatives to develop. In all the cases the firms were able to create an environment characterized by a sense of urgency, upon the existence of a few broad but strong corporate guidelines, the existence of cross-business formal or informal horizontal integration mechanisms and the existence of a culture where collaboration between members of the firm at every level was taken for granted. Although these conditions did not guarantee the emergence of self-organized collaboration, they helped in the cases by motivating the business units to explore the 'market' for joint initiatives offered by the network of businesses that integrate the corporation and also by making easy such exploration process.

In short, we can say that, the distinctive characteristic of complexity theory that differentiates it from other theories related to complex systems such as cybernetics, system dynamics, or chaos theory is that it proposes an explanation of *how novelty unfolds*. That is the reason why complexity theory has received so much attention in the current business literature concerned with understanding co-evolution processes within firms. Such processes are certainly influenced by decisions made at the top of the firm, but are strongly shaped and, in many occasions, strongly altered by unpredictable self-organized behaviour at every organizational level. In Chapter 7 we will analyse how to integrate the analysis of these intra-firm coevolutionary processes with the inter-firm coevolutionary processes that constituted the core of Chapters 2 to 4 of this book.

7 Co-Evolution

7.1 Introduction

Our discussion so far in this book has focused on analysing the dynamics of the external landscape of organizations, where they interact with each other competitively or cooperatively (Chapters 2 to 4) and on the analysis of the internal dynamics of organizations (Chapters 5 and 6).

The conceptual divide between the dynamics of the interactions between firms and the dynamics within them is useful to emphasize the main features and challenges associated with each of these approaches. In the real world, however, firms face the challenge of managing their external and internal landscapes simultaneously. Moreover, both external and internal landscapes are linked creating a complex system where different actors' decisions are mutually interdependent. For example, a change in manufacturing policy made at Firm A is interdependent with other policies made at Firm A, such as Purchases and Marketing. In addition, this new manufacturing policy changes the overall competitive position of firm A (e.g. by lowering its cost), therefore affecting the competitive position of Firm B. Eventually, Firm B will review its policies trying to respond to Firm A's challenge, affecting the position of Firm A. In this way, we can say that the internal and the external landscapes of the firm *co-evolve*. Such co-evolution has been characterized as macro-co-evolution when referred to as the co-evolution between different firms and micro-co-evolution when focused on the co-evolution of the different activities within the firm (McKelvey 1997). The dynamics of these systems show the characteristics referred to in our discussion of complex systems: multilevelness, multidirectional causality, non-linearity, positive feedback, and path dependence.

The study of these complex multi-dimensional dynamics embedded in these micro- and macro-co-evolutionary processes pose several challenges. In this chapter, we propose that such integration on micro- and macro-co-evolution can be pursued effectively through the use of agent-based computational models. As referred to in Chapter 3, these models enable us to provide the formal and systematic treatment of firms' co-evolution in a way that neither economic closed form models nor qualitative work can do.

7.2 **Co-evolution**

The study of firms as complex systems poses the challenge of finding an adequate methodology that enables us to represent firms as systems composed by many interdependent parts and the ability to show emergent behaviour. Moreover, such interdependencies between the different areas of the firm (micro-co-evolution) and between different firms (macro-co-evolution) are not 'a given' but can be manipulated to a great extent by managers. For instance, a multibusiness firm can either be organized in a highly integrated way, with the corporate centre concentrating on 'core activities' benefiting the different units, or it can choose to grant high levels of autonomy to the units and reduce the corporate level to a minimum. For instance, firms such as Sharp or Canon organize their business units around a single highly integrated strategy coordinated by a strong – and expensive – corporate centre. Conversely, Berkshire Hathaway runs its seventy-three businesses without exercising any kind of corporate influence over their operations with the exception of capital allocation. In this way the headquarters can be run effectively by only nineteen people, including Warren Buffet.

Firms may also have variable degrees of interaction within their competitive landscapes. Porter (1980) states that successful firms position themselves strategically within the industries according to a broad generic strategy, also referred to in the strategy literature as value propositions (Treacy and Wieserma, 1995) or strategic options (Hax and Wilde 2001). While these generic strategies are usually characterized rhetorically, for example, as 'cost leadership' or 'customer intimacy', operationally they are the result of a set of specific policy choices made by the firm at the time of organizing their value chains (Rosenkopf and Nerkar 2001). For instance, a 'cost leadership' strategic position is the result of a set of consistent policy choices aimed at increasing the firm's cost efficiency by means such as highly standardized manufacturing, narrow product portfolios, a mature technology base and a 'lean and mean' organizational culture. Each of these policy choices makes its specific contribution to the overall value of the firm's value proposition. When different competitors choose to compete along the same policy choices, such interdependent choices become the *competitive dimensions* of that industry. For instance, as seen in Case Box 7.1, global leading manufacturers of eyeglasses, such as the two Italy-based firms Luxottica or Safilo, pursue 'differentiation' strategies, built around several competitive dimensions such as a strong in-house product design, high profile marketing campaigns, and control – through ownership or licensing – of a strong portfolio of sophisticated brands.

The number of competitive dimensions characterizing competition, as discussed in Chapter 2, not only varies between different industries but also may vary across time within an industry as we show in Case Box 7.2 using the European car components industry as an example of how the number of

---

Case Box 7.1 Competitive dimensions in the eyewear industry

The market of frames for prescription glasses (and sunglasses) had polarized into two sharply differentiated segments in the last years: high-end products and low-end products. By 2005, the global leaders at the high end of the market, based on brand name and design, were two firms of Italian origin: Luxottica and Safilo. These two, besides their own brands, owned licences to use some of the world's most prestigious names. Luxottica sold frames by Bulgari, Chanel, Emanuel Ungaro, Ray-Ban, Versace, Dona Karan, and Vogue. And Safilo had the Gucci, Polo Ralph Lauren, Giorgio Armani, Dior, Pierre Cardin, Burberry, and Max-Mara brands. Controlling those brands gave the two firms access to other distribution channels apart from opticians, mainly stores selling complementary products with the same branding.

The tendency for manufacturers to purchase licences for well-known, medium-high to high-end brands had increased notably in recent years. Luxottica was the only manufacturer in the world that still based a substantial part of its business on its own brands, such as Ray-Ban and Vogue, and even so it had also been very active in acquiring licences for other brands. The frame manufacturers paid the brand owners a royalty that usually consisted of a fixed component and a variable component based on sales. Licences had become so important that there was even competitive bidding for certain brands. For example, Safilo had succeeded in wresting the Armani brand away from Luxottica, while Luxottica had snapped up the Dona Karan brand, previously linked to the U.S. manufacturer Marchon.

The marketing mix of premium manufacturers was completed by high profile advertising based on the endorsement of the firms' brands by worldwide well known celebrities such as top models, movie stars, and figures from sport.

Source: Caldart and Canals (2004)

---

competitive dimensions increase over time leading to a higher competitive intensity.

Qualitative studies adopting a co-evolutionary perspective (Van den Bosch et al. 1999; Huygens et al. 2001; Volberda and Lewin 2003; Madhok and Liu 2006) provide valuable insights for practising managers on how these interdependencies are managed in practice. However, due to the enormous number of micro-level interactions taking place between parts of a firm (micro-co-evolution) and across firms (macro-co-evolution), these studies cannot provide positive accounts of how firms work as complex systems. A robust understanding of the issue of complexity demands a formal research design. Formal economic models would constitute a candidate for such a role. However, these models usually lack the flexibility to represent complex behaviour out of equilibrium.

The challenge is, therefore, to develop a modelling approach that enables us to provide a formal treatment of the problem but without incurring the heroic assumptions that closed form models would require. Caldart and Oliveira (2008) summarized the features that should characterize such a model. First, it must be, by definition, dynamic. A dynamic model is one where the variables at a given time are a function (at least in part) of the same processes at an earlier time (Koput 1992). Second, in order to model

---

Case Box 7.2 The evolution of competition in the car components industry

---

The European Car Component industry experienced substantial changes in its business model between the 1980s and the beginning of the twenty-first century. These changes led to a substantial increase in the competitive dimensions or prerequisites for success of the industry.

By the mid-1980s European car component manufacturers' business was characterized by the following features:

Technological base: mostly mechanical engineering

Market scope: Western Europe for EU countries. National market in European non-EU countries

Products: car components, to be assembled in systems by manufacturers

Contracting practices: spot sales agreed between suppliers and individual plants

Clients: local plants who made decisions on sourcing usually relying on geographically close suppliers. This made logistics quite a straightforward activity.

Competition: EU firms for firms operating within the EU landscape and local firms for firms operating in national protected markets such as Spain or Portugal.

The key competitive dimensions at this time were having competitive manufacturing costs, competence in mechanical engineering for new product development, and developing close links with the car manufacturing plants close to the operations of the component manufacturer.

By 2008, the same business is characterized by quite different features, leading to an increased number of competitive dimensions:

Technological base: mechanical engineering, electronic engineering, and IT

Market scope: Global.

Products: car systems, based on the assembly of components by the manufacturer

Contracting practices: long term 'technology partnerships' with OEMs[1] lasting the whole life of the model for which the systems are manufactured

Clients: Global or regional headquarters of the car manufacturers.

Competition: firms from all over the world

In addition to the competitive dimensions cited earlier, the industry now has new competitive dimensions such as having a competitive global system of plants; managing efficiently capacity allocation per project; assembly engineering; R&D increasingly based on electronics and IT; coordinating with the client; global sourcing and logistics; working in partnership with OEMs; and dealing with increasingly demanding environmental and safety standards.

Source: Caldart and Canals (2002)

[1] Original Equiment Manufacturers.

---

dynamism, we need precise instructions on how the firm's search for a better strategic position unfolds as well as a representation of a well defined environment or 'problem space' in which such an adaptive search takes place. In this context, each of the possible combinations of decisions available for the firm in its problem space constitutes a different strategic position. Third, firms must be considered as heterogeneous entities, as during their co-evolution processes they can evolve and learn in different and path dependent ways. Finally, we must track the performance associated to the different configurations that the firm may adopt during its evolutionary process in order to compare the relative merits of different strategies across time.

Agent-based (simulation) models (ABMs) enable us to address all the requirements stated earlier. In an agent-based model, individual agents autonomously make decisions based on internal rules and local information. Not being constrained by the imposition of equilibrium conditions, these models offer a degree of flexibility that permit key features of complex systems to be addressed, that is, the representation of the firm as a reality composed of many parts interacting non-linearly, the interdependence between such parts and their ability to show emergent behaviour. Additionally, some agent-based models enable the modelling of individuals that can evolve and learn in different ways. This overcomes a limitation of models developed in the tradition of the neoclassical theory of the firm that assumes that all agents have identical behaviour (Arthur 2006).

As discussed extensively in Chapter 3, agent-based models constitute a powerful research method for theory development that allows the flexibility of accommodating out-of-equilibrium behaviour such as the evolution of a firm's strategy over time (Arthur 2006). In their excellent analysis of simulation as a research method in management, Davis et al. (2007) state that simulations are particularly effective for theory development based on research questions that involve fundamental trade-offs, such as short- versus long-run implications of decisions or different structural arrangements. It also enables the development of logically precise and comprehensive theory especially when the theoretical focus is longitudinal, that is, based on observing the evolution of a firm or market through time, non-linear or processual. The increasing adoption of a complex systems perspective within the study of organizations, especially after the irruption of complexity theory, has led to the increasing adoption and diffusion of computational agent-based modelling as a research approach. This approach enables us to address formally the central features of complex systems such as non-linear dynamics, interdependencies between subsystems, and emergent behaviour. Agent-based models have been applied, among many other topics, to the study of the evolution of social norms (Holland 1995), to modelling of organizations (March 1991; Simon 1991; Prietula et al. 1998; van Zandt 1998; Dawid et al. 2001), to the analysis of the formation of economic networks (Weisbuch et al. 1995; Tesfatsion 1997), and to the analysis of strategic decisions (Levinthal 1997; Gavetti et al. 2005; Lenox et al. 2006).

7.3 Modelling co-evolution

In Chapter 3, we showed how agent-based models can be employed to simulate the dynamics of competition. In this section we analyse how these models can be used to simulate simultaneously the micro-co-evolutionary process taking place within the firm and the macro-co-evolutionary processes taking place between firms. Only by combining both the internal and the external dynamics of the firm can we represent the reality of strategic decision making. We discuss the distinct potential of agent-based models to offer insight into issues related to strategic management and organization theory, as well as their limitations. In particular, we first discuss Kauffman's *NK* model, arguably the most frequently used in recent work on organizations based on agent-based modelling. Later we describe Kauffman's *NK(C)* model that enables us to analyse the co-evolution of multiple organizations.

7.3.1 KAUFFMAN'S *NK* MODEL

In this section, we review the *NK* model (Kauffman 1993). This model is particularly versatile for research questions focused on the speed and effectiveness of adaptation within a modular system with different degrees of coupling (Davis et al. 2007).

Work based on the *NK* model has been developed by organizational theorists to provide insights on how important organizational and strategic issues such as understanding the interplay between adaptive and selective forces (Levinthal 1997), why successful strategies are so difficult to imitate (Rivkin 2000), why and to what extent analogical reasoning can inform strategy development in novel industries (Gavetti et al. 2005), why firms need to engage in periodical organizational restructurings in order to improve performance (Siggelkow and Levinthal 2005), and how different ways of managing the headquarters-business unit relationship affects performance (Caldart and Ricart 2007), and how managers' dominant logics affect organizational strategic development processes including the development of capabilities (Gavetti 2005).

In this section, we first review the theoretical roots and main characteristics of the *NK* model. Second we discuss how the model can be applied for the study of issues in strategy and organizing. Finally, we discuss the assumptions of the basic model and explain how organization and strategy scholars extended it in order to address the behavioural and structural issues that characterize organizations.

7.3.2 FOUNDATIONS AND ARCHITECTURE OF THE *NK* MODEL

The *NK* model was originally developed in the field of biology, more precisely, for the study of the evolution of genes. For most of the twentieth century, biologists have assumed that 'order' was due to the effects of selection, as developed under the general label of Darwinian 'selectionist' theory. The intuition behind this idea derived from statistical mechanics, particularly the idea of entropy. Entropy measures the amount of order in a system, with increasing disorder corresponding to increasing entropy. Left to themselves, complex systems such as organizations are inherently disordered and unstructured. Therefore 'selective' work is necessary to achieve and maintain order.[2] In a business context, by operating in a competitive market, the firm is exposed to selective forces that will reward with survival (and profitability) only to those who are able to provide a value proposal that fits with the imperatives of the market.

The biologist Stuart Kauffman challenged the notion that evolution derives exclusively from selection. He stated that, while natural selection is a prominent force in evolution, order can also emerge spontaneously due to the self-organizing properties of complex systems. As the complexity of the system under selection increases, selection is progressively less able to alter the properties of such a system.[3] In these cases we can say that selection is unable to avoid the *spontaneous* or self-organized order derived from the properties of the system. Taken in an organizational context, this idea means that sometimes the competitive forces affecting a firm cannot alter its characteristics due to the existence of internal organizational factors that do not allow the forces of competition to have any effect on the evolution of the firm. These internal factors can be related to the way the firm is structured, its decision system, its governance system, the prevailing power structure, etc.

Kauffman examined the relationship between selection and self-organization and tried to find out under what conditions adaptive evolution is optimized. The variability in behaviour as the structure of a system is altered can be pictured as characterizing the ruggedness of a *fitness landscape*. A fitness or performance landscape consists of a multidimensional space in which each attribute of the entity is represented by a dimension of the space and a final dimension indicates the performance level of the firm as seen in the dynamic competition landscapes in Chapter 3. While trying to improve their fitness, many parts and processes of the agent must become coordinated to achieve some measure of overall success, but conflicting 'design constraints' limit the results achieved (Kauffman 1993). The degree of interdependence between the different attributes that characterize the agent (policies or activities in an organizational context) act as conflicting constraints that affect the ability of the entity to evolve. Increasing the intensity of the interdependencies between policies affects the complexity of the performance landscape and,

---

[2] In the context of strategic management, selection is translated as competition, the force that makes firms keep 'fit' in their quest to survive and develop.

[3] This would be the case, for instance, of a firm stalled as a consequence of excessive bureaucracy or by strong power struggles.

consequently, increases the number of possible emergent patterns of behaviour that the firm can follow. In order to model such webs of complex interdependencies, Kauffman developed the *NK* model.

In the *NK* model, firms are characterized as vectors of *N* bits. The value of each of those bits, either 0 or 1, represents a decision made by the organization. The second structural variable *K* represents the number of other decisions with which a given decision interacts. In an organizational context, *K* can be deemed as a measure of the degree of interdependence of the organization's decisions. The value of *K* ranges between 0 and *N*-1.

The performance landscape of the organization consists of 2^N possible policy choices, being the overall behaviour of the firm characterized by the vector $X\{X_1, X_2, \ldots, X_N\}$ where each X_i takes on the value of 0 or 1. Following Rivkin (2000), we call a strategy to each possible combination of policy choices. When $K = 0$, there are no interactions between the different policy decisions conforming a strategy. In this situation, the mere aggregation of local improvement of performance always leads to global improvement. In these kinds of landscapes, the performance value of similar strategies is highly correlated (Figure 7.1). However, this scenario is not realistic in an organizational setting where the different activities of the value chain (Porter 1985) have interdependencies that create all kinds of conflicting constraints leading to trade-offs. For instance, decisions about the breadth of the portfolio of products of the firm will have an impact on the organization and cost of manufacturing and on the complexity of the purchasing and inbound logistics. In the real world, $K > 0$, as the contribution of an activity to the

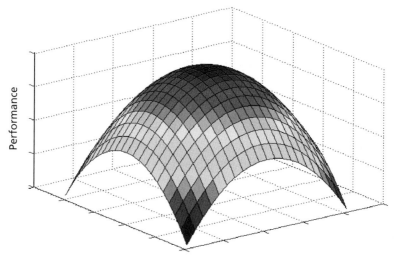

Figure 7.1. A smooth performance landscape
Source: Caldart and Oliveira (2007).

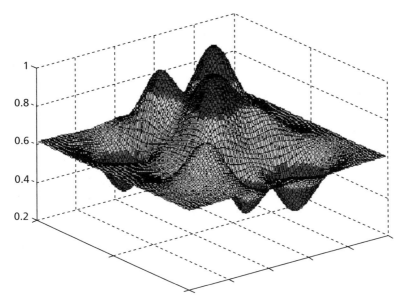

Figure 7.2. A rugged performance landscape
Source: Caldart and Oliveira (2007).

organization's overall performance is affected by other activities. The landscape becomes then more rugged as the number of local maxima or 'peaks' grows and the correlation between similar strategies decreases (Figure 7.2).

It is worth highlighting that, in most of the contributions based on the *NK* model, the organization's adaptive search processes are developed in a fixed performance landscape, that is, the firm is deemed as a complex system that evolves in a (fixed) stationary environment. In the *NK* model, firms evolve facing only the constraints derived from their own structural design in an environment unaffected by other actors' decisions. While this modelling set-up is useful to understand how the internal complexity of the firm affects its ability to evolve (micro-co-evolution), it is not realistic at modelling its response to external changes (macro-co-evolution). We will discuss models that analyse the simultaneous impact of micro- and macro-co-evolution later in this chapter.

7.3.3 THE *NK* MODEL IN THE ORGANIZATIONAL LITERATURE

As we saw in previous chapters, behavioural theory and evolutionary theory (March and Simon 1958; Cyert and March 1963, Nelson and Winter 1982) conceive firms as entities that engage in problem-solving through path-dependent processes of search and discovery. Behavioural theory assumes that, while searching for solutions to their problems, firms adopt some form of adaptive behaviour in response to feedback about their previous performance.

As the previous discussion made apparent, the *NK* model enables us to address many of these organizational characteristics; therefore, it is becoming an increasingly popular research method for recent contributions grounded in the behavioural and evolutionary traditions.

While adapting, under bounded rationality (Simon 1997), agents can identify the positive and negative gradients around and close to their current position, but are not capable of making similar judgements for more distant ones. In the context of the *NK* model, we can observe that in a rugged landscape, such incremental search procedure will lead only to the local maximum or *peak* closest to the starting point of the search process, regardless of its height relative to other peaks in the landscape. As a result of this 'locking in' to the first available solution, a strong form of path dependence is observed and, on average, only modest performance, sometimes referred to as *competency traps*, is achieved (Levitt and March 1988). In these situations, firms achieve the best possible configuration of an unattractive strategy. One mechanism to overcome such 'traps' is to engage in 'long-jumps', random explorations of more distant portions of the landscape. However, though these distant explorations help to prevent falling into 'competency traps', they may result in a deterioration of performance by not exploiting wisdom gained by past experience. So, the problem of adaptation strategies in rugged landscapes can be reframed as a familiar dilemma faced by managers and organization theorists: how to get the benefits of exploring new areas of the landscape, escaping from low local maxima, without losing the advantages of exploiting acquired knowledge (March 1991).

Robertson and Caldart (2008) summarized some central concepts associated with organizational theory that can be operationalized effectively through the *NK* model (see Table 7.1).

7.3.4 KEY ORGANIZATIONAL FEATURES NEGLECTED BY THE 'BASIC' *NK* MODEL

The features described in Table 7.1 show the potential of the *NK* model to represent formally organizational phenomena. However, the model has several strong assumptions that work adequately in the realm of natural science but fail to capture central features of social phenomena. In this section we review the model's limitations and discuss how many of these can be overcome by extending the model.

Table 7.1. Features modelled in agent-based simulations based on the *NK* model

Topic	Operationalization in the *NK* model
Emergent nature of organization behaviour	Performance derives from parallel search by multiple agents
Path dependence in decision-making	Path dependent local search. Risk of 'long jumps'
Interdependence in decision-making	Parameter *K*
Bounded rationality	Firm only aware of neighbouring strategies
Exploitation and exploration	Local search vs. long jumps
Differentiation and integration	Parameter *K*
Difficulty to imitate firms	Low correlation of strategies in highly rugged land-scapes

Source: Adapted from Robertson and Caldart (2008).

In the following section, we discuss a list of major issues that the *NK* model does not contemplate in its original form that require changes in order to make the model suitable for management-related applications.

a) *Non-Full Decomposability of Problems.* First, we need to address the fact that organizations are not fully decomposable systems, as implicitly assumed in the pure form of the *NK* model. Organizational problems tend to have a nearly decomposable structure (Simon 1996). Tasks tend to cluster into subsystems, with interaction within such subsystems, on average, being stronger than interactions across subsystems. For instance, on average, we will always see more interaction *within* the marketing department than between the marketing and operations departments. Recent contributions based on the *NK* model, such as Gavetti et al. (2005) address this issue by clustering decision variables in subgroups or units, and by splitting the parameter *K* in two sub-parameters that track separately interdependence within and between subunits.

b) *Hierarchy of Decisions.* Not only do Kauffman's vectors assume full decomposability of problems but also they neglect another central feature of decisions in organizations: decisions in social groups beyond a minimum level of complexity are also integrated vertically through decision levels. Upper level decisions usually create boundary conditions for lower level decisions. Gavetti et al. (2005) address this issue by defining a hierarchy of decisions in which upper level decisions limit the discretion of lower level decisions. It would also be interesting to see work focused on the fact that influence between decision levels is not entirely hierarchical, as modelled in these contributions, as lower levels can develop ideas that eventually influence top level decisions (Burgelman 1994).

c) *Purposeful Behaviour.* In social systems we cannot neglect the issue of deliberateness of individual and organizational behaviour. Managers may freely choose how to formulate or change the firm's strategy, an ability that the genotypes referred to in biology-inspired models do not have. There-fore, models may include decision rules followed by managers at the time of, for instance, adopting a strategy and deciding whether to maintain it or to modify it. This feature also requires acknowledging the limits of human rationality. Gavetti and Levinthal (2000) used an adaptation of the *NK* model to study the role and interrelationships between search processes based on cognitive representations that are articulated in strategic plans (which they label 'forward-looking') and search processes based on the lessons learnt in previous experience ('backward-looking'). Following the notion of bounded rationality, the authors simulated cognition as a representation of the performance landscape that, being grounded on the actual landscape, has a lower dimensionality. In this way, as firms know the expected performance values associated with certain strategies that the firm may follow, they are able to identify more or less attractive sub-areas of the problem space. However, as their representation has a lower dimensionality than the real problem, they cannot foresee the most attractive peaks within each of those sub-areas, therefore suffering the risk of falling in a competency trap. Gavetti et al. (2005) further developed the study of the relationship between managerial cognition and strategic decision making through the development of a highly sophisticated model of how managers reason by analogy. They show how the depth and the breadth of managers' 'portfolio' of experiences can help them to make sense of novel situations and develop superior strategies reasoning by analogy.

d) *Learning through Experience.* Social agents also have the ability of learning through experience. *NK* vectors only evolve according to their rules of behaviour and do not increase their understanding of the landscape through experience. *NK* simulations developed in the realm of social science rather than natural science should address this fact by, for instance, progressively refining the quality of the firm's cognitive representation of the landscape as it evolves.

e) *Weight of Decisions on Performance.* Each X_i refers to a particular policy decision within the firm, such as advertising, product development, research on product line extensions, or production planning. In the *NK* model, it is assumed that all policies have an equal weight on performance. This contradicts the reality marked by the existence of 'core' and 'periph-eral' areas of the firm and the dynamism of such relative importance due to the environmental change.

f) *The Social Agent's Environment is Dynamic.* In the *NK* model, the organ-ization's adaptive search processes are developed in a fixed performance landscape, that is, the firm is deemed as a complex system that evolves facing only the constraints derived from its own complexity captured by the interaction parameter K in a stationary environment. Siggelkow and Rivkin (2005) addressed this limitation of NK models by introducing exogenous 'shocks' that alter the topography of a focal organization's performance landscape. However, these shocks do not capture the impact on the shape of the performance landscape resulting from specific decisions made by other firms whose actions are interdependent with those of the focal firm. Kauffman's $NK(C)$ model addresses this issue by modelling the co-evolution of many agents and capturing the interdependence of their decisions through the parameter C. It is worth reminding ourselves that we have already discussed a co-evolutionary model of the competitive landscape in Chapter 3. The $NK(C)$ model discussed here introduces dynamism in the performance landscapes of the interacting agents, enabling us to integrate the analysis of micro- and macro-co-evolution, therefore linking the competitive and the organizational landscape. In the following section, we discuss the $NK(C)$ model.

7.4 Modelling the co-evolution of multiple firms: the NK*(C)* model

Models of adaptive search processes as in the NK model, that assume stationary environments, are useful to analyse the internal complexity of the organization but neglect the complexity associated not only to the fact that firms interact with others, modifying the payoffs of their problem spaces, but also they do it along multiple activities. Firms try to create competitive advantage through their decisions along a range of competitive dimensions such as manufacturing cost, financial cost, R&D talent, marketing insight, or lobbying. In order to address this phenomenon, we need to model networks of firms whose strategic decisions are interdependent, therefore mutually affecting each other's performance. The $NK(C)$ model (Kauffman 1993) provides a path for such an endeavour. Interdependence between firms is captured in this model by the parameter C that represents the number of a firm's decisions that are interdependent with those of other firms. This C connects the different decisions of the agents in the environment. For example, if $C = 1$ the firm's strategy co-evolves with those of other firms along one dimension. If $C = 2$ the outcome of each strategy is contingent to other firms' decisions along two dimensions. When moving to co-evolutionary simulations the topography of the performance landscape is a function not only of the structural complexity of the firm but also of the interdependencies of decisions between different firms. This increases, dramatically, the complexity of the system of decisions and therefore that of the model.

7.4.1 ANALYSING THE COMPLEXITY OF CO-EVOLUTIONARY DECISIONS

In the *NK(C)* model, each firm can implement 2^N different strategies. Then, as the firm's performance is interdependent with the actions of other firms as well, the size of the performance landscape is equal to 2^{NP} where *P* represents the number of firms in the model (see Table 7.2).

In a simple example with $N = 10$, the size of the performance landscape grew from about 1,000,000 possible combinations of decisions, for $P = 2$, to about 1,000,000,000,000,000,000,000,000,000,000 for $P = 10$. Even in the simplest co-evolution model, a case of a duopolistic industry, where $P = 2$, the size of the landscape would increase from 1,024 possible strategies in the *NK* model to about one million.

We mentioned earlier, interdependencies between firms do not happen at a 'firm versus firm' level but at the level of the different activities of the firm that constitute competitive dimensions in a particular industry. For instance, manufacturers of sunglasses can compete at a premium end or at a low cost end. Each of these segments has different competitive dimensions. As seen in Case Box 7.1, premium frames for sunglasses require a strong brand image (based on licensing a fashionable brand and endorsing well known celebrities), design, and sophisticated channels of distribution such as opticians and fashion houses. Low cost or 'value' frames require a business model that privileges high manufacturing volume (in low cost countries) and mass distribution channels (supermarkets, magazines, discount stores, holiday resort shops). The activities supporting these business models constitute the competitive dimensions of the industry.

As we can see in the following, the impact of considering the impact of the number of competitive dimensions on the complexity of the decision problem faced by each firm is very important. As the number of competitive interactions (*C*) increases, the number of possible alternatives grows

Table 7.2. Relationship between the number of firms *N* and the size of the performance landscape ($N = 10$)

Number of Firms	Size of the Landscape
2	1.05×10^6
3	1.07×10^9
4	1.10×10^{12}
5	1.13×10^{15}
6	1.15×10^{18}
7	1.18×10^{21}
8	1.21×10^{24}
9	1.24×10^{27}
10	1.27×10^{30}

Table 7.3. Total number of decision alternatives for each strategy ($N = 10$, $P = 5$)

K	C					
	0	1	2	3	4	5
0	20	320	5,120	81,920	1,310,720	20,971,520
1	40	640	10,240	163,840	2,621,440	41,943,040
2	80	1,280	20,480	327,680	5,242,880	83,886,080
3	160	2,560	40,960	655,360	10,485,760	167,772,160
4	320	5,120	81,920	1,310,720	20,971,520	335,544,320
5	640	10,240	163,840	2,621,440	41,943,040	671,088,640
6	1,280	20,480	327,680	5,242,880	83,886,080	1,342,177,280
7	2,560	40,960	655,360	10,485,760	167,772,160	2,684,354,560
8	5,120	81,920	1,310,720	20,971,520	335,544,320	5,368,709,120
9	10,240	163,840	2,621,440	41,943,040	671,088,640	10,737,418,240

exponentially.[4] Table 7.3 represents the sensitivity of computational complexity for our example with $N = 10$ and $P = 5$. Table 7.3 shows the number of decision alternatives per strategy for a given firm.

For the simple case where decisions have no interdependencies within the firm and between firms ($K = 0$ and $C = 0$), the total number of alternatives that the firm must consider is only 20, equal to 2 alternatives per decision (0 or 1) for a total of 10 decisions. However, as the degree of interdependencies grows, we observe how the number of possible alternatives increases very rapidly as the impact of interdependencies within the firm and of the decisions from other firms comes into consideration. The total number of evaluations that would be required in order to optimize these decisions following an algorithmic approach becomes impracticable in reasonable time.[5] In other words, strategic decision making becomes an *intractable* problem (Rivkin 2000).

This analysis illustrates the views of the firm developed by behavioural theory, evolutionary theory, and Thompson's analysis of the institutional/strategic level of the firm (see Chapter 5). Firms do not solve problems through optimization but follow processes of search and discovery. In doing so, they consider only a limited number of decision alternatives due to the bounded rationality of decision makers. Being managers who are unable to write an algorithm that will enable them to locate the optimal set of choices in reasonable time, as neoclassical economics assumes, they instead make decisions trying to satisfy a limited number of criteria they judge as relevant.

---

[4] In the coevolutionary model the number of decisions that needs to be evaluated by each firm, for each one of its strategies, is equal to $N2^{K + 1 + C(P - 1)}$.

[5] Even for computers able to solve 1 million operations per second, it would take about 383 trillion years to evaluate all the strategies for the case when $K = 9$ and $C = 5$ (Caldart and Oliveira, 2008).

7.5 **Analysing the impact of complexity on industry performance**

The analysis of the structure of industrial sectors has been at the forefront of the strategic management field during the last three decades (Porter 1980, 1985; White 1986; Murray 1988). This analysis has been mostly based on the Structure-Conduct-Performance (S-C-P) paradigm (Mason 1939; Bain 1956) originally developed in Industrial Organization Economics. The S-C-P paradigm suffers however from strong limitations, notably the employment of static analysis focused on equilibrium conditions and the assumption of homogeneity of firms within the industry (McWilliams and Smart 1993). An analysis of industry profitability based on the use of the *NK(C)* model enables us to overcome these limitations by adopting a systemic and longitudinal perspective to analyse the dynamics of competitive interaction within an industrial sector. While the model is too simple to consider the varied profiles and capabilities characterizing the different players in the industry, it enables us to study the impact of the structural complexity of the industry as a driver of its performance. Such complexity is associated with the number of competitors in the industry and the numbers of competitive dimensions that characterize their interactions. Caldart and Oliveira (2008*a*; 2009) analysed the impact on complexity of industry performance modelling different types of industries (monopoly, duopoly, oligopoly, and fragmented industries) and different numbers of competitive dimensions. In the following sections, we review and discuss some of the main findings from this work.

7.5.1 COMPETITIVE INTENSITY AND PERFORMANCE

Figure 7.2 represents the evolution of the average industry performance for the cases of two, three, and ten competitors. In all the cases, three different degrees of competitive complexity ($C=1$; $C=2$; and $C=4$) were modelled. A case with $C=0$, a situation in which firms evolve only constrained by their own internal complexity but in isolation from external forces (there is no competition). Overall results show that the performance of the industry is lower as the number of competitors increases and as competitive complexity increases. In a $C=0$ situation, (no competition) firms obtain the highest performance. Such performance is matched in the long term also by firms competing in a duopoly situation with low degrees of interdependence ($C=1$). Even markets with three firms and $C=1$ achieve similar levels of performance. The reason for this is that when competitive complexity is low, competitors' moves only alter minimally the competitive landscapes of each firm. In this competitive scenario, the landscape's payouts associated with the different strategies – or peaks in the landscape – are relatively stationary enabling firms to benefit from their incremental efforts to learn and improve their strategies. The situation is different when competitive complexity is high ($C=4$). As the number of interdependent competitive dimensions increases, the firms' landscapes become more dynamic as there are now many decisions from each firm that affect the performance contribution of decisions from the others. Firms' efforts to learn to improve their strategies incrementally ('peak climbing') are less effective as the likelihood that such peaks will shift increases. In other words, the attractiveness of a particular strategy is likely to be affected due to 'emergent' changes derived from competitors' actions. These emergent changes prevent firms from pursuing their intended strategies through a learning process that incrementally refines a certain strategy or business model.

Figure 7.3 represents the differences in performance between the different cases versus the $C=0$ 'happy world' of evolution in isolation from competition. When a low number of competitors (2 and 3) and low competitive complexity ($C=1$) are combined, we notice that firms can benefit from learning through time, improving their profitability and that of the industry. This is reflected by the notable narrowing of the gap between the profitability of the 'no competition' case ($C=0$) and that of the cases mentioned earlier. Oppositely, differences in profitability become substantial for cases with $C=2$ arriving at a maximum for industries with ten players and high competitive complexity ($C=4$). In these cases, the gap in profitability versus the $C=0$ case widens and stabilizes in the long run. As the number of interdependent dimensions multiplies, firms cannot, even in the long run, take advantage of

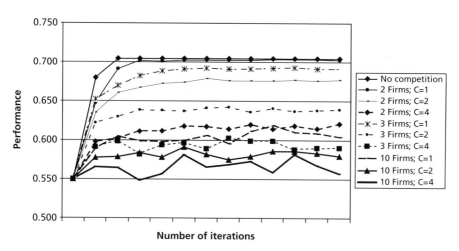

Figure 7.3. Evolution of industry performance (2, 3, and 10 players; $C = \{0, 1, 2, 4\}$)

Source: Caldart and Oliveira (2009).

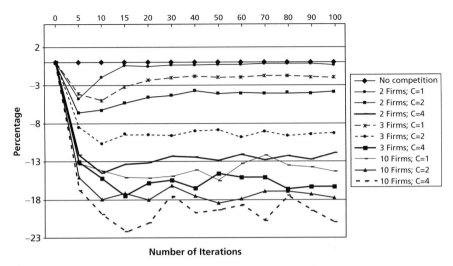

Figure 7.4. Differences in industry performance (2, 3, and 10 players; C = {0, 1, 2, 4})
Source: Caldart and Oliveira (2009).

their learning as their competitive game changes too frequently to let them improve gradually their strategic positioning through incremental search.

The variance in each industry's performance is also positively linked with competitive intensity. For the cases of duopoly and oligopoly – with $C = 1$ – the standard deviation falls from an initial 7–8 per cent to 5 per cent in the long run. For the rest of the cases, standard deviation remains in a range between 7 and 9 per cent throughout the simulation.

7.5.2 ANALYSIS OF THE INDIVIDUAL EFFECTS

a) Number of players. The next simulation focuses only on understanding how the complexity associated with the interaction of different firms affects the performance of the industry. In all the cases, differences between industries with a different number of firms and the same number of competitive dimensions were computed. In this way, only the impact on complexity associated with the number of firms is computed. Figure 7.4 shows the results of the simulation. Results are consistent with the economics literature as they show that increases in the number of competitors, keeping competitive complexity constant, reduce industry profitability. Interestingly, differences in performance between industries with 2 and 10 players are lower for the highest level of complexity ($C = 4$). The reason for this is the already low performance of the two players industry with $C = 4$. These results suggest that

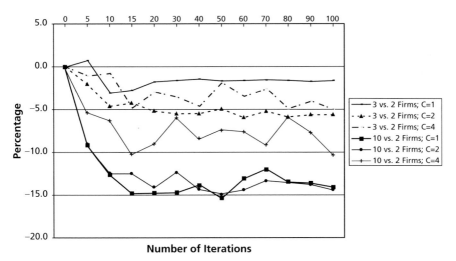

Figure 7.5. Differences in industry performance for different numbers of players (% variation for 3 firms vs. 2 firms; % variation for 10 firms vs. 2 firms)

Source: Caldart and Oliveira (2009).

increases in the number of competitors in an industry with high competitive complexity are not as harmful for industry profitability as increases in industries where competition is based on a lower number of interdependent competitive dimensions.

b) Number of Competitive Dimensions. Figure 7.5 analyses the differences in profitability due to differences in the number of competitive dimensions for industries with the same number of players. In all the cases industries with a higher level of competitive complexity show a lower performance than those with a lower complexity, for a constant number of players. Moreover, the magnitude of differences in performance due to the number of competitive dimensions is similar to that due to differences in the number of players. Interestingly, the magnitude of this reduction is lower when the number of players in the industry is higher. In industries with ten firms, increases from low to high competitive complexity only decrease performance in a range between 3 and 7 per cent throughout the simulation. Instead, industries with more competitive dimensions $(C=4)$ perform much less well than low complexity ones $(C=1)$ for concentrated industries, duopolies, and oligopolies, with differences reaching between 12 and 14 per cent.

Caldart and Oliveira (2009) state that two important insights derive from these analyses. The first insight is that the higher the number of competitive dimensions characterizing competition within an industry, the lower the profitability of such industry. Decreases in performance associated to in-

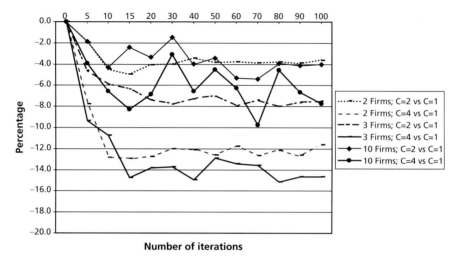

Figure 7.6. Differences in industry performance due to different number of competitive dimensions (percentage variation of two competitive dimensions vs. one; percentage variation of four competitive dimensions vs. one)

Source: Caldart and Oliveira (2009).

creases in the number of competitive dimensions are comparable to those associated to increasing the number of competitors. This evidence has important implications when assessing the intensity of rivalry within an industry. The number of competitive dimensions constituting bases of competition within an industry is as important as the number of firms competing in such industry when explaining industry profitability. As the number of interdependent competitive dimensions multiply, (see Case Box 7.2) firms become competitors along more activities, making their strategic choices vulnerable to more of their competitors' moves. The mere multiplication of potential emergent changes derived from competitors' moves makes it more difficult for firms to pursue their intended strategies and make strategic management more a dialectic process than a long-term plan or pattern. In this way, these results help to shed new light on the debate on deliberatedness versus emergence (Mintzberg 1990; Ansoff 1991; Porter 1996). They suggest that in industries with low competitive intensity, Porter's advice (1996: 77) to top managers to resist 'constant pressures to compromise, relax trade-offs, and emulate rivals' is sound. Given the relative stability of their performance landscapes due to the small number of competitors and the low competitive intensity, these firms can learn incrementally how to make their strategies more efficient and eventually achieve high performance, as shown in Figure 7.2. This situation is consistent with the rational tradition of strategic planning embedded in the design, planning, and positioning schools of strategy (Mintzberg et al. 1998).

As the environment becomes more dynamic due to the combination of an increasing number of players and an increase in the number of competitive dimensions linking them, the competitive situation changes dramatically. The multiplication of the possible competitive responses along several different competitive dimensions makes each of the firm's decisions more subject to uncertainty. High competitive dynamism limits managers' ability to build incrementally on their current strategy, therefore obliging managers to alter their initial plans and explore new strategic directions as a response to these emergent changes. Given the widespread agreement among academics and practitioners that business environments are becoming increasingly dynamic and complex (D'Aveni 1994; Day and Reibstein 1997; Brown and Eisenhardt 1998; Brews and Hunt 1999; Normann 2001; Galbraith 2002), these conclusions are especially relevant, as what we have labelled as landscapes with high competitive intensity represent the kind of environments that we find in an increasing number of industries today.

The second insight is that the damage to performance resulting from a higher number of competitive dimensions is moderated as the number of players increases. Despite the fact that a decrease in performance associated with an increased number of competitive dimensions was observed 'across the board', it is worth reminding ourselves that effects were lower the higher the number of competitors. Caldart and Oliveira's models show that duopolies and oligopolies showed higher damage in their profitability from the increase in the number of competitive dimensions than firms operating in fragmented industries with ten players. Fragmented industries were already less profitable due to the impact of intense competition, being therefore relatively less affected by increases in the number of competitive dimensions. Therefore, firms willing to alter their value propositions by improving their offering around new competitive dimensions, should be more worried about the potential backlash derived from competitive responses based on matching my value proposition if they compete in a concentrated industry than if they do in a more fragmented one.

7.5.3 ORGANIZATIONS' SIZE AND PERFORMANCE

We now discuss a set of experiments focused on analysing the impact of the size of the co-evolving organizations on the performance of the firms in the industry. For this purpose, it is assumed that the number N of decisions made by the firm represents the size of such a firm. Simulations were run for $N = 4$, 10, 20, 30, and 40, with $C = 1$ and $K = 3$. It can be observed that firms in industries populated by smaller firms tend to achieve the highest performance (Figure 7.6). However, they also tend to show higher risk, as shown by the

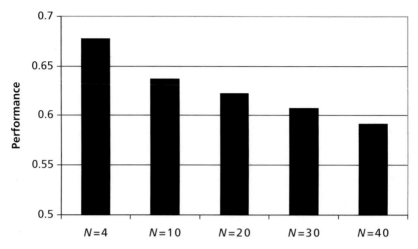

Figure 7.7. Size of the firms and performance ($P = 5$; $K = 3$; $C = 1$; $N = \{4, 10, 20, 30, 40\}$)
Source: Caldart and Oliveira (2008*a*).

standard deviation of returns (Figure 7.7). These results are explained by the trade-off between complexity and learning abilities. Whereas a larger number of possible decisions represents an increase in the potential ability to learn more combinations of strategies, it also leads to an increase in the complexity of the competitive interaction and, therefore, to lower performance overall. Therefore, the increase in the size of the performance landscape associated with a higher N increases the options available but hinders the firm's ability to converge towards the most rewarding strategic configurations.

7.5.4 EQUILIBRIA IN A NETWORK OF MULTIPLE FIRMS

The $NK(C)$ model can also be used to analyse the important issue of whether and how the co-evolutionary processes modelled can lead to any form of equilibrium. As discussed in Chapter 2, in the context of game theory we say that a game has a *Nash equilibrium* when in a given state of the game no player can improve his reward by unilaterally changing his actions (Fudenberg and Tirole 1993). In the context of the $NK(C)$ model, we can define a *local-Nash* equilibrium, in which for a given state of the state space no firm can improve its performance by unilaterally changing one of the decisions in its policy vector.

The higher the number of firms in the environment, the longer it will take until pure local-Nash equilibrium is reached (if one exists). Moreover, as we have seen earlier, another important factor influencing the long-term dynamics of an industry is the number of competitive dimensions that link the different firms. If a firm decides to move into a given strategic position, there

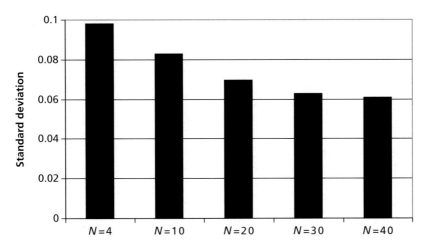

Figure 7.8. Size of the firms and variation of industry performance ($P = 5$; $K = 3$; $C = 1$; $N = \{4, 10, 20, 30, 40\}$)

Source: Caldart and Oliveira (2008*a*).

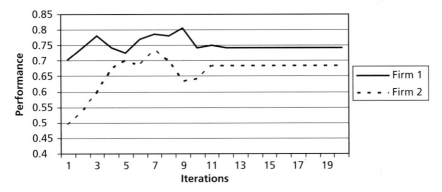

Figure 7.9. Co-evolution. Two firms model

Source: From Caldart and Oliveira (2008*a*).

is no guarantee that the other firms will not alter its performance landscape by making their own strategic decisions. If the players are rational, once local-Nash equilibrium is reached no player has an incentive to deviate from it. However, most of these equilibriums are local only. Within the context of the *NK(C)* model, equilibrium is local-Nash when no firm can improve its performance by unilaterally moving to a neighbouring state. These local-Nash equilibriums are more common than the Nash equilibriums, as it is possible for equilibrium to be local-Nash but not Nash. Figure 7.9 illustrates the co-evolution of a two firm industry, with $N = 10$, $K = 3$, and $C = 1$.

Figure 7.9 illustrates the behaviour of two co-evolving firms. The dynamics of the game showed that in the performance landscapes of the two firms there is at least a Nash equilibrium in which Firm 1 has a performance of 0.74 and Firm 2 a performance of 0.69. Given the very different initial conditions, Firm 2 presented the biggest improvement in performance. Moreover, this example also shows that possible solutions or local optima of the *NK* evolutionary game, such as iteration seven for Firm 2 and iteration nine for Firm 1, were not sustainable under co-evolution. As this simulation progresses the performance of any firm can go up or down, as it is not in complete control of its own performance landscape.

7.5.5 COMBINING THE NK MODEL WITH TRADITIONAL MODELS FROM ECONOMICS

An alternative co-evolutionary model, based on a combined application of the *NK* model and more traditional models from economics such as the Cournot model (discussed in Chapter 2) has been developed by Lenox et al. (2006). Their focus, as in other contributions based on the *NK* model (Levinthal 1997; Rivkin 2000), is to understand how the coordination of interdependencies between firms explains the heterogeneity in capabilities amongst them. They extend the analysis by explicitly modelling competition among firms in an industry. For this purpose they use the Cournot model, discussed in Chapter 2. This model enables us to model competition assuming that firms recognize their interdependence and choose output quantities that maximize their profits given the expected output from their rivals. In this way, the *NK* model is used to determine the relative cost of the firm given its interdependencies (micro-co-evolution), and the Cournot model captures the macro-co-evolution between the competing firms. They found that the highest expected averages in the industry's profits are produced by intermediate levels of interdependence between activities. These moderate levels of interdependence permit firms to benefit from the ability to find preferable competitive positions (or sets of practices) and at the same time reduce the likelihood that all the firms will be able to discover how to copy these practices. This leads to a small set of profitable competitors.

7.6 **Summary**

In this chapter, we integrated the analysis of the external and internal dynamics of the strategy of a firm. We relied on agent-based simulations based on Kauffman's *NK* and *NK(C)* models for this purpose. After explaining the architecture of these models and discussing their strengths and limitations when applied to social science, we applied the simulations to give a fresh look at the classic topic of industry structure. The simulations enabled us to analyse how the complexity associated with different structural parameters of an industry, such as the size and number of players, and the number of competitive dimensions linking them, affects the performance of such industry. This analysis enabled us to enhance our idea of competitive intensity by showing that not only the number of players of the industry but also that of the competitive dimensions that characterize competition in such industry have a strong impact on its performance.

8 Conclusion

Strategic management has evolved from a consideration of the situation a firm faces at the immediate time to one where firms should consider their position and strategy in a dynamic environment, where the decisions they make influence other firms, and their reactions change the nature of competition.

8.1 Dynamics within strategic management

In the early days of strategic management, little attention was paid to the dynamics of strategy. Markets were considered to be static, and the resource-based view was also in its infancy. Both the market approach (Porter 1980) and the resource-based view (Barney 1991; Wernerfelt 1984) trace their roots back to early industrial organization economics (Bain 1956; Penrose 1959) where assumptions of equilibrium were made in the economic models of that time. In more recent years, the assumptions of equilibrium have been tested by strategy researchers; Porter (1991) was aware of this fact when he wrote his article 'Towards a Dynamic Theory of Strategy'. Dynamic capabilities (Teece et al. 1997) focus on the rearrangement of firm resources, where learning about the firm's environment can be a source of competitive advantage. However, despite these advances, the dynamic approach to strategic management is in its early stages, a fact that makes research in this area both contemporary and exciting. Mintzberg et al. (1998) considers dynamic strategy:

[Dynamic strategy] is...the most comprehensive and therefore the most difficult form of research, so it is not surprising that it has probably received the least attention.

We have viewed this as an opportunity rather than a restriction. It is true that most of the contemporary approaches to strategic management are ill-equipped to cope with these non-linear, dynamic views. In the book, we have analysed classic literature but also have gone beyond that, setting out new approaches that can be used to help with considering the dynamics of strategy. In 1991, when Porter was considering the nature of dynamic strategy, three main contenders for 'the' theory of dynamic strategy were cited: game theoretic models, the resource-based view, and commitment under uncertainty. While each remains active within strategic management research, game theory appears to have gone out of fashion as *the* framework for dynamic strategy. The rise of the resource-based view[1] has certainly been prevalent in redefining the focus of strategy research, and with the recent attention to dynamic capabilities, it has indeed featured in contemporary research in the dynamics of strategy. But more recent advances have also been relevant in shaping the field, and these have been described in the book. Some of these will be more relevant than others, and we describe several models and frameworks in order that the reader can be exposed to several views, and to understand that there is not 'one' dynamic theory of strategy, but several.

8.2 **Connected strategy**

A central theme of this book is that strategic decisions should not be taken in isolation. The firm, and the people within it, all make up a complex system of interactions within the firm and between firms. Assuming that the firm is 'well behaved' and that strategic decisions can be made on an assumption of the firm being an isolated, closed system, will lead to decisions that may not be optimal. We have considered the competitive landscape and the organizational landscape as separate sections within the book, but this is for ease of reading rather than being our view that they are separate. In reality, these cannot be seen as detached: intra-firm decisions influence and affect inter-firm competition. As we have seen, organizations interact with their environment and need to be considered as such. Bounded rationality rather than strict rationality prevails, and organizations behave as natural systems as opposed to strictly economically rational systems. Social networks between individuals, networks between buyers and suppliers, and networks between firms skew the decisions that need to be made, and treating individuals or firms in isolation may cause a reaction that is stronger (or weaker) than expected. These networks of firms may mean that firms do not evolve in isolation, but instead may co-evolve.

Strategic decisions may also behave in a way that re-enforces their effect, as recent events in the banking sector in 2008 show. We have shown that seemingly simple decisions, such as the level of orders to make in a factory, may have significant effects at later times in the system, that may be difficult to attribute to the initial decision. Conceptualizing strategic decisions as contributing to

---

[1] 'a framework that has the potential to cut through much of this confusion is now emerging from the strategy field ... The resource-based view ... will be as powerful and as important to strategy in the 1990s as industry analysis was in the 1980s' (Collis and Montgomery 1995).

feedback loops emphasizes the connected nature of strategy. Of course, this may work in positive or negative ways: both virtuous as well as vicious circles: we may be able to harness the power of social networks, or they may act against us. What is clear is that effects may be emphasized in a way that is non-linear and therefore may be difficult to predict. The recent rise of complexity science approaches to systems holds great promise to the field of strategic management as it does for many other disciplines such as natural science or other socially-based sciences. For this reason, we have allowed this book to contain a wide range of inter-disciplinary approaches. Looking at the problem of strategic management from a purely economically-based perspective is bound to produce blinkered and myopic perspectives and hence outcomes. Complexity science, unlike economics, is at a relevant infancy. However, there is a great deal of research being conducted in this area, where problems that are considered different may have surprisingly similar solutions, or at least methods of analysis. We have introduced these tools in the book, to show that strategic analysis has gone far beyond the rational industrial organization models of the 1970s.

8.3 Consolidating the field: dynamic views within the book

In Chapter 1, we introduced our framework for dynamic strategy. Strategic initiatives, strategic intent, and strategic organizing all co-exist within the firm to make up its strategic posture. But the firm does not act alone, instead it acts within a competitive environment to gain competitive advantage over other firms that are setting their strategy based on similar, but reconfigured bases.

We introduced Chapter 1 with our framework for viewing organizations in a dynamic context. Chapters 2–4 concentrated on the inter-firm dynamics (the interactions with other firms in Figure 8.1), while Chapters 5–7 concentrated on the intra-firm dynamics (on the left of Figure 8.2).

We can treat the levels of interaction of the firm within a complex system of other firms independently, but this is more of a tool for organizing the chapters of the book. If as managers or as researchers we consider the strategic intent, strategic organization, and strategic initiatives level as independent silos, we are acting not as a strategist but as a tactician or an operational manager. The true challenge for a manager is to be able to hold several, often conflicting, models as to how the system will change as a result of their strategic action, and to make the decisions as to which is the most appropriate behaviour as a result of these analyses.

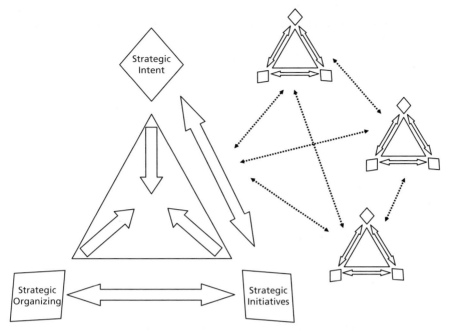

Figure 8.1. The dynamics of the strategy process

Figure 8.2 shows some of the areas we have covered in the book. While we have presented certain frameworks in Part I and some in Part II, in fact all these frameworks go together to understand the complex question that underpins strategic management. We classified the frameworks according to two dimensions. The first dimension (the horizontal axis) is whether the focus is on the internal (intra-firm) or the external (inter-firm) dynamics of the firm. The second dimension (the vertical axis) relates to the epistemology that characterizes the model, where we find a continuum ranging between models based on the assumptions of complete rationality and those based on an open system perspective assuming bounded rationality, path dependence, and recursive dynamics. We should not treat these frameworks as independent – far from it. This breaking down of strategy into constituent parts is the way that strategy is traditionally studied – individuals will become experts in population ecology, or economic modelling. We think that this is a mistake, as the interdependencies of the organizational landscape and the competitive landscape are such that treating strategy as a closed system will produce less than optimal strategies.

By using the tools in this book, we are able to view these connections in more detail, and go beyond treating each of these decisions as independent or isolated. Strategic management is not a field to be considered in isolation or

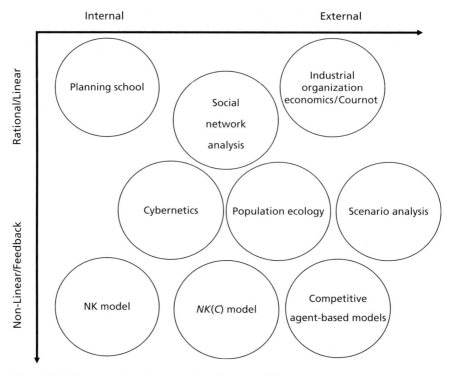

Figure 8.2. The dynamics of strategy. Classification of frameworks.

by using only one model or framework. For many years, MBA classes have been taught models of strategy and MBA students have produced reports on the competitive position of an industry or the internal positioning of a firm using simplified tools that are appropriate either in a static environment or where other, potentially critical, behavioural or competitive pressures are ignored or abstracted away. Whittington (2001) notes the similarity of strategic management text books, while Mintzberg (2004) criticizes contemporary business education. Perhaps this is indeed due to the inconsistency of thinking that competitive advantage can be achieved by using often tired frameworks that are 'explicit knowledge' in the parlance of the resource-based view and therefore *cannot* be a source of competitive advantage. The one-size-fits-all approach to strategy is inherently false. We have deliberately taken a different view. Instead, it allows the reader to understand *why* carrying out traditional analyses will not be sufficient to maintain competitive advantage: it is precisely due to the fact that the world in which we (and firms) live is inherently complex and dynamic that requires us to embrace new ideas that are better suited to this changing environment.

Moves from a view of an industry attractiveness to an individual firm's resources and capabilities has gone some way to considering the individual firm's perspective. But this can be criticized for abstracting away the competitive nature of the industry in which firms are situated.

The firm within an industry and the resources and capabilities within the firm are an inherently complex system (Robertson 2004). It would be facile to believe that considering one technique or tool from this book will give the reader a strategy for gaining and maintaining competitive advantage. But by going through the process of model-building, by considering which are the most important drivers of a firm's behaviour, the reader can begin to understand the areas which can be studied in more detail in order to understand the complex interactions within a firm and within an industry. We would also advocate using the models within the book not in isolation but together. This may run the risk of producing an overly complicated model, one that is not easily tractable, but instead of making an overly complicated model, by using *elements* of the models, we can construct a model that is more easily used for decision making.

Examples where this may be taken forward, as corporate research within organizations, or as academic research include the following. We set out in Conceptual Box 8.1 some of the areas that we feel may give new insights into the future of the field and that may provide valuable research outputs.

Conceptual Box 8.1 A roadmap for future work on the dynamics of strategy

---

Combining Agent-Based Models and Social Network Analysis

In Chapter 3, we reviewed the application of agent-based models to modelling firms within a competitive environment. In Chapter 4, we further discussed the applicability of social network analysis to determine the social structure of individuals which, when combined, create a social structure which can influence firms' market share and profitability. While these techniques are traditionally used separately, we can develop agent-based models that model social interaction, or agent-based models that include an element of connections between customers. This is a largely untapped research area that could yield improvements of our understanding of interactions that influence firm profitability in what may be a non-linear and, without using such combinations of models, seemingly intractable manner.

Combining Agent-Based Models with Economic Models

In Chapter 7, we show how economic models and agent-based models have been combined in order to develop simulations of how economic agents travel over *NK* fitness landscapes. In Chapter 2, we see how the Hotelling model of competition has been combined with an agent-based approach to extend equilibrium-based approaches. The inherently dynamic nature of agent-based modelling allows us to investigate systems of interacting agents in a non-equilibrium system. With increased computing power, and simpler to use agent-based toolkits being produced, this promises to be an interesting area for future research in the field.

The quest to understand the dynamics of strategy, and the research proposals listed earlier are by no means trivial: they require skills in the consideration and the interpretation of complicated interacting systems, and the ability to use a wide range of techniques to truly understand the mechanisms of interaction. This is in contrast to traditional approaches, where one becomes an expert in mastering a particular technique or tool. It is also different from corporate approaches where traditionally models are constructed developing 'strategy by spreadsheet'. We require strategists to look beyond economics, with broad interests and skills to answer that most elusive question: the quest for sustainable competitive advantage.

⬚ REFERENCES

Aldrich, H. E. and Kim, P. H. (2007). Small Worlds, Infinite Possibilities? How Social Networks Affect Entrepreneurial Formation and Search, *Strategic Entrepreneurship Journal*, 1(1–2), 147–65.

Amit, R. and Schoemaker, P. J. H. (1993). Strategic Assets and Organizational Rent, *Strategic Management Journal*, 14(1), 33–46.

Ansoff, H. I. (1979). *Strategic Management*. London: MacMillan.

—— (1988). *The New Corporate Strategy*. New York NY: John Wiley & Sons.

—— (1991). Critique of Henry Mintzberg's The Design School: Reconsidering the Basic Premises of Strategic Management, *Strategic Management Journal*, 12(6), 449–61.

Argyris, C. (1982). *Reasoning, Learning, and Action: Individual and Organizational*. San Francisco CA: Jossey Bass.

—— (2004). *Reasons and Rationalizations. The Limits to Organizational Knowledge*, Oxford: Oxford University Press.

—— Putman, R., and McLain Smith, D. (1985). Action Science: Concepts, Methods, and Skills for Research and Intervention. San Francisco: Jossey-Bass.

—— and Schon, D. (1978). *Organizational Learning. Reading*. MA: Addison-Wesley.

Ariño, A., de la Torre, J., Doz, Y., Ring, P. and Lorenzoni, G. (2002). Process issues in Alliance Management: A panel discusión in Advances in International Management: Managing Transnational Firms, Vol. 14, pp. 306–25. Edited by Michael Hitt. Oxford: Elsevier.

Ariño, A. and De la Torre (1998). Learning From Failure: Towards an Evolutionary Model of Collaborative Ventures, *Organization Science*, 9, 306–25.

Arthur, B. (2006). Out-of-equilibrium economics and agent-based modeling. In: K. Judd and L. Tesfatsion (eds.) *Handbook of Computational Economics*. Elsevier/North Holland.

Ashby, W. (1952). *Design for a Brain*. New York: John Wiley & Sons.

Axelrod, R. (1997). The Complexity of Cooperation: Agent-Based Models of Competition and Collaboration, Princeton Studies *In Complexity*, Princeton NJ: Princeton University Press.

Bain, J. (1956). *Barriers to New Competition*, Cambridge MA: Harvard University Press.

Bak, P., C. Tang, and K. Wiesenfeld (1988). Self organized Criticality, *Phys. Rev.* A, 38. 364–74.

—— Chen, K., and Tang, C. (1990). A Forest-Fire Model and some Thoughts on Turbulence, *Physics Letters A*, 147(5–6), 297–300.

—— Tang, C. and Wiesenfeld, K. (1987). Self-Organized Criticality: An Explanation of $1/f$ Noise, *Physical Review Letters*, 59(4), 381–4.

Barabási, A. L. (1999). Emergence of Scaling in Random Networks, *Science*, 286(5439), 509–12.

Barnard, C. (1938). The Functions of the Executive. Harvard University Press.

Barney, J. B. (1991). Firm Resources and Sustained Competitive Advantage, *Journal of Management*, 17, 99–120.

Barton, A. H. (1955). The Concept of Property-Space in Social Research. In: Lazarsfeld, P. F. and Rosenberg, M (eds.), *The Language of Social Research: A Reader in the Methodology of Social Research*. Glencoe, IL: Free Press, pp. 40–53.

Bar-Yam, Y. (1998). *Dynamics of Complex Systems*, Westview Press.

Bass, F. (1969). A New Product Growth Model for Consumer Durables, *Management Science*, 15(5), 215–27.

Beer, M. (1997). Allentown Materials Corporation. The Electronic Products Division (A). Harvard Business School Case Study 9-498-023. Harvard Business Publishing.

Benner, M. J., and Tushman, M. L. (2003). Exploitation, Exploration, And Process Management: The Productivity Dilemma Revisited. Academy of Management Review, 28(2), 238–56.

Bertrand, J. (1883). Review of 'Théorie mathématique de la richesse sociale' and 'Recherche sur les principes mathématiques de la théorie des richesses', Journal de Savants, **48**, 499–508.

Besanko, D., Dranove, D.,Shanley, M., and Schaefer, S (2003:223). *The Economics of Strategy.* 3rd edn., John Wiley & Sons, Inc.

Bethel, J. and Liebeskind, J. (1993). The effects of ownership structure on corporate restructuring, Strategic Management Journal, **14**: 15–31.

Boisot, M. (1996). Preparing for Turbulence: The Changing Relationship Between Strategy and Management Development in the Learning Organization. In: Garratt, R. (eds.), *Developing Strategic Thought: Rediscovering the Art of Direction-Giving.* London: McGraw-Hill (first published in 1995 by McGraw-Hill International, London).

Boulding, K. (1956). General Systems Theory. The Skeleton of Science, *Management Science,* **2,3**: 197–208.

Bourgeois, L. J. and Eisenhardt, K. M. (1987). Strategic Decision Processes in Silicon Valley: The Anatomy of a 'Living Dead', *California Management Review,* 30(1), 143–59.

—— —— (1988). Strategic Decision Processes in High Velocity Environments: Four Cases in the Microcomputer Industry, *Management Science,* 34(7), 816–35.

Brandenburger, A. and Nalebuff, B. J. (1997). *Co-opetition.* New York NY: Doubleday.

Braybrooke, D. and Lindblom, C. E. (1963). *A Strategy of Decision,* New York NY: Free Press.

Brews, P. and Hunt, M. (1999). Learning to Plan and Planning to Learn: Resolving the Planning School/Learning School Debate, Strategic Management Journal, **20**, 889–913.

Brown, S. L. and Eisenhardt, K. M. (1997). The Art of Continuous Change: Linking Complexity Theory and Time-Paced Evolution in Relentlessly Shifting Organizations, *Administrative Science Quarterly,* 42(1), 1–34.

—— —— (1998). *Competing on the Edge: Strategy as Structured Chaos,* Boston MA: Harvard Business School Press.

Buckley, W. (1967). Sociology and Modern Systems Theory. New Jersey: Englewood Cliffs.

Bura, S., Guerin-Pace, F., Mathian, H., Pumain, D., and Sanders, L. (1995). Cities can be Agents Too: A Model for the Evolution of Settlement Systems. In: Gilbert, N., and Conte, R. (eds.), *Artificial Societies: The Computer Simulation of Social Life.* London UK: UCL Press, pp. 86–102.

Burgelman, R (1994). Fading memories: A process theory of strategic business exit in dynamic environments, *Administrative Science Quarterly,* 39(1): 24–56.

—— (2002). Strategy as Vector and the Inertia of Coevolutionary Lock-in, *Administrative Science Quarterly,* **47**: 325–57.

Burt, R. S. (1988). The Stability of American Markets, *American Journal of Sociology,* **93**, 356–95.

—— and Carlton, D.S. (1989). Another Look at the Network Boundaries of American Markets, *American Journal of Sociology,* **94**, 723–53.

Caldart, A. (2006). The challenge of constant change – Nokia. (Case update). In "Distance Learning MBA Notes (Strategy & Practice)". Warwick Business School.

—— and Canals, J. (2002). Ficosa International. International Expansion, *IESE Business School Case Study DG-1415-E.* Barcelona: IESE Publishing.

—— and Canals, J. (2004). Indo Internacional 2004, *IESE Business School Case Study DG-1474-E,* Barcelona: IESE Publishing.

—— and Ricart, J. E. (2007). Corporate Strategy: an agent-based approach, *European Management Review,* **4**: 107–20.

—— and Canales, J. (2008). Creating Corporate Advantage from Unsuspected Places, Working Paper.

—— and Oliveira, F. S. (2007). The Impact of Organisational Complexity in the Strategy Development Process', in Frances O'Brien and Robert Dyson(eds.), Supporting Strategy: Frameworks, Methods and Models, Wiley, 2007, 191–210.

—— —— (2008a). The Complexity and Equilibrium Properties of an Agent-Based Model for the Analysis of Strategic Decisions, Working paper.

—— —— (2009) 'Analyzing Industry Profitability. A "complexity as cause" perspective', Forthcoming European Management Journal.

Camerer, C. F. (1991). Does Strategy Research Need Game Theory?. *Strategic Management Journal*, **12**, 137–52.

Campa, J. and Kedia, S. (2002). Explaining the Diversification Discount, *Journal of Finance*, 57, 1731–62.

Carley, K. (2002). Simulating Society: The Tension Between Transparency and Veridicality, *Proceedings of the Agent 2002 Conference*. Chicago IL, USA.

Carroll, G. R. (1985). Concentration and specialization: Dynamics of niche width in populations of organizations, *American Journal of Sociology*, 90, 1262–83.

—— and Hannan, M. T. (2000). *The Demography of Corporations and Industries*, Princeton NJ: Princeton University Press.

Chackravarthy, B., Zaheer, S., and Zaheer, A. (2001). Knowledge sharing in organizations, A field study. Working paper.

Chaffee, E. E. (1985). Three Models of Strategy, *Academy of Management Review*, **10**(1), 89–98.

Chakravarthy, B. (1997). A New Strategy Framework for Coping with Turbulence, *Sloan Management Review*, **38**(2), 69–82.

Chakravarthy, B. S. and White, R. E. (2002). Strategy Process: Forming, Implementing, and Changing Strategies. In: Pettigrew, A., Thomas, H., and Whittington, R. (eds.), *Handbook of Strategy and Management*. London: Sage.

Chandler, A. D. (1962). Strategy and Structure: Chapters in the History of the American Industrial Enterprise, Cambridge MA: MIT Press.

Checkland, P and Scholes, J. (1990). Soft Systems Methodology in Action. New York: John Wiley and Sons.

Christaller, W. (1966). *Central Places of Southern Germany*. Englewood Cliffs NJ: Prentice Hall.

Clar, S. B. Drossel, and F. Schwabl, (1994). Scaling Laws and Simulation Results for the Self Organized Critical Forest-Fire Model, *Physics Review E*, 50, 1009–18.

Clippinger, J. (1999). The Biology of Business. Decoding the Natural Laws of the Entreprise. San Francisco: Jossey Bass.

Collier, N. (2001). RePast: An Extensible Framework for Agent Simulation, *University of Chicago Social Science Research Computing Working Paper*.

Collis, D. J. (1994). Research Note: How Valuable Are Organizational Capabilities, *Strategic Management Journal*, **15**, 143–52.

Collis, D. and Montgomery, C. (1995). Competing on Resources: Strategy in the 1990s. Harvard Business Review, 73 (July–August), pp. 118–28.

—— —— (1998). 'Creating Corporate Advantage', HBR, May–Jun 1998, 71–83

Conyon, M. J. and Muldoon, M. R. (2006). The Small World of Corporate Boards, *Journal of Business Finance and Accounting*, **33**(9–10), 1321–43.

Cournot, A. (1838). *Recherches sur les Principes Mathematiques de la Theorie des Richesses*. Paris: Hachette.

Cyert, R., and March, J. 1963. A Behavioral Theory of the Firm. New Jersey: Prentice Hall.

D'Aspremont, C. J., Gabszewicz, C. J. J., and Thisse, J.-F. (1979). On Hotelling's 'Stability in Competiton', *Econometrica*, **47**, 1145–50.

D'Aveni, R. A. (1994). *Hypercompetition: Managing the Dynamics of Strategic Maneuvring*, New York NY: Free Press.

—— (1995). Coping with Hypercompetition: Utilizing the new 7S's Framework, *Academy of Management Executive*, **9**(3), 45–57.

—— (1999). Strategic Supremacy through Disruption and Dominance, *Sloan Management Review*, **40** (3), 127–135.

Daft, R. (1983). Organizational Theory and Design. New York NY: West.

Darwin, C. (1859). On The Origin of Species by Means of Natural Selection, London: John Murray.

Davis, J., Eisenhardt K., and Bingham C.(2007). Developing Theory Through Simulation Methods, Academy of Management Review, **32**, 480–99.

Dawid, H., Reimann, M., and Bullnheimer, B. (2001). To innovate or not to innovate?, *IEEE Transactions on Evolutionary Computation*, 5: 470–81.

Dawkins, R. (1982). The Extended Phenotype: the Gene as the Unit of Selection. Oxford: W. H. Freeman.

Day, G. and Reibstein, D. (1997). *Wharton on Dynamic Competitive Strategy*. New York: John Wiley & Sons.

Denis, D., Denis, D., and Sarin, A. (1997). Agency problems. Equity Ownership and Corporate Diversification, *Journal of Finance*, **52** (1), 135–60.

Dess, G. G. and Beard, D. W. (1984). Dimensions of Organizational Task Environments, *Administrative Science Quarterly*, **29**(1), 52–73.

Dosi, G., Nelson, R. R., and Winter, S. G. (eds.) (2000). The Nature and Dynamics of Organizational Capabilities, Oxford: Oxford University Press.

Downs, A. (1957a). *An Economic Theory of Democracy*, New York NY: Harper & Row.

—— (1957b). An Economic Theory of Political Action in a Democracy, *Journal of Political Economy*, **65**(2), 135–50.

Drossel, B., and Schwabl F. (1992). Self-Organized Criticality in a Forest-Fire Model, *Physica A*, **191**, 47–50. ISSN 0378–4371.

Drucker, P. (1994). The Theory of the Business, *Harvard Business Review*, **72**, 95–104.

Dunban, R. and Starbuck, W. (2006). Learning to Design Organizations and Learning from Designing Them, *Organization Science*, **17**, 171–8.

Duncan, R. B. (1972). Characteristics of Organizational Environments and Perceived Environmental Uncertainty, *Administrative Science Quarterly*, **17**(3), 313–27.

Dyer, J. H. and Nobeoka, K. (2000). Creating and Managing a High-Performance Knowledge-Sharing Network: The Toyota Case, *Strategic Management Journal*, **21**, 345–67.

Edgeworth, F. Y. (1881). *Mathematical Psychics: An Essay on the Application of Mathematics to the Moral Sciences*, London: Kegan Paul & Co.

Eisenhardt, K. M. (1989). Making Fast Strategic Decisions in High-Velocity Environments, *Academy of Management Journal*, **32**, 543–76.

—— and Martin, J. A. (2000). Dynamic Capabilities: What Are They?, *Strategic Management Journal*, **21**, 1105–21.

Emery, F. E. and Trist, E. L. (1965). The Causal Texture of Organizational Environments, *Human Relations*, **18**(1), 21–32.

Epstein, J. and Axtell, R. (1996). *Growing Artificial Societies: Social Science from the Bottom Up*, Cambridge MA: MIT Press.

European Economic Community (1957). *Treaty Establishing the European Economic Community (Treaty of Rome)*.

Facebook (2007*a*). Press Room, http://www.facebook.com/press/info.php?statistics, accessed 14 December 2007.

—— (2007*b*). Opening Up the Facebook Platform Architecture, http://developers.facebook.com/news.php?blog=1&story=60, accessed 14 December 2007.

—— (2007*c*). 'Application Directory', http://www.facebook.com/apps/, accessed 14 December 2007.

Fayol, H. (1916). General and Industrial Management. Pitman, London.

Ferber, J. (1989). Des Objets aux Agents, *Unpublished Doctoral Dissertation*, University of Paris VI.

Financial Times (2008). GM and Toyota Share Top Carmaker Crown, http://www.fr.com/ accessed 1 February 2008.

Forrester, J. (1958). Industrial Dynamics: A Major Breackthrough for Decision Makers, *Harvard Business Review*, **36**(4): 37–66.

—— (1968). *Principles of Systems*, Cambridge MA: MIT Press.

—— (1961). *Industrial Dynamics*, Portland OR: Productivity Press.

Frischknecht, F. (1993). *Dirección Recursiva. De las ideas a la acción y de la acción a las ideas*, Buenos Aires, El Ateneo.

Fruchterman, T. M. J. and Reingold, E. M. (1991). Graph Drawing by Force-Directed Placement, *Software – Practice and Experience*, **21**(11), 1129–64.

Fudenberg, D., and Tirole, J. 1991. Game Theory. Cambridge: The MIT Press.

Galbraith, J. (2002). *Designing Organizations: An Executive Guide to Strategy, Structure, and Process*, San Francisco: Jossey Bass.

Galunic, D. C. and Rodan, S. (1998). Resource Recombinations in the Firm: Knowledge Structures and the Potential for Schumperterian Innovation, *Strategic Management Journal*, **19**(12), 1193–201.

Garvin, D. and Levesque, L. (2004). Emerging Business Opportunities at IBM (A), *Harvard Business School Case Study*, 9–304–075, Cambridge: HBS Publishing.

Gary, S. (2005). Implementation Strategy and Performance Outcomes in Related Diversification, *Strategic Management Journal*, **27**: 643–64.

Gavetti, G. (2005). Cognition and Hierarchy: Rethinking the Microfoundations of Capabilities Development, *Organization Science*, **16**, 599–617.

—— and Levinthal, D. (2000). Looking Forward and Looking Backward: Cognitive and Experiential Search, *Administrative Science Quarterly*, **45**, 113–37.

Gavetti, G., Levinthal, D. and Rivkin, J. (2005). Strategy-Making in Novel and Complex Worlds: The Power of Analogy. Strategic Management Journal 26, 691–712.

Gavetti, G., and Rivkin, J. (2005). "How Strategists Really Think: Tapping the Power of Analogy." *Harvard Business Review* 83, no. 4: 54–63.

Ghemawat, P. (1995). *Games Businesses Play: Cases and Models*, New York NY: Wiley.

Gilbert, N. and Terna, P. (2000). How to Build and Use Agent-Based Models in Social Science, *Mind and Society*, **1**, 57–72.

—— and Troitzsch, K. G. (1999). *Simulation for the Social Scientist*, Buckingham: Open University Press.

Gilbreth, F. and Gilbreth, L. (1924). Classifying the Elements of Work, *Management and Administration*, **8**(2): 151–4.

Gouldner, A. (1959). Organizational Analysis. In: *Sociology Today.* Merton, R., Broom, L., and Cottrell Jr. L (eds.). New York: Basic Books, pp. 400–28.

Granovetter, M. (1985). Economic Action and Social Structure: The Problem of Embeddedness, *The American Journal of Sociology,* **91**(3), 481–510.

Grant, R. M. (1996). Prospering in Dynamically-competitive Environments: Organizational Capability as Knowledge Integration, *Organization Science,* **7**(4), 375–87.

Gulati, R. (1995). Social Structure and Alliance Formation Pattern: A Longitudinal Analysis, *Administrative Science Quarterly,* **40**, 619–42.

—— (1998). Alliances and Networks, *Strategic Management Journal,* **19**(4), 293–317.

—— Nohria, N. and Zaheer, A. (2000). Strategic Networks, *Strategic Management Journal,* Special Issue: Strategic Networks, **21** (3), 203–15.

Gupta, A. Anil K., Smith, K. & Shalley, C. (2006). 'The interplay between exploration and exploitation', *Academy of Management Journal,* 49 (4), pp. 693–706.

Hamel, G. and C. K. Prahalad (1989). To Revitalize Corporate Performance, We Need a Whole New Model of Strategy. Strategic intent, *Harvard Business Review,* **67** (3), pp. 63–76.

Hannan, M. T. and Freeman, J. (1974). Environment and the Structure of Organizations, Paper presented at the Annual Meeting of the American Sociological Association, Montreal, Canada.

—— —— (1977). The Population Ecology of Organizations, *American Journal of Sociology,* **82**(5), 929–64.

Hannan, M. T. and Freeman, J. (1989). *Organizational Ecology,* Cambridge MA: Harvard University Press.

Hatten, K. J. and Hatten, M. L. (1987). Strategic Groups, Asymmetrical Mobility Barriers and Contestability, *Strategic Management Journal,* **8**(4), 329–42.

Hax, A. and Wilde, D. (2001). *The Delta Project. Discovering New Sources of Profitability in a Networked Economy,* New York: Palgrave.

Hayes, R. (1985). Strategic Planning: Forward in Reverse, *Harvard Business Review,* **63**(6), 111–19.

Hofbauer, J. and Sigmund, K. (1998). *Evolutionary Games and Population Dynamics,* Cambridge: Cambridge University Press.

Holland, J. H. (1995). Hidden Order: How Adaptation Builds Complexity, Reading MA: Addison-Wesley.

Holland, J. H. (1998). *Emergence: From Chaos to Order,* Reading MA: Addison-Wesley.

Hotelling, H. (1929). 'Stability in Competition', *Economic Journal,* **39**, 41–57.

Huff, A. S. (ed.) (1990). *Mapping Strategic Thought,* Somerset NJ: Wiley.

Hunt, M. S. (1972). *Competition in the Major Home Appliance Industry, 1960–1970,* Unpublished doctoral dissertation, Harvard University.

Hutchinson, G. E. (1957). Concluding Remarks, Cold Harbor Symposium on Quantitative Biology, 22, 415–27.

Huygens, M., Baden-Fuller, C., Van Den Bosch, F., and Volberda, H. (2001). Coevolution of Firm Capabilities and Industry Competition: Investigating the Music Industry 1877–1997, *Organisation Studies,* **22**, 971–1011.

Karlgaard, R. and Gilder, G. (1996). Talking with Intel's Andy Grove, *Forbes,* **26** February: 63.

Kauffman, S. (1993). *The Origins of Order: Self-organization and Selection in Evolution,* New York NY: Oxford University Press.

Knott, A. M. (2003). Persistent Heterogeneity and Sustainable Innovation, *Strategic Management Journal,* **24**, 687–705.

Koput, K. (1992). *Dynamics of New Idea Generation in Organizations: Randomness and Chaos in the Development of a New Medical Device,* Ann Arbour MI: UMI Press.

Kossinets, G. and Watts, D. J. (2006). Empirical Analysis of an Evolving Social Network, *Science*, **311**(5757), 88–90.

Krackhardt, D., and Hanson, J. "Informal Networks: The Company Behind the Chart." Harvard Business Review, 71 (July/August (4)): 104–11.

Kunc, M. and Morecroft, J. (2007). System Dynamics Modelling for Strategic Development. In: *Supporting Strategy: Frameworks, Methods and Models*. O'Brien F. and Dyson, R. (eds.). Chichester: John Wiley & Sons, pp. 157–90.

Lancaster, K. J. (1966). A New Approach to Consumer Theory, *Journal of Political Economy*, **74**(2), 132–57.

Lang, L. and Stultz, R. (1994). Tobin's q, Corporate Diversification, and Firm Performance, *Journal of Political Economy*, **102**(6), 1248–80.

Lant, T. and Mezias, S. (1990). 'Managing Discontinuous Change: A Simulation Study of Organizational Learning and Entrepreneurship', *Strategic Management Journal*, **11**(Summer Special Issue), 147–79.

Lawrence, P. and Lorsch J. (1967). *Organization and Environment: Managing Differentiation and Integration*, Cambridge MA: Harvard Business School Press.

Lazarsfeld, P. F. (1937). Some Remarks on the Typological Procedure in Social Research, *Zeitschrift für Sozialforschung*, **VI**.

Lee, J., Lee, K., and Rho, S. (2002). An Evolutionary Perspective on Strategic Group Emergence: A Genetic Algorithm-Based Model, *Strategic Management Journal*, **23**, 727–46.

Lenox, M., Rockart, S., and Lewin, A. (2006). Interdependency, Competition, and the Distribution of Firm and Industry Profits, *Management Science*, **52**, 757–72.

Levinthal, D. A. (1997). Adaptation on Rugged Landscapes, *Management Science*, **43**(7), 934–50.

—— and March, J. (1981). A Model of Adaptive Organizational Search, *Journal of Economic Behavior and Organization*, **2**, 307–33.

Levitt, B. and March, J. (1988). Organizational Learning. Annual Review of Sociology, 14, 319–40.

Lieberman, M. B. and Montgomery, D. B. (1988). First-Mover Advantages, *Strategic Management Journal*, **9** (Special Issue: Strategy Content Research), 41–58.

Lösch, A. (1967). *The Economics of Location*, New York NY: John Wiley & Sons.

Madhok, A. and Liu, C. (2006). A coevolutionary theory of the multinational firm, *Journal of International Management*, **12**, 1–21.

Mailath, G. J. and Samuelson, L. (2006). *Repeated Games and Reputations: Long-Run Relationships*, Oxford: Oxford University Press.

Makadok, R. (2001). Toward a Synthesis of the Resource-Based and Dynamic-Capability Views of Rent Creation, *Strategic Management Journal*, **22**, 387–401.

March, J. (1991). Exploration and Exploitation in Organizational Learning, *Organization Science*, **2**, 71–87.

March, J. and Simon, H. (1958). *Organizations*, New York: John Wiley & Sons.

Markides C., Williamson, P. (1994). Related diversification, core competencies and corporate performance. *Strategic Management Journal* 15(special issue): 149–67.

Mason, E. (1939). Price and Production Policies of Large-Scale Entreprise, *American Economic Review*, Supplement **29**.

Mayo, E. (1933). *The Human Problems of and Industrial Civilization*, New York: The Macmillan Company.

McGee, J. and Thomas, H. (1986). Strategic Groups: Theory, Research and Taxonomy, *Strategic Management Journal*, **7**, 141–60.

McKelvey, B. (1997). Quasi-natural Organization Science, *Organization Science*, 8(4), 352–80.

—— (1999). Complexity Theory in Organization Science: Seizing the Promise or Becoming a Fad?, *Emergence: A Journal of Complexity Issues in Organizations and Management*, 1(1), 5–32.

McNamara, G., Vaaler, P. M., and Devers, C. (2003). Same As It Ever Was: The Search for Evidence of Increasing Hypercompetition, *Strategic Management Journal*, 24(3), 261–78.

McPherson, J. M. (1983). 'An Ecology of Affiliation', *American Sociological Review*, 48(4), 519–32.

McWilliams, A. and Smart, D. (1993). Efficiency vs. Structure-conduct-Performance: Implications for Strategy Research and Practice, *Journal of Management*, 19, 63–78.

Mezias, S. and Eisner, A. (1997). Competition, Imitation, and Innovation: An Organizational Learning Approach. In: Walsh, P., Huff, A., and Shrivastava, P. (eds.) *Advances in Strategic Management*. 14. Greenwich, CT: JAI Press, pp. 261–94.

Milgram, S. (1967). The Small World Problem, *Psychology Today*, 1(1), 60–7.

Miller, D. (1990). The Icarus Paradox: How Exceptional Companies Bring about their Own Downfall. In: Segal-Horn, S. (eds.) *The Strategy Reader*. Oxford: Blackwell Publishing, pp. 461–76.

Minar, N., Burkhart, R., Langton, C., and Askenazi, M. (1996). The Swarm Simulation System: A Toolkit for Building Multi-Agent Simulations, Working Paper *96*, *06–042*, Santa Fe NM: Santa Fe Institute.

Mintzberg, H. (1973). *The Nature of Managerial Work*, New York: Harper & Row.

—— (1990a). Strategic Formation: Schools of Thought. In: Fredrickson, J. (eds.) *Perspectives on Strategic Management*. Grand Rapids. Philadelphia: Harper Business, 105–236.

—— (1990b). The Design School: Reconsidering the Basic Premises of Strategic Management, *Strategic Management Journal*, 11(3), 171–95.

—— (1990c). The Design School. Reconsidering the Basic Premises of Strategic Management, *Strategic Management Journal*, 11, 171–95.

—— (1991). Learning 1, Planning 0: Reply to Igor Ansoff, *Strategic Management Journal*, 12, 463–6.

—— (1993). The Pitfalls of Strategic Planning, *California Management Review*, 36(1), 32–47.

—— (1994). The Rise and Fall of Strategic Planning, Englewood Cliffs NJ: Prentice Hall.

—— (2004). Managers not MBAs: A Hard Look at the Soft Practice of Managing and Management Development, San Francisco CA: Berret-Koehler.

—— Alhstrand, B., and Lampel, J. (1998). Strategy Safari, *A Guided Tour Through the Wilds of Strategic Management*, New York: Free Press.

Morck, R., Shleifer, A., and Vishny, R. (1990). Do Managerial Objectives Drive Bad Acquisitions?, *Journal of Finance*, 15, 31–48.

Murray, A.1. (1988). A contingency view of Porter's 'generic strategies', *Academy of Management Review*, 13, 390–400.

Nelson, R. and Winter, S. (1982). *An Evolutionary Theory of Economic Change*, Cambridge MA: Belknap Harvard.

Newell, A. (1990). *Unified Theories of Cognition*, Cambridge: Harvard.

Noboa, F. (2004). Estrategia de la Subsidiaria: Influir en el nivel de embeddedness, *Tesis Doctoral IESE Business School*, Universidad de Navarra.

Nohria, N. and Berkley, J. D. (1992). Amgen, Inc.: Planning the Unplannable. Harvard Business School Case Study 492052. Harvard Business Publishing. Garcia-Pont, C., Canales, J. and Noboa, F. (2009). "Subsidiary Strategy: The Embeddedness Component," Journal of Management Studies, 46(2): 182–214.

Nonaka, I. (1988). Toward Middle-Up-Down Management: Accelerating Information Creation, *Sloan Management Review*, 29, 9–18.

—— and Takeuchi, H. (1995). *The Knowledge Creating Company*, Oxford: Oxford University Press.

Normann, R. (2001). Reframing Business, *When the Map Changes the Landscape*, Chichester: John Wiley & Sons.

OED *(1989). Oxford English Dictionary, 2nd Edition, Oxford UK: Oxford University Press.*

Parsons, T. (1960). *Structure and Process in Modern Societies*, Glencoe IL: Free Press.

Pascale, R. (1999). Surfing the Edge of Chaos, *Sloan Management Review*, **40**(3), 83–94.

—— (1990). Surfing the Edge of Chaos: The Laws of Nature and the New Laws of Business. New York. Three Rivers Press.

Péli, G. and Nooteboom, B. (1999). Market Partitioning and the Geometry of the Resource Space, *American Journal of Sociology*, **104**, 1132–53.

Penrose, E. G. (1959). *The Theory of the Growth of the Firm*, New York NY: Wiley.

Porter, M. (1979). How Competitive Forces Shape Strategy, *Harvard Business Review*, **57**(2), 137–45.

—— (1980). *Competitive Strategy. Techniques for Analyzing Industries and Competitors*, New York: The Free Press.

—— (1985). Competitive Advantage, *Creating and Sustaining Superior Performance*, New York: Free Press.

—— (1996). What is strategy?, *Harvard Business Review*, **74**(6), 61–78.

Porter, M. (1991). Towards a Dynamic Theory of Strategy, *Strategic Management Journal*, **12**, 95–117.

Prahalad, C. K. and Hamel, G. (1990). The Core Competence of the Corporation, *Harvard Business Review*, 68(3), 79–91.

Priem, R. L., Rasheed, A. M. A., and Kotulic, A. G. (1995). Rationality in Strategic Decision Processes, Environmental Dynamism and Firm Performance, *Journal of Management*, **21**(5), 913–29.

Prietula, M. J., Carley, K. M., and Glasser, L. (1998). *Simulating Organizations: Computational Models of Institutions and Groups*, Cambridge, MA: The MIT Press.

Quinn, J. B. (1978). Strategic Change: "Logical Incrementalism", *Sloan Management Review*, **20**(1), 7–21.

—— (1980). *Strategies for Change: Logical Incrementalism*, Homeward IL: Irwin.

Richardson, G. (1994). *Feedback Thought in Social Science and Systems Theory*, Philadelphia: University of Pennsylvania Press.

Rigby, D. and Rogers, P. (2000). Winning in Turbulence – Strategies for Success in Turbulent Times, *European Business Journal*, **12**(2), 76–86.

Rivkin, J. W. (2000). Imitation of Complex Strategies, *Management Science*, **46**(6), 824–44.

Robertson, D. A. (2003*a*). Agent-Based Models of a Banking Network as an Example of a Turbulent Environment: The Deliberate vs. Emergent Strategy Debate Revisited, *Emergence: A Journal of Complexity Issues in Organizations and Management*, 5(2), 56–71.

—— (2003*b*). The Strategy Hypercube: Exploring Strategy Space using Agent-Based Models. In: D. Hales *et al.* (eds.) *Multi Agent Based Systems III*. Berlin: Springer-Verlag, pp. 182–92.

—— (2004). The Complexity of the Corporation, *Human Systems Management*, **23**(2), 71–8, Special Issue: Corporation: An Intelligent Complex Adaptive System.

—— (2005). Agent-Based Modeling Toolkits, *Academy of Management Learning and Education*, **4**(4), 525–7.

—— and Collet, F. H. (2008). The Small and Not Small Worlds of Strategic Management: A Dynamic Social Network Study, Working Paper.

Robertson, D. A. and Fan, T. (2008). Mutualistic Entrepreneurship: The Case of Facebook, Paper presented at the Strategic Management Society Annual Conference, Cologne, Germany.

—— and Siggelkow, N. (2005). The Value of Search and Change Capabilities: A Multi-Agent Simulation Model of Competition, Strategic Management Society Conference, Vienna, Austria.

Robertson, D. and Caldart, A. (2008). Natural Science Models in Management: Opportunities and Challenges, *Emergence: Complexity and Organisations*, **10**, 61–75.

Romme, G. (1995). Non-Participation and System Dynamics, *System Dynamics Review*, **11**, 311–19.

—— (2003). Making a Difference. Organization as Design, *Organization Science*, **14**, 558–73.

Rosenkopf, L. and Nerkar, A. (2001). Beyond Local Search: Boundary-spanning, Exploration, and Impact in the Optical Disc Industry, *Strategic Management Journal*, **22**, 287–306.

—— and Schilling, M.A. (2007). Comparing Alliance Network Structure Across Industries: Observations and Explanations, *Strategic Entrepreneurship Journal*, **1** (3/4), 191–209.

Rumelt, R. (1974). Strategy, Structure, and Economic Performance, Boston, MA: Division of Research, Graduate School of Business Administration, Harvard University.

Salop, S. C. (1979). Monopolistic Competition with Outside Goods, *Bell Journal of Economics*, **10**, 141–56.

Schelling, T. C. (1978). *Micromotives and Macrobehavior*, W. W. Norton and Co., 147–55.

Schmidt, E. (2005). Google 2004 - A Retrospective: Annual Meeting with Shareholders of Google, http://home.blarg.net/~glinden/Google-shareholders-meeting-slides-2005–05–12.html, accessed 14 January 2008.

Schweitzer, F. and Troitzch, K. G. (2002). *SocioPhysics Conference Abstracts*, Bielefeld Germany: Universität Bielefeld – Zentrum für interdisziplinäre Forschung.

Scott, R. (1998). *Organizations. Rational, Natural and Open Systems*, New Jersey: Prentice Hall.

Selznick, P. (1957). Leadership in Administration, *A Sociological Interpretation*, New York: Harper & Row.

Senge, P. (1990). The Fifth Discipline, *The Art and Practice of the Learning Organization*, New York: Doubleday Currency.

Shah, S. K. and Tripsas, M. (2007). The Accidental Entrepreneur: The Emergent and Collective Process of User Entrepreneurship, *Strategic Entrepreneurship Journal*, **1**(1–2), 123–40.

Shell (2005). Global Scenarios for 2025. www.shell.com/scenarios.

Siggelkow, N. and Levinthal, D (2005). Escaping Real (Non-Benign) Competency Traps: Linking the Dynamics of Organizational Structure to the Dynamics of Search, *Strategic Organization*, **3**, 85–115.

Siggelkow, N. Levinthal, D and Rivkin, J. W. (2005). Speed and Search: Designing Organizations for Turbulence and Complexity, *Organization Science*, **16**, 101–22.

Simon, H. (1947). *Administrative Behaviour: A Study of Decision-Making Processes in Administrative Organizations*, New York NY: Free Press.

—— (1957). *Administrative Behaviour*, Second edn., New York NY: Macmillan.

—— (1957*a*). 'A Behavioral Model of Rational Choice', In: Models of Man, Social and Rational New York NY, John Wiley.

—— (1991). *Models of my Life*, New York NY: Basic Books.

—— (1996). *The Sciences of the Artificial*, Cambridge: MIT Press.

—— (1997). *Administrative Behavior*, Fourth Edition, New York: Free Press.

Slater, S. F. and Narver, J. C. (1999). Market Oriented is More than being Customer Led, *Strategic Management Journal*, **20**, 1165–8.

—— —— (1998). Customer-led and market-oriented: let's not confuse the two, *Strategic Management Journal*, **19**, 1001–6.

Smith, C. H. Commentary on Wallace, A. R. On the Tendency of Varieties to Depart Indefinitely from the Original Type (543: 1858), http://www.wku.edu/~smithch/Wallace/S043.htm, accessed April 2009.

Spence, M and Zeckhauser, R. (1971). Insurance, Information and Individual Action, *American Economic Review*, **61**(2), 380–7.

Spender, J.-C. (1989). *Industry Recipes: An Enquiry into the Nature and Sources of Managerial Judgment*, Oxford: Blackwell.

Stacey, R. (1993). Strategy as Order Emerging from Chaos, Long Range Planning, **26**(1), 10–17.

Stuart, T. E. and Sorenson, O. (2007). Strategic Networks and Entrepreneurial Ventures, *Strategic Entrepreneurship Journal*, **1**(3–4), 211–27.

Sull, D. and Eisenhardt, K. (2001). Strategy as Simple Rules, *Harvard Business Review*, **79**(1), 106–16.

Taylor, F. (1911). *The Principles of Scientific Management*, New York: Harper.

Teece, D., Pisano, G., and Shuen, A. (1997). Dynamic Capabilities and Strategic Management, *Journal of Strategic Management*, 509–33.

Tesfatsion, L. (1997). A Trade Network Game with Endogenous Partner Selection. In: Amman, H., Rustem, B., and Whinston, A. B. (eds.) *Computational approaches to economic problems*. Dordrecht. The Netherlands: Kluwer Academic Publishers.

Thompson, J. (1967). *Organizations in Action, Social Science Bases of Administrative Theory*, New York: McGraw-Hill.

Times, (2007). Analysts Deferd $15 billion Facebook Valuation, Times Online, http://technology.timesonline.co.uk, Accessed January 2008.

Treacy, M. and Wieserma, F. (1995). *The Discipline of Market Leaders, Choose your customers, narrow your focus, dominate your market*, Reading: Addison-Wesley Publishing Company.

Tushman, M. and O'Reilly, C. A. (1996). Ambidextrous organizations: Managing evolutionary and revolutionary change. California Management Review, 38(4), 8–29.

United States (1890). Sherman Antitrust Act, 15 U.S.C, §§ 1–7.

United States Generel Accounting Office (1987), Food and Drug Administration, 'Food Additive Approval Process followed for Asportane'.

Van den Bosch, F., Volberda, H., and de Boer, M. (1999). Coevolution of Firm Absorptive Capacity and Knowledge Environment: Organization Forms and Combinative Capabilities, *Organization Science*, 10, 551–68.

Van Witteloostvijn, A. (1993). 'Multimarket Competition and Business Strategy', *Review of Industrial Organization*, **8**(1), 83–99.

Van Zandt, T. (1998). Organizations with an Endogenous Number of Information Processing Agents. 239–305. In: Majumdar, M., (eds.) Organizations with Incomplete Information. Cambridge, UK: Cambridge University Press.

Verhulst, P.F. (1845). Recherches Mathématiques sur la Loi d'accroissement de la Population Nouv. mém, de l'Academie Royale des Sci. et Belles-Lettres de Bruxelles, **18**, 1–41.

—— (1847). Deuxième Mémoire sur la loi d'Accroissement de la Population, Mém. de l'Academie Royale des Sci., des Lettres et des Beaux-Arts de Belgique, 20, 1–32.

Vickrey, W. S. (1964). *Microstatics*, New York NY: Harcourt, Brace, and World.

Vilallonga, B. (2004). Does Diversification Cause the 'Diversification Discount'? *Financial Management*, 33, 5–27.

Visscher, K. (2005). How to Frame an Organization: A Study of Organizational Design Practices in Management Consulting, EGOS colloquium 2005.

Volberda, H. and Lewin, A. (2003). Coevolutionary Dynamics within and between Firms: From Evolution to Coevolution, *Journal of Management Studies*, 40, 2111–36.

von Hippel, E. (1986). Lead Users: A Source of Novel Product Concepts, *Management Science*, **32**(7), 791–805.

von Neumann, J. (1928). Zur Theorie der Gesellschaftsspiele, *Mathematische Annalen*, **100**(1), 295–320.

—— and Morgenstern, O. (1944). *Theory of Games and Economic Behavior*, Princeton NJ: Princeton University Press.

Waldrop, M. (1992). Complexity: The Emerging Science at the Edge of Order and Chaos, New York: Touchstone.

Watts, D. J. (1999*a*). *Small Worlds: The Dynamics of Networks Between Order and Randomness*, Princeton NJ: Princeton University Press.

—— (1999*b*). Networks, Dynamics, and the Small-World Phenomenon, *American Journal of Sociology*, **105**(2), 493–527.

—— and Strogatz, S. H. (1998). Collective Dynamics of 'Small-World' Networks, *Nature*, **393**, 440–2.

Weisbuch, G., Kirman, A., and Herreiner, D. (1995). Market organization, *Economic Journal*, **110**, 411–36.

Wellman, B. (1988) Structural analysis: from method and metaphor to theory and substance. In Wellman, B. & Berkowitz, S. D. (eds) *Social Structures: A Network Approach*. Cambridge. Cambridge University Press. 19–61.

Wernerfelt, B. (1984). A Resource-Based View of the Firm, *Strategic Management Journal*, **5**(2), 171–80.

Westphal, J. D., Boivie, S. and Ching, D. H. M. (2005). The Strategic Impetus for Social Network Ties: Reconstituting Broken CEO Friendship Ties, *Strategic Management Journal*, **27**(5), 425–45.

White, R. E. (1986). Generic Business Strategies, Organizational Context and Performance: An Empirical Analysis, *Strategic Management Journal*, 7:2, 17–23.

Whittington, R. (1993). *What is Strategy – and Does It Matter?*, London: Routledge.

Wicks, A. and Freeman, E. 1998: Organization studies and the new pragmatism: Antipositivism, and the search for ethics. *Organization Science*, 9(2), 123–40.

Wilensky, U. (1999). *NetLogo: http://ccl.northwestern.edu/netlogo/*, Center for Connected Learning and Computer-Based Modeling, Northwestern University, Evanston, IL.

Wilson, D. (2003). Strategy as Decision Making. In Cummings, S. and Wilson, D. (eds.), *Images of Strategy*. Oxford: Blackwell, pp. 383–410.

Winter, S. G. (2003). Understanding Dynamic Capabilities, *Strategic Management Journal*, **24**, 991–5.

Yoo, Y., Boland, R., and Lyytinen, K (2006). From Organization Design to Organization Designing, *Organization Science*, **17**, 215–29.

INDEX

Figures and tables are indexed in bold.